The Secret Lives of
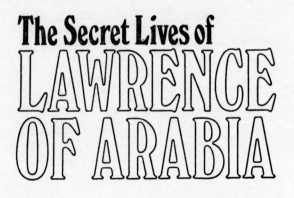
LAWRENCE OF ARABIA

The Secret Lives of

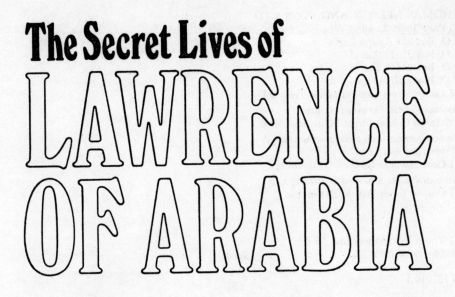

LAWRENCE OF ARABIA

Phillip Knightley and Colin Simpson

Nelson

THOMAS NELSON AND SONS LTD
36 Park Street London W1
P.O. Box 336 Apapa Lagos
P.O. Box 25012 Nairobi
P.O. Box 21149 Dar es Salaam
P.O. Box 2187 Accra
77 Coffee Street San Fernando Trinidad

THOMAS NELSON (AUSTRALIA) LTD
597 Little Collins Street Melbourne 3000

THOMAS NELSON AND SONS (SOUTH AFRICA)
   (PROPRIETARY) LTD
51 Commissioner Street Johannesburg

THOMAS NELSON AND SONS (CANADA) LTD
81 Curlew Drive Don Mills Ontario

© Times Newspapers Ltd, 1969
First published 1969

17 135010 3

Made in Great Britain at the Pitman Press, Bath

Contents

Plates

Acknowledgements

We are greatly indebted to Miss Parin Janmohamed and Arabella Rivington who carried out most of the research for this book. We would also like to thank Mr Suleiman Mousa for research on the chapters dealing with the Arab Revolt and its aftermath. (Our researchers are, however, not responsible for any of our conclusions.) We are grateful to Miss Anne Dark who cheerfully carried the secretarial side of the project single-handed; to Miss Wendy Hughes and Mrs Monica Foot; to Miss Dora Bryen for her exhaustive photo-research; to Mrs Sevinc Kislali for help in Turkey; to Mr Targan Haccim Carikli for access to his father's papers; to Mr Tom Beaumont for his recollections of Lawrence; to Mrs April Hersey for work in Australia; to Dr Sourin Roy for research in the Government of India Archives; to Mr Geddes Wood; Mr Arthur Lippett; Mr Charles Boutagy; and Col. R. V. C. Bodley.

We owe a special debt to Dr Denis Leigh, BSc, MD, FRCP, Secretary-General of the World Psychiatric Association, and a distinguished psychiatrist, for advice on the book in general and Chapter 15 in particular.

We wish to thank the Public Record Office for access to Crown copyright material, which is published by permission of H.M. Stationery Office. (Reference to this material in the footnotes is indicated by the following abbreviations: PRO (Public Record Office); FO (Foreign Office); CAB (Cabinet papers).) Lord Trenchard for his generous permission to use material from his collection of his father's papers; the Bodleian Library, Oxford; the Library of the School of Oriental Studies, University of Durham, for Clayton and Wingate papers (Wingate Papers in the footnotes); the Scottish Record Office, Edinburgh; the Centre of Middle Eastern Studies, St Antony's College, Oxford, for Hogarth's and Allenby's papers (and Mrs Grace W. Hogarth for copyright permission);

All Souls Library, Oxford, for Lionel Curtis's material; Mr Meyer W. Weisgal, chairman of the Board of Trustees, for access to the Weizmann Archives, Rehovoth, Israel.

The letters of Mrs Bernard Shaw to T. E. Lawrence are printed by permission of the Trustees of the will of Mrs Shaw; Lady Nancy Astor's letters by permission of her literary executors; the Kipling poem by permission of Mrs George Bambridge. We thank the London Library and *The Sunday Times* Library for their tolerant and helpful attitude to difficult requests; and Mr Nicolas Bentley, of Nelson's, for his sympathetic guidance. The book would not, of course, have been possible to write without the support, advice and encouragement of the editor of *The Sunday Times*, Mr Harold Evans, and the associate editor, Mr Leonard Russell.

All men dream: but not equally. Those who dream by night in the dusty recesses of their minds wake in the day to find that it was vanity: but the dreamers of the day are dangerous men, for they may act their dream with open eyes, to make it possible—*Seven Pillars of Wisdom, introductory chapter.*

Introduction: Legend and Reality

Lawrence of Arabia, who died in 1935, is one of the most fascinating and at the same time perplexing men of our age. To two generations he has represented all that is finest in the English Imperial Hero, a man of integrity, wise, fair-minded and courageous, who took up his country's burden in the Middle East and led his faithful Arabs to victory over the Turks. Rightly honoured, he moved with kings and poets, generals and ministers of state. Then, believing that the Arabs had been betrayed, that his word pledged as an Englishman had been dishonoured, he retired from public life and buried himself in the ranks of the army and then of the Royal Air Force, living strangely and dying sadly, a white Arab, Prince of Mecca, and uncrowned King of Damascus.

It is an attractive legend and as a result of it Lawrence is, except for Winston Churchill, probably the best known Englishman of this century. His bust stands in St Paul's Cathedral with those of Nelson and Wellington. His cottage, Clouds Hill in Dorset, is like a place of pilgrimage. His book, *Seven Pillars of Wisdom*, describing the Arab Revolt, is one of the most widely read works in the English language. Some thirty books in at least four languages have been written about him, and a film, *Lawrence of Arabia*, was one of the most successful money-makers in cinema history.

How is it that the British, supposedly an unromantic race, have developed so grand a passion for this small man? True, he had a magical personality, a sparkling intellect, energy and charm. Churchill, Bernard Shaw, and many others fell under his influence. (At his funeral Churchill wept, called him 'one of the greatest beings of our time' and prophesied that 'whatever our need we shall never see his like again'.) The answer is perhaps to be found in the fact that to a generation reared in Flanders with its mud and slaughter, Lawrence and the desert campaign were exhilarating and romantic.

The Bedouin were brave, unspoiled primitives fighting a just war of liberation—men on camels against planes and machine guns. Lawrence, the blue-eyed young man from Oxford, with courage, endurance, and a strong emotional attachment to the Arabs and their way of life, inspired them to overthrow their oppressors and take Damascus. If the war had not ended and the politicians had not betrayed him, he might well have conquered Constantinople with half the tribes of Asia Minor at his side.

Any attempt to take a cool look at this legend dissolves into a quicksand of hearsay, rumour and fantasy, where even the simplest enquiry evokes a complicated response. To take one example: among a variety of important posts reputedly offered to Lawrence to lure him back into public life after he had buried himself in the Royal Air Force, was that of secretary of the Bank of England. It was said that Montagu Norman, the governor of the Bank, made the offer in 1934. But in a letter in answer to our enquiries the Bank makes it plain that at no time did it offer Lawrence the job of secretary, a post which, by tradition, is filled from the Bank's own staff. The letter states that Lawrence had, however, once been considered for the position of night porter, a job in which he had expressed some interest as it would have given him time to write.

Did the story grow by itself, helping to achieve for Lawrence the importance that it was felt he deserved, or—unlikely though it seems—was Lawrence perhaps approached unofficially to see if he would be interested if the offer were made to him? It is this difficulty in trying to separate fact from fantasy that bedevils anyone trying to write about Lawrence and which has resulted in a certain sameness in the writings already published about him. We were fortunate in that a decision by a man who had kept silent for more than forty years unlocked a part of Lawrence's life which had remained secret and this in turn led us to discover vital new material about him.

Our interest began early in 1968, when *The Sunday Times* was approached by Mr John Bruce, who said that he had known Lawrence from 1922 until his death. He told us of a relationship with Lawrence that was so surprising and which seemed to involve such strange ramifications that it was decided to try to check the authenticity of his story. This investigation then expanded as it became clear that much of what had been accepted as fact about Lawrence's career was really legend, in the sense ascribed to it in the *Oxford English Dictionary*— 'an unauthentic story handed down by tradition and popularly regarded as historical'.

Next, Lawrence's brother, Professor A. W. Lawrence, agreed to allow us access to Lawrence's papers in the Bodleian Library at Oxford. These consisted mostly of letters written by Lawrence. On his death, the recipients had lent them for copying on the understanding that they would not be published without their consent before the year 2000.

But much the most important source of new material was the Public Record Office in London. Until 1968 it was the government's policy to keep state documents secret for fifty years after they had been written. Allowing time for classification and indexing, this would have meant that much of the material concerning Lawrence— his reports, his papers to the Foreign Office, telegrams to and from him, minutes of meetings he attended, instructions from various ministers of state—would not have been available until about 1970. Then in 1968 the period of official embargo was altered to thirty years, and a variety of documents concerning Lawrence have been released at irregular intervals since then.

With these documents as a basic source it became possible to trace complementary material at Durham University, the Scottish Record Office, St Antony's College at Oxford, the Government of India archives in New Delhi, and in several private collections. With the world-wide facilities of *The Sunday Times* at our disposal it was possible to locate and interview people who could add their personal recollections to the story of Lawrence. In Australia we found one of the first agents recruited by him when he was concerned with an espionage network in Cairo in 1915; in Turkey the family—and through it the diaries—of the Bey of Deraa, the man whom Lawrence accused of having buggered him; in Israel a record of a vital meeting between the Arab leader, Emir Feisal and the Zionist, Dr Chaim Weizmann, one of the founders of Israel.

From all this material, much of it hitherto inaccessible, there emerges a new picture of Lawrence's life, both private and professional. It is now possible to see that in each of the four phases into which his career divides itself there was a dominant figure whose influence had a profound effect on his actions and his emotions. As a youth at Oxford it was D. G. Hogarth, the scholar and archaeologist, whom Lawrence saw as a sustaining parent, and who saw in Lawrence an instrument through which to realize his dream of expanding the British Empire in the Middle East. In the desert it was S.A. the person to whom Lawrence dedicated *Seven Pillars of Wisdom*, an enigmatic figure whose identity has remained until now a mystery, and with whom Lawrence seems to have established a deeper emotional relationship than with anyone else. During the years he spent in the ranks of the Royal Air Force and the Tank Corps it was to a young and unknown Scotsman, John Bruce, that Lawrence turned for the release of feelings which could only be expressed through an elaborate ritual involving fantasy, pain and humiliation. Finally, in the last decade of his career, his friendship with Mrs Bernard Shaw, in whose company and correspondence he found a unique satisfaction, became a predominating influence, partly fulfilling the natural intimacy between mother and son that Lawrence felt he had lacked.

Clues to an understanding of the complex and sometimes contra-dictory factors in Lawrence's personality may be found in these four relationships, each of which served in turn to counterpoint separate and distinct phases of his public life. For, from the new material un-covered by our researches, there emerges a picture of Lawrence of Arabia no less remarkable than the legend, though almost the antithesis of it. It is now clear that, far from having a deep emotional attachment to the Arabs, as a race Lawrence did not care for them. Far from devoting himself to uniting their divided tribes so that an Arab nation would emerge, he believed that it was in Britain's interests to keep the Middle East divided. Far from furthering the cause of Arab freedom and independence, he was intent on making them part of the British Empire. In our view it is clear that Lawrence promised the Arabs freedom because he knew it was the best way of getting them to fight, but all along he knew that British policy would never allow them the independence they imagined they were fighting for. ('I had to join the conspiracy. . . . I risked the fraud, on my conviction that Arab help was necessary to our cheap and speedy victory in the East, and that better we win and break our word than lose.') This betrayal gave him a lasting sense of guilt which was the main reason for his refusal to profit from the sales of his book *Seven Pillars of Wisdom*. ('It's part of my atonement for the crime of swindling the Arabs to continue to lose money over my share of the adventure.'*)

Lawrence's main role in the Arab Revolt is now shown as being not that of a military leader but a political officer attached to Feisal with the object of influencing him and so ensuring the success of British policy. His main motivation throughout the Revolt, apart from patriotism, was ambition and hatred of the French; a hatred so powerful that in some of the papers he wrote early in the war it is difficult to tell whether the Turks or the French were the enemy.

This bitter distrust continued after the war. During the Paris

* Letter to Charlotte Shaw, 19 March 1924.

Peace Conference, far from devoting himself to fighting for a fair deal for the Arabs, Lawrence was working on a scheme to upset the French position in the Middle East by arranging for international Jewry to finance Feisal, and perhaps all Arabia, at 6 per cent. The intrigue this involved played a part in creating Israel, which can hardly be said to have turned out to be in the Arabs' best interests.

Lawrence withdrew from public life after the war not because he felt that the Arabs had been betrayed, but because he was disgusted that his plan for the Middle East had been abandoned in favour of another. Not that there was a great deal of difference between the two plans as far as the Arabs were concerned. Both denied them real independence, both placed British interests first, and both placed heavy emphasis on maintaining British influence in the area indefinitely. In fairness, let it be said that Lawrence's plan did at least give the Arabs a façade of independence, and no doubt he must have felt a certain satisfaction when the plan he opposed rapidly went wrong.

What, then, is left of the popular conception of Lawrence? His military role, though it was not his main one, undeniably had a certain importance. The Revolt in which he played a part, though not that of the leader, diverted considerable Turkish forces and supplies to the Hejaz and protected the right flank of the British armies in their advance through Palestine. Lawrence himself was a tough and resourceful soldier, but to attribute the entire success of the Revolt to him is to ignore the facts. His account in *Seven Pillars of Wisdom*, indisputably a great book, must not be taken as history. Lawrence himself, in a note written en route to Cairo in 1919, gave warning that '. . . no one should mistake this narrative of mine for history. This book is the bone of history, not history herself'.*

It is easy to overlook the fact that the Revolt occupied only two years of Lawrence's life and that the whole of his Arabian period, from Carchemish to the Cairo Conference, only eleven years. The rest of his life tends to be smothered in the legend of the Prince of Mecca. Yet as an ordinary aircraftman, using his influence in high places, and with the taste for intrigue that he had acquired from his intelligence days, he achieved a range of reforms which influenced the progress of the Royal Air Force, and in a role far removed from that of Arabia he devoted himself to the development of high-speed launches and a forerunner of the hovercraft.

It is in this post-war section of the book that the most controversial part of Lawrence's private life is recounted. We make no apology

* Bodleian Library.

for what some may consider to be an intrusion. The actions of a public figure may be influenced by his private behaviour. When a man has been acclaimed as a national hero it is historically important to present every facet of his life, warts and all, in the hope, as Lord Vansittart remarked, that this will provoke not only interest but anger, and in the clang a balance may be struck.

We deal, therefore, at some length, with a series of emotional crises which Lawrence, with the help of the Scots youth we have mentioned, attempted to solve in a highly personal way. It is possible that the source of these troubles goes back to the guilt Lawrence felt over the fate of his beloved S.A., or to Deraa, the night when according to Lawrence, he was tortured and buggered by the Turks. Some of the material we have found casts doubt on Lawrence's version of what really happened at Deraa, but clearly something occurred during the war which later caused these periods of emotional turmoil. Whether the practices to which he resorted during these periods were intended, as Professor Lawrence believes, to achieve a subjection of the body 'by methods advocated by the saints whose lives he had read', or whether they were the manifestation of an incipient masochistic side to his character, is open to debate.

Professor Lawrence has written: 'One of his [Lawrence's] friends . . . holds that he was a man perfectly clear in his way of life, who had achieved a balance between spirit, intellect, and body to a degree few even imagine . . . in my opinion he neglected the body's claims unfairly. He maintained this "balance" at a cost so terrible in waste and suffering, that its author would himself, I believe, have agreed that it was a failure.'* Psychiatric examination, so far as it is feasible at this date, of Lawrence's difficulties, offers another view. Whichever argument one accepts, it is clear that in his later life Lawrence went through spells of torment that were connected with his desert days, and which, all things considered, can only evoke for him a measure of sympathy. For the emotional wounds that Lawrence suffered in the war were in the service of his country, and there is no doubt that he did his best to further Britain's aims. He was the Imperial Hero, after all, and in this respect the legend has, if anything, understated Lawrence. His importance, we suggest, lies in the fact that he was not only, as Richard Aldington has said, representative of his time and his class, but also of the policy and tactics adopted by an imperial power to protect its interests. It is in this role that history will judge him.

* Editor's postscript to *T. E. Lawrence by his Friends*. Jonathan Cape, London, 1937.

1 Boyhood of an Outsider

Lawrence's father, heir to an Irish baronetcy, leaves his wife and four daughters and runs away with their governess. They cannot marry, but they have five sons, the second of whom is T. E. Lawrence. He is an intelligent boy, interested in archaeology. He begins to grow into an outsider, and at seventeen, as a result of tensions in the family, runs away and joins the Army, from which he is soon bought out by his father. He wins a scholarship to Jesus College, Oxford, where D. G. Hogarth, Keeper of the Ashmolean Museum, agrees to keep a friendly eye on him.

In County Meath, Ireland, in the latter part of the last century there lived an Anglo-Irish landowner called Thomas Robert Tighe Chapman. The Chapmans, who numbered among their ancestors Sir Walter Raleigh, tended, like most Anglo-Irish families, to draw their faith from Canterbury, to buy their guns and their claret from London, and to select their wives from the English shires. Chapman had married in 1873 and his wife, Edith, bore him four daughters. He was a modest, retiring man who had no interests apart from the running of his estate, shooting, fishing, sailing and, in general, enjoying the life of an Irish country gentleman. But behind a Victorian façade of righteousness and respectability Thomas Chapman concealed physical passions of considerable strength and, finding them unreciprocated by his wife, looked elsewhere for their satisfaction. He might well have continued indefinitely the deception this involved, but in 1884 his extra-marital activities were brought into the open and his entire life was altered.

There are several versions of how this occurred. Ours comes from a distant relative of Mrs Chapman's, a young girl at the time, who emphasizes that although her memory is good the story is not necessarily complete because 'people in those days never discussed marital matters in front of their children'. As she understands it, the Chapmans at one time employed a Scots girl called Sarah Maden or Sarah Junner as a nursery governess to their four daughters. After a while she gave notice, saying she was needed at home. Apparently she left on amicable terms because Mrs Chapman gave her as a gift a locket containing a photograph of the girls. Some time afterwards, the Chapmans' butler, while in a Dublin grocer's shop, heard a young woman give her name as Mrs Thomas Chapman. At first he thought that someone was pledging his employer's credit and was about to object when he realized that the young woman was the ex-governess, Sarah Maden. The butler turned his back so that he would not be recognized and when Sarah left the shop he followed her to a house which he saw her enter. As he stood nearby wondering what to do, he heard a man's voice greeting Sarah in affectionate terms. It was the voice of Chapman. The butler returned home and told Mrs Chapman what he had discovered. Chapman's secret was out.

Whether this story is correct in all its details is not important; what is certain is that Chapman left Edith and his daughters, set up house with Sarah Maden, and changed his name. He and Sarah were never able to marry, but they had five sons. The second was T. E. Lawrence, later to be known as Lawrence of Arabia.

Chapman's involvement with Sarah Maden had not resulted from a casual or irresponsible decision. He had come to regret bitterly having married Edith, who had turned out to be a truly ferocious spouse. Such was her fanatical Evangelicalism and so violent her reaction to the cloistered atmosphere of Irish Roman Catholicism that in Dublin circles she became known as 'the Holy Viper'. She considered any form of amusement to be a sin, said prayers three times a day, and could carry on a conversation consisting almost entirely of biblical quotations. There is no doubt that she made life for the tolerant and easy-going Chapman both an embarrassment and a misery.

Her harsh, humourless attitude was such that on one occasion she would not allow the two elder girls to return home after their aunt had taken them to a pantomime because she feared they would 'contaminate' the younger girls; another time she locked up one daughter on a five-day diet of bread and water as punishment for a childish misdemeanour.

Mrs Chapman seldom went to Dublin, which she believed to be a city of sin. She kept herself busy with good works in the village, distributing tracts and presiding over interminable prayer meetings of her servants and those of her husband's tenants who, despite their native faith, knew better than to resist their mistress's attempts to win them from the embrace of Popery. The result was that the running of the house was left to Miss Maden, who managed it with precision and affection, soon becoming more like one of the family than a governess. She was a small girl, neat and beautiful, with blue eyes, a gentle manner, a passionate nature, and a lively and inquiring mind. The Chapmans' house had given her strong roots for the first time in her life, and these she strengthened with her own brand of the Christian faith—she had been recommended to the family by a visiting Anglican Priest as 'a true daughter of God'. Her background is obscure and even her surname Maden is perhaps not that of her parents. Her mother was English, her father Norwegian. She was probably illegitimate, for she had been brought up in the north of Scotland by an aunt and an uncle, who was a Church of England priest in a Presbyterian parish. Sarah was sufficiently pious to satisfy Mrs Chapman, and had the intelligence and adaptability to elevate herself from the obscurity of her Highland existence into the more promising if ambiguous situation of governess to the Chapman family. More important, she established an atmosphere of ordered living, which was what Thomas Chapman needed above all else. Obviously, he made his comparisons, and in 1884, when Sarah was twenty-three, he rented a small terraced house in an outlying suburb of Dublin, where she became installed and he could visit her.

Their first child, Robert, was born in Dublin, but soon afterwards they left Ireland for England, changed their names by deed poll to Lawrence, and began to erect a façade of married respectability which they maintained for the rest of their lives. But they never seemed to feel sufficiently secure to settle in one place. Their second son, Thomas Edward, was born in the early hours of 16 August 1888 at Tremadoc in Caernarvonshire, Wales. Thirteen months later the Lawrences left Wales for Kirkcudbright in Scotland, where their third son William was born. Eighteen months later, after short stays in the Isle of Man and in Jersey, the family settled in Dinard on the northern coast of France.

There the two elder boys, Bob and T.E. (known to the family as Ned), went to the Frères school every morning for an hour or so and twice a week joined three other English boys at a private gymnastic class in St Malo. The reports that have survived indicate that T.E. was the brighter of the two brothers, a robust little boy with a quick and lively intelligence; his mother claimed that he knew the alphabet before he was three. Despite what numerous biographers have written, he was neither a prodigy nor a prig.

A fourth son, Frank, was born in February 1893, the Lawrences having travelled to St Helier in Jersey to ensure English nationality for the child. The following spring they all returned to England and rented a small cottage—Langley Lodge—on the edge of the New Forest. Here they lived a normal and healthy family life. A governess came to give them lessons, and the local schoolmaster coached Bob and T.E. in Latin before they went away to school. T.E. learnt to ride a pony, swim and climb trees, and to experiment in pottery-making, firing his moulded clay pots in the kitchen oven.

Lawrence's father was now well established in his role as Thomas Lawrence, and Langley was near enough to the Solent for him to indulge in his favourite sport of sailing. Often he would take his three elder sons down to the edge of the Solent at Lepe and point out the racing yachts from Cowes as they dipped past. Occasionally he took them to the Isle of Wight, where he had joined a yacht club, and they were allowed to roam the slipway and play about in boats belonging to members of the club. Lawrence was proud of his sons. He took them fossil hunting, taught them to recognize the house flags of the ocean-going ships that came up Southampton Water and took them on expeditions to see the coloured cliffs at Alum Bay in the Isle of Wight, to Tennyson's house at Farringford and monument at Freshwater, and to Carisbrooke Castle, with its unhappy memories of Charles the First's imprisonment.

Thomas Lawrence had had to trim his expenditure when he opted for Sarah Maden and exile from Ireland. By the time he had settled funds on his wife and made provision for the education of his four daughters his remaining capital brought him an income of about £300 a year. Occasionally he sold something to provide a little extra ready money. His pair of sporting guns went when he realized he would no longer be shooting grouse, but he still managed to sustain the life of a simple country gentleman, though one whose pursuits were on a reduced scale. Photography replaced grouse shooting and ocean-racing; a bicycle his hunters. By 1896 his financial commitments to his daughters were diminishing and he now felt justified in moving the family and sending the boys to school. In September of that year the family went to live in Oxford. This was a logical choice from Thomas Lawrence's point of view because there were several schools there well endowed with scholarships. He himself had little learning, though he had had a traditional classical education. (T. E. Lawrence said years later to Captain—now Sir Basil—Liddell Hart, 'He never touched a book, or wrote a cheque.') Oxford had another important attraction for Thomas and Sarah

Lawrence—it was the home of Canon Alfred Christopher, the rector of St Aldate's church and a force in the Evangelical movement. They had met him briefly when he had preached at Ryde in the Isle of Wight in 1895, and the message of love that was to earn him a place in the history of the Church of England had appealed very strongly to them. Mrs Lawrence was troubled in conscience by her illicit union; she could never bring herself to use the words 'my husband' and referred to Lawrence instead as 'Tom', or 'the boys' father'. In this state of mind the words of Evangelicals like Canon Christopher gave her comfort and the five 'R's' of the Evangelization Society—Ruin, Redemption, Regeneration, Righteousness and Responsibility—came to mean a lot to her. She believed that if she could regenerate her life, then God with his love and understanding would surely forgive her. This consoling thought was her great strength and when she was nearing death in a nursing home in Oxford, she kept murmuring, 'God hates the sin but loves the sinner'.

The family lived in Oxford at 2 Polstead Road, a modest red-brick villa with a long back garden flanked by acacia trees. They kept to themselves and Mrs Lawrence discouraged all but one or two of her neighbours. Those who did know her and Thomas recall the contrast between the quiet easy-going father, with his birthright of dignity and charm, and the tense and strict but loving mother. The family worshipped at St Aldate's and it was not long before Thomas Lawrence became a member of the church committee. The four boys all attended Oxford High School, cycling to and fro in line, with the eldest, Bob, leading and Frank, the youngest, bringing up the rear. They were neatly dressed in striped jerseys and the neighbours could—and did—set their clocks by them as they rode off in the morning to school. For the first few summer holidays they returned to Langley Lodge, which they took for the occasion, and later Thomas Lawrence rented for a couple of years a small house called Myrtle Cottage near Yarmouth in the Isle of Wight.

Ernest Cox, an assistant master at Oxford High School, who later became Vicar of Steyning in Sussex, remembered the boys clearly:

'The eldest of the family was Bob—conscientious, solicitous, always kind; one in whom even in those early days spiritual values had a place. And then there was Ned—one of few words, self-possessed, purposeful, inscrutable. He was just like other boys in most things, but differed from them mainly in that he gave rise to a sense of hidden possibilities—a feeling that there was a latent something just out of reach. He was clear of mind and not readily perturbed; but he was self-reliant and one could feel in him an instinctive recoil when he was being pressed into a way that he did not feel inclined to go. There was no robustness of body to suggest those future powers of physical endurance; but that short quick step with which he walked told of an alertness of mind and body; whilst there was depth and seriousness of purpose in that steady and unyielding gaze with which, with head slightly bowed, he looked up into the eyes of those who spoke with him.

'And next after him came Will—one beautiful to look upon; and already as a boy possessed of a certain gravity of mind and character which gave full promise of that fine early manhood which was cut off so early in the War.

' And then last of the four was Frank—a dear boy; lovable and greatly loved; one whose happiness and radiant smile remain an enduring and ever helpful memory. He joined the Army in August 1914, and was killed in France on the 9th of the following May.

'Here then was an ideal family of boys, a very band of brothers— united, conscientious, strong in character, clean alike in limb and in life; each influencing and shaping the others in ways that he knew not of.'*

The boys' headmaster, A. W. Cave, shared similar memories, but more intimate reminiscences are those of two schoolfellows, T. W. Chaundy, who became a lecturer and tutor in mathematics at Christ Church, Oxford, and C. F. C. ('Scroggs') Beeson, who was T.E.'s bosom companion at school and shared in many of his early escapades. Chaundy remembers the Lawrence family by the regularity with which, as term succeeded term, yet another Lawrence seemed to join the school. Best of all he remembers T.E., known at school as Lawrence II and characterized by a 'spareness of body and a pithy energy of speech'. On some occasions he went brass rubbing with Lawrence, but his main recollection is of an arrangment they worked out together whereby he did Lawrence's algebra and Lawrence helped Chaundy with his English composition. Chaundy says neither was a great scholar. (Lawrence was later to remember school as 'an irrelevant and time-wasting nuisance which I hated and condemned'.†)

* *T. E. Lawrence by his Friends.*
† Robert Graves and Liddell Hart, *T. E. Lawrence to his Biographers*. Cassell, London, 1963.

Beeson was closer to Lawrence and as scavengers of antiquities the pair achieved local notoriety. Now retired after a distinguished career as forester and ecologist, Beeson recalls Lawrence with sympathy, clarity and insight.

As boys they went to meetings of the Oxford Archaeological Society. To Beeson's surprise, Lawrence on one occasion refused to take part in a pageant organized by the city authorities. Beeson had expected him to relish a chance to act because acting seemed an integral part of Lawrence's temperament. 'One could never be sure whether he was serious, or merely being affected for affectation's sake.' This was due partly to Lawrence's craving to be liked which he himself described as 'so strong and nervous that never could I open myself friendly to another'.* Yet he was not unpopular and many of his school friends found him fascinating. His pockets were likely to hold a piece of early pottery, some materials for brass rubbing, or some mechanical part of the racing bicycle to which he was devoted. He was not simply a moody schoolboy shunning his fellows, but a youngster who seemed to be trying deliberately to play the part of an unfathomable outsider.

While he was still at school, probably when he was about twelve or thirteen, Lawrence got into an argument with another boy and fell, breaking a bone in his leg. The leg was put into plaster but the fracture took a long time to heal. It has been suggested that this accident affected Lawrence's growth, but if his growth was stunted it is more likely to have been as a result of mumps which he caught when he was adolescent.

Lawrence was 5 feet 5½ inches in height, which, although short for his social class (Oxford undergraduates at that time averaged 5 feet 9½ inches), was about the national average. He no doubt looked smaller than he was because his head was large in proportion to his body.

When Lawrence's leg healed he took to bicycling more and more, partly to strengthen the injured muscles, but also because he and 'Scroggs' Beeson were interested in making rubbings from monumental brasses, and together they rode to villages for miles around. Beeson has written:

'It was no collector's hobby. There were experiments in the technique of rubbing with different grades of heelball and paper, assisted by friendly advice from shoemakers and paperhangers whose shops

* *Seven Pillars*, Chapter CIII.

supplied our raw materials. There was much searching in libraries for the histories of those priests and knights and ladies, which narrowed into a study of armour and costume.

'The Wallace Collection and the Tower Armouries became familiar, and the manufacture of camail and jointed plate armour was gravely projected as a means of interpreting the conventions of early illustrators ... Heraldry displayed an alluring field that resulted in the compilation of rolls of arms, painted in their proper tinctures ... a herald's jargon was permanently acquired, which, with many another special terminology, eventually enriched the vocabulary of the *Seven Pillars*. We ranged from palaeography to the Kelmscott Press and thence to ideal book-making: a new Froissart's Chronicles illustrated only by contemporary art, a school history, cleansed of anachronisms.

'Many a trespass was committed in Lawrence's company. The artistry of his tact in convincing irate guardians of the honesty of our purpose was often put to test; it extricated us from such compromising positions as the middle of a rhododendron-covered tumulus, suspected of rabbit snaring, and the crypt of St Cross in possession of human bones. ....

'A bicycle tour of the country north of the Loire was planned for the summer vacation of 1906. In August of that year I was able to join him in the exploration of parts of Brittany. We met at St Malo, each equipped for the venture with a small American-cloth covered basket (handiwork of our respective mothers) on the rear carrier, a waterproof cape and spare boots on the handlebars, and, wherever handiest, a volume of Viollet-le-Duc's *Dictionnaire Raisonné*. The Côtes du Nord and Finisterre were covered closely in search of cathedrals and the less known fortifications. ....

'Lawrence's main preoccupation was with the minds of the designers of these defensive works and the extent to which history had tested their intentions. He talked little of campaigns and military art in general. ....

'There was little time spared for megaliths or the *pêcheurs* of Pierre Loti or other Breton attractions; these were out of date with our mood. Search on the sea-coast discovered a long flat beach of hard sand that satisfied Lawrence as a site for speed trials on his latest bicycle, a model with dropped racing handles and an unusually high ratio to the top gear. With the full force of a Channel gale behind ... the results were mightily pleasing.'*

* *T. E. Lawrence by his Friends*, pp. 53–4.

In the summer of 1908 Lawrence set out on a cycling tour of France that took him as far south as Carcassonne, mostly to study medieval military architecture. He rode strenuously and ate frugally, and described himself as being 'as brown as a Jap and as thin as paper'. Lawrence and Beeson also found plenty to occupy their interests in Oxford. They searched for Roman relics on farmland and in woods and in 1906, when during excavations for building work in Oxford medieval pottery and glass began to be turned up, they were quickly on the scene. They were worried that the value of these discoveries would not be appreciated by the workmen, so they toured the sites offering the men a few pence each for their finds. This system—Lawrence was later to use a similar incentive scheme at Carchemish in Asia Minor—lasted for about two years and produced pipes, coins, tokens and pottery vessels. The best of these finds were presented to the Ashmolean Museum and listed as 'Found by C. F. C. Beeson and presented by T. E. Lawrence'.

Up to this stage Lawrence appears as a normal, healthy youth: intelligent, somewhat introspective, well-adjusted to school and its demands, and absorbed in medieval history. But what of his home life? It is clear that his mother rather than his father was in charge of his upbringing and that the basis of her system was strong adherence to biblical and Protestant values. Lawrence went to classes held by Canon Christopher, where he learnt the gospels. He was for some years an officer of the St Aldate's branch of the Boys' Brigade and took Sunday school classes himself. His mother instilled in him the importance of respect for one's parents and the necessity for unquestioning obedience, any resistance to this being dealt with by beating her son on his bare buttocks.

It is difficult to discover how Lawrence reacted to all this. His brother, Professor A. W. Lawrence, believes his biblical upbringing and the inculcation of Protestant values shaped his life almost to the same extent as his later classical and medieval reading and his experience of austerity in the desert. Lawrence himself gave few clues. His letters to his mother are normal until the war. Yet there were obviously certain barriers between them and thereafter neither succeeded in re-establishing contact. Many years later in a letter to Bernard Shaw's wife, Charlotte, Lawrence said that his mother had made impossible demands on him for love, that there was not a subject on which they dared to be intimate, and that she had given him a terror of family life.

Here, his feelings about his illegitimacy may have been a factor, depending on when he discovered this. The evidence is contradictory.

He told Charlotte Shaw in 1927 that he knew before he was ten, 'and they never told me'. Other authorities say he became aware of his father's other family when he was only four; alternatively that he found out about it when he was seventeen, perhaps as a result of his researches into heraldry. How he found out is not important. Its significance, however, can hardly be exaggerated. Much has been written about it. Some say it did not matter to him, others that it influenced him greatly. The fact is that his attitude remained ambivalent throughout his life. He was able to write to Lionel Curtis in 1926, 'Your remark about ancestry, for which you apologised, I've entirely forgotten. So what can it have been? Bars sinister are rather jolly ornaments. You feel like a flea in the legitimate prince's bed!' But the following year, in another letter to Curtis about a proposed entry in *Who's Who*, he said '. . . write anything you please so long as you don't give away . . . my original family'. Sometimes he considered it did not matter, at others that people were talking about it behind his back. (In this he was correct. King George V's secretary, Lord Stamfordham, for example, wrote to Sir Reginald Wingate, the soldier and Arabist, from Buckingham Palace in 1927 enclosing a private report on Lawrence's illegitimacy which said, in part, 'When they [the sons] were told that their mother was not married, it appears to have embittered their lives . . . the eldest is the celebrated Colonel Lawrence.')

Such evidence as there is about Lawrence's early life suggests that it was not his illegitimacy that caused the tensions that existed in his family. That there were tensions seems indisputable. When Lawrence was seventeen he slipped away overnight, bicycled to St Just-in-Roseland in Cornwall, and enlisted as a private soldier in the training battalion of the Royal Artillery. What prompted his flight is not known, but whatever it was he made his point. His father went to Cornwall, bought him out of the army and brought him back to the family; but important adjustments were made to avoid further domestic discord and to give Lawrence the quiet he needed for his studies during his last and most important term at school. His father built a small two-roomed bungalow for him at the bottom of the garden. Here Lawrence, who had turned from studying mathematics to history, worked diligently. He narrowly failed to win a scholarship to St John's College, but the next year, 1907, won a Jesus College history exhibition reserved for students born in Wales. His father, however, was still worried about him. He consulted Canon Christopher, who in turn spoke to two scholars with whom he was on close terms and both agreed to help Lawrence through what seemed

likely to be a difficult period of his life. One of these was David
Margoliouth, Laudian professor of Arabic at Oxford; the other,
D. G. Hogarth, Keeper of the Ashmolean Museum, who already
knew Lawrence through his interest in medieval pottery. They
kept a friendly eye on him and agreed that when he came up to
Jesus College they would do what they could to help him. This
arrangement was to have major repercussions on Lawrence's career.
Hogarth was to become for Lawrence 'the parent I could trust,
without qualification, to understand what bothered me'.

2 The Recruit

At Oxford Lawrence comes under the influence of D. G. Hogarth, who is, among other things, a political intelligence officer specializing in the Middle East. Hogarth, an autocrat by conviction, imbues Lawrence with those ideals of imperialism originally formulated by an organization, the Round Table. Lawrence, outwardly a reserved youth interested in medieval history, studies military tactics and also begins to train his body to resist pain and exhaustion. He makes a 1,000-mile walking tour of Syria and becomes fascinated by the country and its people. When he comes down from Oxford he prepares to accompany Hogarth on an archaeological dig in Asia Minor, where they believe they have a part to play in a new era of the Empire.

When Lawrence went up to Oxford in the autumn of 1907 it was still too early to detect the shadows of war soon to threaten Europe. There was an uneasy calm in the Balkans, and ominous stirrings in Russia, while in Turkey, Germany had already established a political and military ascendancy. In Britain, however, the security of Victorian imperialism lingered on. The Empire, *Pax Britannica*, and the civilizing influence of cricket and the English language were still supreme. One in five of the earth's population owed allegiance to the King Emperor, whose protection, it was said, extended not only to the British, but to all who valued law and order. Little had changed in fact, since Kipling had written of the King's mother:

> Walk wide o' the Widow at Windsor,
> For 'alf o' Creation she owns:
> We 'ave bought 'er the same with the
>   sword an' the flame,
> An' we've salted it down with our bones. . . .

> Hands off o' the sons of the widow,
> Hands off o' the goods in 'er shop,
> For the Kings must come down an' the
>   Emperors frown,
> When the widow at Windsor says "Stop"!

For the privileged it was a golden age. Oxford, an oasis of upper middle-class learning, was still unsullied by the tourist, the motor car, or the multiple store. In this academic lagoon of unknown depth, its surface barely disturbed by the various fashionable idiosyncrasies cultivated by its more eccentric or irresponsible members, Lawrence arrived without a ripple and neither Jesus College nor Oxford was more than barely aware of the event.

Outwardly, Lawrence was little different from the mass of undergraduates beginning their university careers. The legends that he was the darling of the unorthodox, the navigator—with his mother, on one occasion—of the Trill Mill stream, one of the more accessible of the city's underground sewers, aroused no comment until he became the hero of Arabia. A more balanced picture of Lawrence in his early Oxford days is that of a modest and tractable undergraduate. He had rooms only for the first term and was then given a special dispensation to live at home, his mother undertaking to see that during the term he was in by midnight. He showed no interest in games, and instead spent his spare time exploring Oxford with an archaeological thoroughness that merits admiration. He continued with his photography and read voraciously. But as time passed, Lawrence developed, probably as a defence mechanism, several outward characteristics some of which were to mark his behaviour in later life. The first and most obvious was a shrill, nervous—and, to some people, effeminate—giggle, with which he often punctuated his conversation. Secondly, he began to show off, at first discreetly, but effectively. He would walk his bicycle downhill and ride it up, pole a canoe like a punt, and once a week in hall, while the rest dined heartily, he would refuse to eat at all. He became a practical joker and a regular participant in college battles, in which his favourite weapon was a bicycle pump filled with water and his favourite defence an inverted hip-bath, used like a tin helmet, to ward off lumps of coal. Thirdly, he cultivated a ready tongue and was quick to denigrate and eager to display his newly acquired scholarship. He became adept at turning the conversation, if it seemed to be veering towards a subject of which he knew little, towards ground on which he felt unassailable. His contemporaries remember him as elusive, contrivedly enigmatic, yet generous with offers of reconciliation if his sarcasm cut too deep. In short, he was now adopting the defences of an intelligent, shy and acutely sensitive boy beginning to feel his way in a world which was dominated by men who were endowed with a depth of masculine maturity that—as perhaps he realized—he would never attain.

At this remove it is difficult to probe into what must have been an attractive but complex mind. It is possible, however, to peel away some of the sentiment and half-truths which have grown round Lawrence during this period. He was not the golden child of a golden age, as his mother believed and wrote. Nor was he the long-haired homosexual that Aldington imagined. He was a slightly-built young man, with a weak leg, conscious of his illegitimacy and of his relative poverty; and with an abnormal attitude to the physical side of life. At an age when most young men were enjoying the delights of the senses, he was deliberately withdrawing himself from them. In short, T. E. Lawrence was different. His contemporaries knew it, he knew it, but none of them knew why.

One man, however, had a shrewd idea of what made him tick. This was David George Hogarth, author, archaeologist and orientalist, then Keeper of the Ashmolean Museum at Oxford. It was Hogarth who encouraged Lawrence as a schoolboy to collect pottery fragments. It was to Hogarth that Canon Christopher had sent a note—after Lawrence had been bought out of the Royal Artillery— asking him to stand, when necessary, *in loco parentis* to Lawrence. It was of Hogarth that Lawrence was later to write: 'He is the man to whom I owe everything I have had since I was seventeen',* and, 'he was like a great tree, a main part of the background of my life: and till he fell I hadn't known how much he had served to harbour me'.†

In his first year at Oxford Lawrence was nineteen. Hogarth was forty-five. He became Lawrence's mentor, confessor, and patron, and it is no exaggeration to say that without Hogarth there might have been no Lawrence of Arabia. Since he was of such importance in Lawrence's life it is worth looking closely at him. He was a formidable, bearded figure with enormously long arms and he gave the impression, as a woman who met him at a party described it, 'of being a cynical and highly-educated baboon'. In fact, he was a remarkable man of a type that Britain seldom seems to produce nowadays. He was an intellectual, a man of letters with immense knowledge of a wide range of subjects, and yet, when the moment required it, a man of action. He spoke French, German, Italian, Greek, Turkish and Arabic; he was an archaeologist of note and an orientalist whose opinion was respected throughout Europe; as a conversationalist he was as much appreciated in London society as in academic circles at Oxford. And, like many of his kind, when

* Letter to Charlotte Shaw.
† *The Letters of T. E. Lawrence*, edited by David Garnett. Jonathan Cape, London, 1938, No. 347.

the opportunity presented itself he carried out political intelligence work for the British government. There has not yet been a biography of this remarkable man, possibly because most of his papers, when they referred to his government work, appear to have been destroyed. Hogarth was, in short, one of the first 'backroom boys', men of special talents who are not officially part of government, but upon whose information and advice contemporary leaders seem more and more frequently to rely.

Hogarth was born at Barton-on-Humber on 23 May 1862. He was educated at Winchester, where he had a reputation for greater ability than he cared to show, and at Magdalen College, Oxford, where he took a First in Classical Moderations and then in *litterae humaniores* in 1885. By the time he met Lawrence he was a Fellow at Magdalen, had been on archaeological expeditions to Asia Minor, Cyprus and Egypt, and had held appointments as director of the British School of Archaeology at Athens and as correspondent for *The Times* in Crete during the revolution in 1897 and in Thessaly on the eve of the Greco-Turkish war—an incredible career for a man of forty-five. When he was thirty-two he had married a Miss Laura Uppleby, but their life was not one of complete compatibility. She showed little interest in his work and during his long absences abroad his letters suggest that she was not so close to him in this respect as was his son. Of cool temperament himself, he was irritated by her nervous anxiety and impatient at her lack of understanding. He was a man of single-minded purpose, sardonic and with few illusions. The Middle East had an emotional attraction for him and its people 'appealed to every romantic and lawless instinct in his nature'.* As a result, he spent a large part of his life there, read innumerable books in various Western languages about its people and was deeply involved in their destiny. He had a strong contempt for democracy, which was by no means confined to what he considered to be the absurd idea of introducing it to lesser nations. He was strongly patriotic, convinced of Britain's greatness, and certain of the best way to keep her great. He saw the world as a huge gaming table with a number of powerful adversaries each out to further his own interests and increase his own stake. Play, he believed, was continuous and, as there were no alliances of a lasting nature, went on against current friends as well as against current enemies— exactly the way of thinking that informs the *modus operandi* of most modern intelligence services.

In a game of this nature the processes of parliamentary democracy

* Memoir by C. R. L. Fletcher, *Geographical Journal*, April 1928.

were, Hogarth believed, useless. The nation needed dedicated men of special knowledge, 'in it neither for pay nor honours',* men who understood historical trends and could interpret intelligence, and from all this form an opinion on policy and, if need be, push that policy through the right channels. These dedicated men naturally came to the fore in wartime, but they also had a part to play in peace. Although outwardly most of them were scholars, archaeologists, consuls, or in commerce, they could continue to serve their country— secretly, in a way that the ordinary citizen would never know and could never understand—by gathering information, observing trends, interpreting intelligence, arranging, fixing, manipulating persons and events, formulating policy, shaping, on however small a scale, a part of history.

Many people recognized men of this type as dangerous to the democratic tradition. Churchill complained in 1920—about some- one not unlike Hogarth himself—that no one who did not hold a leading position in the state should be permitted to exercise so much influence on policy. But in Hogarth's day many men in government were quite happy to allow a clique of academics, mostly from Oxford, to help to plan the future of the Empire. As, presumably, this future was limitless, these academics were quick to recruit likely young men to carry the torch, and this is how Hogarth viewed Lawrence. He recognized the extent of Lawrence's ability, his ambition, his determination, and he set out to channel Lawrence's thinking in the right direction. How thoroughly Hogarth studied Lawrence, how completely he knew him and how, in many respects, he moulded Lawrence in his own image, is best demonstrated by a report he wrote about him in 1920:

'The things he wants not to be are quite numerous; but things he could be, if he wanted, are more numerous still. He is not fond of being anything, and official categories do not fit him. He can do most things and does some; but to expect him to do a particular thing is rash. Besides being anti-official, he dislikes fighting and , Arab clothes, Arab ways, and social functions, civilized or uncivilized. He takes a good deal of trouble about all things but quite a great deal about repelling people whom he attracts, including all sorts and conditions of men and some sorts and conditions of women; but he is beginning to be discouraged by consistent failure, which now and then he does not regret. He has as much interest as faith in

* Letter to his mother, 20 September 1918, in Hogarth Papers, St Antony's College, Oxford.

himself: but those who share the last are not asked to share the first. He makes fun of others or kings of them, but if anyone tries to make either of him, he runs away. Pushing (not himself) he finds more congenial than leading and he loves to push the unsuspecting body: but if it does not get on as fast as he thinks it should, he pushes it into the gutter and steps to the front. What he thinks is his Law. To think as fast or as far as he thinks is not easy, and still less easy is it to follow up with such swift action. He can be as persuasive as positive; and the tale of those he has hocussed into doing something they never meant to do and are not aware that they are doing, is long. It is better to be his partner than his opponent, for when he is not bluffing, he has a way of holding the aces: and he can be ruthless, caring little what eggs he breaks to make his omelettes and ignoring responsibility either for the shells or for the digestion of the mess. Altogether a force felt by many but not yet fully gauged either by others or by himself. He should go far; but it may be driving lonely furrows where at present few expect him to plough.'*

What did Hogarth have in mind for Lawrence? He cannot, at this early stage have foreseen the role both he and Lawrence would play in the Arab Revolt. But, like other academics at Oxford, he had given a lot of consideration to the future of the Empire and had been influenced by the ideas of Lord Milner and his 'kindergarten', best expressed by Lionel Curtis and his strange *Round Table*, a periodical† and also a study group 'which have played a role in British imperial affairs that has never yet been properly analysed or described'.‡ (One of the reasons for this has been a certain secrecy which the group maintained ever since its founders agreed that 'as little as possible should be said about its existence or the objects of its activities ... When asked, men should explain that a number of individuals were making a study of imperial relations and conducting a magazine to communicate ideas and information'.§)

Curtis, who later became a close friend of Lawrence's, was a racist and a Francophobe; he once wrote 'some Brahmins are as white as Frenchmen'.‖ He was also a fanatical supporter of the English-speaking countries as the main civilizing influence in an

* William Rothenstein, *Twenty-four Portraits*, Allen and Unwin, London, 1920.
† Founded in 1910 and still published as a quarterly.
‡ Elizabeth Monroe, *Britain's Moment in the Middle East, 1914–1956*. Chatto and Windus, London, 1963, p. 134.
§ Lothian Manuscripts, Scottish Record Office, Edinburgh.
‖ Arnold J. Toynbee, *Acquaintances*. Oxford University Press, London, 1967, p. 144.

otherwise irredeemable world. He told Arnold Toynbee in 1925 that
if Christ were to return to earth he would find that his precepts were
being best practised in the British Commonwealth. The Round
Table's main aims, taken from Milner's teachings as described in
the *Round Table*, were Federation (union of all the white people
in the Empire) and Imperialism ('The work of British imperialists during my lifetime has been to hold the fort ... to get over
the dangerous interval during which imperialism, which for long
appealed only to the far-sighted few, should become the accepted
faith of the whole nation ... in another twenty years it is reasonable to hope that all Britons, alike in Motherland or overseas, will
be imperialists').*

John Buchan,† who became a friend of Lawrence's, believed in the
Round Table and in a fictional essay called 'Lodge in the Wilder-
ness', outlined the ideas for which it stood. This summary is from
Elizabeth Monroe (*op. cit.*):

'It describes a group of imaginary people born within the political
and social pale (some of the prototypes are obvious), who are hand-
picked by a hero modelled on Rhodes for a house-party on an escarp-
ment in East Africa. They represent the whole range of empire
builders—politicians, pro-consuls, traders, men who can pass as
natives or stay *impis* [Zulu armies] with a word. They spend the day
shooting lions and visiting chieftains, but as soon as night falls settle
to the real business of their meeting, which is to decide how to fire
the empire with their spirit. "The average man [says one of them],
may be described as a confused imperialist. He wants to make the
most of the heritage bequeathed to him; his imagination fires at its
possibilities; but he is still very ignorant and shy, and he has no idea
how to set about the work. The first of imperial duties is to instruct
him".'

The Round Table might have been written off as an esoteric,
jingoist political movement (it grew out of Lord Milner's group
called a Moot—which held symposia called 'eggs', the policies of
which, if adopted, were launched as 'omelettes') had it not been for
the wealth, scholarship, patronage and class consciousness of many
of its disciples. This combination enabled it to exert considerable

---

* *Round Table*, March 1954.
† John Buchan, 1st Baron Tweedsmuir (1875–1940). Best known as a novelist;
engaged in intelligence and propaganda work, 1916–17. Governor-General of
Canada, 1935–40.

pressure on the decision-making élite of government. Milner at a Round Table dinner in 1912 said that Philip Kerr* (later to become another friend of Lawrence's) 'had altered the whole course of the last Imperial Conference and the immense advance in the attitude of the imperial governments in the Dominions in the matter of foreign policy was due to his efforts'. Professor A. P. Thornton, however, says that men like Kerr and Curtis spent much of their time 'trying to add cubits to the stature of their contemporaries; if never quite failing to influence, never quite succeeding in guiding'.† Suffice it to say that there was a member of the Round Table in Lloyd George's 'Garden Suburb' (a brains trust installed in huts in the garden of No. 10 Downing Street in the later stages of the war, attached to the War Cabinet and with direct access to ministers); that there were at least two Round Table men in the British delegation to the Peace Conference; that it was a Round Table member who got Lawrence his fellowship at All Souls; that one of these knights of the Round Table was editor of *The Times*; that they used to meet in each others' houses, where the guests often included the Prime Minister, the Foreign Secretary, and other ministers of State. As will emerge later, a walk in the garden with the Foreign Secretary or breakfast with the Prime Minister is sometimes a far more successful way of advancing a scheme or propagating an idea than any number of meetings, letters or petitions.

Where did Lawrence fit into all this? He absorbed, via Hogarth, some of the precepts of the Round Table, and these came to be among his main motivations in Arabia. As he himself wrote later, 'You know how Lionel Curtis has made his conception of Empire—a commonwealth of free peoples—generally accepted. I wanted to widen that idea beyond the Anglo-Saxon shape, and form a new nation of thinking people, all acclaiming our freedom, and demanding admittance into our Empire. There is, to my eyes, no other road for Egypt and India in the end, and I would have made their path easier, by creating an Arab Dominion in the Empire'.‡ Lawrence greatly admired Curtis and, in common with other friends of Curtis's, often referred to him as 'The Prophet'—one feels only half in jest. In fact, the Round Table was among the first organizations to express fear of German influence in the Middle East and was constant

* Philip Henry Kerr, 11th Marquess of Lothian (1882–1940). Co-founder and first editor of the *Round Table*. His career as a politician achieved its climax by his becoming British Ambassador at Washington in 1939.

† A. P. Thornton, *The Imperial Idea and Its Enemies*. Macmillan, London, 1959, p. 81.

‡ Letter to Foreign Office official, Paris, 1919, Bodleian Library.

in expressing its strong disapproval of Turkish behaviour; perceptive views which Lawrence certainly absorbed.

Arnold Toynbee has written of Curtis, 'Lionel . . . needed, and recruited, a supply of younger assistants for his successive public activities. . . . These human tools of his were valuable to him primarily as instruments for getting on with the particular job that he had in hand at the time.'* The same could have been said of Hogarth, who recognized in young men like the poet, James Elroy Flecker, H. Pirie-Gordon† and T. E. Lawrence, the qualities that would make them ideal disciples, and later ideal recruits for what became, unofficially, Hogarth's Political Intelligence Service.

This is not to suggest that Hogarth or any of his young men were formally on any intelligence department's payroll. The sort of relationship he enjoyed with Whitehall and Westminster, until he emerged during the war as director of that formidable British intelligence operation, the Arab Bureau—with the rank of Lieutenant-Commander in the RNVR—was an informal one, and probably went no further than a conversation at a dinner party, a meeting in a club, or occasionally, an anonymous but telling paper prepared for ministerial attention. For Hogarth's knowledge of the Arab provinces of the Ottoman Empire was unrivalled and for years before the war—although principally an archaeologist—he devoted a considerable amount of time to gathering and assessing information, especially on political trends, in that area. National sentiments, underground movements, potential leaders, activities of German and French agents, topography, military leaders, and possible battle tactics, were all of interest.

Lawrence, as a new recruit to this Great Game, was prepared for his role by Hogarth with meticulous attention to detail. He began by disciplining Lawrence's reading, especially that relating to military history. How this affected him is described in a letter from Lawrence to Liddell Hart. He started with 'the usual school-boy stuff—Creasy, Henderson, Mahan, Napier, Coxe: then technical treatises on castle-building and destruction: Procopius, Demetrius, Poliorcetes and others which I have forgotten. I already read nearly every manual of chivalry. Remember that my "period" was the Middle Ages, always.'

According to Liddell Hart, dissatisfied with Clausewitz, he worked back to Napoleon ploughing through the twenty-five volumes of despatches, and from them to Bourcet, Guibert and Saxe in that

---

* *Acquaintances*, p. 132.
† An archaeologist and later a member of the Arab Bureau in Cairo.

order. From there he devoured most of the eighteenth-century manuals of arms.* Procopius, a Roman military secretary, advocated indirect means for avoiding pitched battles and described the hit-and-run tactics which broke the morale of the Gothic lancers and archers, so it is interesting to speculate as to what use Lawrence later made of this information. Saxe was the source for the idea that war could be won without fighting battles and Bourcet for the belief that every plan must have flexible alternatives.

In the summer before he came up to Oxford, and again in 1908 during his first long vacation, Lawrence went to France, largely at Hogarth's instigation. His purpose was to study castles and battle-fields and draw and photograph what he saw. He wrote to Liddell Hart: 'I made a series of maps (of battlefields) and visited Rocroi, Crecy, Agincourt, Sedan, and two other Franco-German war places whose names I forget.' Lawrence then explained that his interests were mainly medieval, and that in pursuit of this, 'I went to every 12th century castle in France, England and Wales, and went elaborately into siege manoeuvres . . . I also tried to get an idea of the bigger movements, and saw Valmy and its neighbour-hood, and tried to re-fight the whole of Marlborough's wars.'

This was a very broad field of study for a young undergraduate, even for one whom Hogarth recognized as being exceptionally single-minded. But the spectrum of scholarship was from Hogarth's palette, and when it came to re-fighting wars Lawrence did not always re-fight them alone. It was Hogarth's habit to hold occasional meetings either at his home or at his room in Magdalen. Each meeting had a theme, which was to re-fight and re-think some decisive political or military battle. The leadership, the strategy, and the motives of history's greatest leaders were dissected and analysed. Time would also be given to the intellectual 'spin-off' of each event. Thus the poetry and romance of the French medieval chroniclers was discussed equally with the tactics of Henry of Navarre, and Ronsard would rank equally with any of the great marshals of France. Lawrence was frequently invited to these meetings and the breadth of knowledge that he gained from these discussions deeply impressed his tutor at Jesus, Dr Lane-Poole, who noted that Lawrence was drawn towards the fanciful and the romantic; that during tutorials he would espouse an unfashionable theory or defend the romantics of history against the pragmatists. It was Dr Lane-Poole's contention that for Lawrence to be really interested, the idea or cause would have to be either against all current thought

* *T. E. Lawrence to his Biographers*, p. 50.

on the subject, or steeped in mystery, mysticism and romance. His essays, on the rare occasions they were written, instead of being made up on the spur of the moment, almost invariably opened with a challenging statement or drew heavily upon the more romantic passages of medieval chroniclers.

Perhaps it was due to Lawrence's natural inclination, perhaps to Hogarth's encouragement, but increasingly the Crusades became the subject of his special interest. The semi-religious aura of Richard Coeur de Lion, Saladin, and, for good measure, the mystical and poetic conception of the Order of Knighthood, became something in which he could immerse himself and with which he eventually identified himself completely. He was to be a Knight, a crusading Knight, fighting for good against evil, searching for his own personal Sangrail, and in his life he began to strive to be the epitome of Knighthood, clean, strong, just and completely chaste.

It was a poetic and an understandable posture. Popular authors of the day dwelt almost exclusively on England, home and beauty, upon the immeasurable superiority of the clean-limbed, lantern-jawed young Englishmen who laboured for an empire on which the sun never seemed likely to set. For Lawrence this empire became an almost spiritual concept, a divine order in which Britain was destined to extend her law, her culture, and her protection to the lesser nations of the world, in the process of which the knights of the period would play a major part.

What one sees of Lawrence at this period of his life are two different yet complementary pictures. The first of these was of Lawrence, the intellectual idealist, a young man of taste and discernment, the Lawrence best known to his closest friend at Oxford, Vyvyan Richards, an Anglo-American undergraduate. Richards has proved invaluable to us in reconstructing not only details of Lawrence's life but the ambience in which he lived at the time. At considerable emotional cost to himself Richards has for the first time discussed this period in Lawrence's life and his own involvement with him freely and frankly. His motivation has been simple and honest: Lawrence gave him so much pleasure and so much happiness that he feels he owes it to Lawrence's memory to try to set the record straight.

Richards and Lawrence together explored the Arts and Crafts movement, spending most of their time on the work of its founder, William Morris. Together they planned a Utopian house to be built at Poles Hill in Epping Forest (where, as a child, Morris had played at being a medieval knight) and assiduously collected material for its construction. The house was to be a Pre-Raphaelite hall, with all Morris's associative visions of knights, tourneys and chivalry. Ensconced in their hall, Lawrence and Richards would produce hand-printed books of exquisite workmanship and live a life devoted to the appreciation of quality, craftsmanship, and all that was just and pure. It was an idealistic concept, not very different from that which many intellectually-inclined young men conceive in early manhood. But as Richards and Lawrence explored the byways of chivalry, as they retraced the career of their hero, William Morris, there grew up between them a relationship that probably provided the first opportunity either had had to reveal himself completely to another. Richards is open about this relationship. 'Quite frankly', he said, 'for me it was love at first sight.' The love they had for each other was, on Lawrence's side, uncomfortably and irritatingly pure.

'He had neither flesh nor carnality of any kind; he just did not understand. He received my affection, my sacrifice, in fact, eventually my total subservience, as though it was his due. He never gave the slightest sign that he understood my motives or fathomed my desire. In return for all I offered him—with admittedly ulterior motives—he gave me the purest affection, love and respect that I have ever received from anyone... a love and respect that was spiritual in quality. I realise now that he was sexless—at least that he was unaware of sex.'

The other view of Lawrence was of the potential intelligence agent, the latter-day Crusader, preparing for his life's mission not only by sharpening his intellect but also punishing his body by a physical regime not unlike a commando course. C. F. C. Beeson, Lawrence's friend from his Oxford school days, tells of Lawrence testing his endurance by going for two or three days without food; of his making midwinter cross-country treks by compass to test his stamina; of his swimming or climbing every obstacle during these marches; of his spending long, lonely evenings on the Cadet Force pistol range practising until he became equally adept with either hand; and of riding his bicycle non-stop until exhaustion made him collapse by the roadside.

At the end of 1908, Lawrence told Dr Lane-Poole that he intended to submit a thesis for his degree on the premise that the Crusaders had taken *to* the Middle East those principles of military architecture that all scholars had said the Crusaders brought *from* the Middle East. Cocking a calculated snook at authority was typical of Lawrence, but Hogarth supported his protégé and when Lawrence sailed for the Middle East in June 1909, he took with him a sheaf of instructions from Hogarth, a camera with a powerful telephoto lens, a pistol and ammunition, and irades (letters of authority requesting safe conduct) signed by Lord Curzon. Hogarth was hoping perhaps that his recruit was ready to be fired with the same enthusiasm for the Middle East that he himself felt. Lawrence later wrote of this enthusiasm: 'He had a delicate sense of value, and would present clearly to us the forces hidden behind the lousy rags and festering skins which we knew as Arabs'. Lawrence had prepared for the journey by taking lessons in Arabic from a Syrian clergyman living in Oxford, the Reverend N. Odeh, a friend and confidant of Professor Margoliouth, and had also talked to Charles Doughty, the famous Arabian explorer. (Hogarth described Lawrence to Doughty as 'a boy of extraordinary aptitude both for archaeology and a wandering life among the Arabs'.*) Lawrence had been given some maps, in need of updating, by Pirie-Gordon, another protégé of Hogarth's, who was then a leading intelligence operative in the Middle East. Lawrence arrived at Beirut on 6 July. His plan was to walk 1,000 miles through Syria (which then included the countries now known as Israel, Jordan, and the Lebanon) by stages, studying various Crusaders' castles on the way. From Beirut he went on foot to Sidon, making his first acquaintance with Arab food, then on to Banias, Safad, Lake Huleh, Tiberias, Nazareth and Haifa, returning to Sidon by way of Acre and Tyre. Then he headed north to Tripoli, Latakieh, Antioch, Aleppo, Urfa and Harran, whence he returned through Damascus. It was, he wrote, 'a most delightful tour . . . on foot and alone all the time, so that I have perhaps, living as an Arab with the Arabs, got a better insight into the daily life of the people than those who travel with caravan and dragomen'.†

Three points about this trip are worth noting. First, that Lawrence was beaten and robbed. There are many accounts of what happened, all different in detail, but what seems to have occurred is that a Turkoman villager attacked him to steal his watch, believing it to be made of gold. A shepherd intervened and saved Lawrence from being severely injured. Lawrence used his irade to persuade a Turkish official to arrest the Turkoman and his watch was recovered. The second point to note is a comment made by Lawrence on Palestine: 'The sooner the Jews farm it all the better',‡ a view he

* Letter, 21 August 1911, quoted in Hogarth's *Life of Doughty*. Oxford University Press, London, 1928.

† *Letters*, No. 17.

‡ *Letters*, No. 13.

was later to help to put into practice. And the third, that through his journey Lawrence, as Hogarth had hoped, gained his first enrapturing taste of the Levant. He shared the bread, the water, the milk, the honey, and the fleas of the ordinary people; he travelled as St John the Baptist and Paul of Tarsus had done: and he became intoxicated—like many a European before and after him—with the dazzling light, the harsh landscape, and the sense of time-lessness of desert life. He also achieved the main purpose of his journey—material for his thesis on 'The Military Architecture of the Crusades', since published as *Crusader Castles*.* At Oxford on his return he took first-class honours in history. B. H. Hutton, who was his examiner, said later that Lawrence's ten papers and a translation paper were all good and some very good. His thesis, which was optional, was 'most excellent'.

Lawrence came down from Oxford in the summer of 1910. Hogarth recommended him for a senior demyship at Magdalen (a form of postgraduate award) so that he could join an archaeo-logical dig at Carchemish in Asia Minor, which Hogarth was supervising for the British Museum. Hogarth's archaeological expeditions are something of a mystery. There were always excellent reasons for them, but also they always seemed to be in politically or militarily interesting areas. When one also learns that some of Hogarth's 'archaeological' activities were financed by unlikely government departments, it is tempting to compare him, in modern terms, with a cultural foundation sponsored and financed by the American Central Intelligence Agency.

By this time the empathy between Lawrence and Hogarth was such that Lawrence, looking back on this period, was able to write: 'He was my background, in a curious sense; the only person to whom I never had to explain, the "why" of what I was doing.' Their relationship was later to grow more distant, but at this stage their aims were identical: the Middle East was stirring after a four-hundred-years' sleep. If the Turks were pushed out, who should replace them? The Germans, the French, the Russians, or the British? Hogarth and Lawrence were in no doubt. Their vision was that these ancient lands could be coloured red—not by conquest, but by example and persuasion. If this could be accomplished, then Lawrence, the young outsider, and Hogarth, the middle-aged Oxford don, could each claim a share in the writing of a new chapter in Britain's imperial history.

* The Golden Cockerel Press, London, 1936.

3 The Game Begins

Germany, France and Russia prepare to enter the power vacuum which a dissolution of the Ottoman Empire will create. The strategic importance of the Suez Canal and the discovery of oil in the area make it imperative for Britain to protect her own interests and her agents in the Middle East help to prepare for a war which now seems inevitable. One of these agents is Lawrence, who, at the Carchemish dig overlooking a vital section of the Berlin–Baghdad railway, gets his first taste of the Great Game. A major political passion is aroused in him during this period: dislike and distrust of the French. With Hogarth's approval he spends his summers increasing his knowledge of Arabia and its peoples, noting likely allies—and enemies—and taking part in two military surveys. In 1914 Hogarth gets him into military intelligence. When Turkey joins Germany in the war against the Allies he is posted to Cairo, where he runs an intelligence operation, recruiting his own agents.

The Middle East in which Lawrence and Hogarth were about to become embroiled had been dominated for four hundred years by the Ottoman Empire, a vast and powerful hegemony extending to three continents—Africa, Asia and Europe. At one stage it had stretched from the Adriatic to Aden and from the eastern border of Morocco to the Persian Gulf, and by the skill of its generals and the bravery of its soldiers had reached as far as the outskirts of Vienna. But from about the middle of the nineteenth century the technology of the Western world, rudimentary though it still was, began to make itself felt, and the Ottoman Empire started to flake at the edges.

The nations that had once felt threatened by Turkey now turned on her. France took Algeria and Tunisia. Britain occupied Egypt. Austria-Hungary annexed Bosnia and Herzegovina (now part of Jugoslavia), Italy seized Libya, and the Balkan provinces broke away.

The collapse of the Ottoman Empire had been envisaged as a possibility by European statesmen since the remark made by Czar Nicholas I in 1853: 'We have on our hands a sick man—a very sick man. He may suddenly die....' Early in this century the death of the sick man looked more likely than ever and the big powers—Britain, France, Russia and Germany—all began to look to their separate interests. These were complicated and various, and the four countries were motivated as much by fear of each other as by a common desire to expand their empires. Britain, for example, had good reason for viewing the decline of Turkey with alarm. The Ottoman Empire was a religious unity with the Sultan as caliph and head of the Muslim world; in India Britain controlled about seventy million Muslim subjects and the possibility that they might side with Turkey if for some reason the Sultan were to embark on a Holy War, was a permanent and anxious preoccupation of the British government: a power that Britain knew was far safer, ricketty though it might be, than the dangerous vacuum that the disintegration of Turkey would create.

On the other hand, if Turkey were to collapse Britain would have a duty to protect her own military and economic lines of communication with India, where half the British army was stationed and which was unquestionably Britain's best customer. The Suez Canal therefore had to be defended and the only way of ensuring this was for Britain to control Syria and Arabia.

France, for her part, had only recently given up trying to fulfil the Directory's dictum, which even Napoleon had found beyond him: 'Drive the English out of their possessions in the East .... Destroy their trading stations in the Red Sea, cut the isthmus of Suez, ensure free and exclusive possession of the Red Sea to the Republic.' But her sentiment for Syria, dating back to the Crusades, remained a strong factor in French policy.

Then there was Germany. With her rapidly expanding economy she wanted to turn Mesopotamia into a 'German India', and with the aim of eventually making it a protectorate was insinuating herself into Turkey. Russia had moved into Armenia and the Caucasian countries and had persuaded the Turks to allow her to build railways in the north-east of Turkey. She yearned to dominate Constantinople, terminus for all caravan routes in the Middle East and, most important of all, the centre from which the exit from the Black Sea to the Mediterranean was controlled.

For all these countries there was an additional exciting prospect—oil. Although the importance of the internal combustion engine was not fully realized until the last stages of World War I, as early as 1904 Britain's First Sea Lord, Admiral Fisher, had anticipated that oil would supersede coal as fuel for warships and had started to look for a cheap source not too far from Europe and in an area which Britain could dominate.

At 4.30 a.m. on 26 May 1908 it looked as if this source had been found. A company later to become known as British Petroleum (or BP) struck oil at Masjid-i-Salaman in the Zagros mountains in Persia. The British government, pressed to recognize the strategic importance of oil by its new First Lord of the Admiralty, Winston Churchill, became part-owner of the company in 1914. Germany, too, was seeking oil in the Middle East. In 1888 the German-controlled Ottoman Railway Company, whose officials were planning to build a railway to link Berlin with Baghdad, secured oil concessions for twelve miles on both sides of the projected line.

As the Ottoman Empire grew more senile, it became increasingly clear that in the struggle to replace the vacuum that its passing would create Britain stood to lose—or gain—most, and it was debatable from which of her rivals she had most to fear.

The Germans had been modernizing the Turkish army since the 1890s. German influence was growing among the Young Turks, who by 1908–9 had overthrown Abdul Hamid, the last of a long line of despotic Sultans. Now the Turks were trying to rebuild their country on Western lines. German engineers were engaged in improving communications, German geologists were seeking oil and the German-controlled Baghdad railway was being pushed forward.

In the eighteenth century France had tried to induce the Czar of Russia, Paul I, to invade India. His assassination put an end to the plan, but in the nineteenth century Russian advances into Central Asia continued to haunt Britain. This long-standing fear of a Russian attack on India caused her to maintain a constant surveillance of Russia's southern frontiers. Generations of young Englishmen, working from Delhi, Lahore, Kabul, Tehran, Tabriz, Erzerum and Samarkand, played 'The Great Game' for King, Country and the safety of India. Kipling wrote of it in *Kim*, but the truth was equally fascinating. Eric Newby describes how, in the abandoned offices of the British Consulate in Meshed, in the province of Khurasan in north-east Persia in 1956, he found a map of central Asia heavily marked in coloured pencil and on some sand dunes in the Kara-Kum desert, well inside Russian territory, the mystic inscription 'Captain X, July '84?'*

By the early 1900s this struggle between Asiatic Russia and British India had shifted ground slightly, but was still being pursued to the same end. In Afghanistan, Persia, Mesopotamia, Syria and

---

* *A Short Walk in the Hindu Kush.* Secker and Warburg, London, 1958.

the Persian Gulf a network of British agents, ostensibly consuls, travellers, merchants and archaeologists, working for the army, the Admiralty, the Foreign and India Offices, or the Intelligence Service, collected fragments of information in the hope that to someone, somewhere, they would form a pattern. Their aims were to influence chieftains, win over tribes, settle disputes and disparage the Russians and the French—all in the cause of protecting the Empire.

These men and women believed passionately in the British right to impose law and order on lesser tribes and that the end—peace, prosperity and civilization—could be held to justify the means. They saw their calling as honourable and noble, and if the nature of the work meant that the rewards could never be made public, the knowledge of having served the cause was sufficient. (Buchan's Brigadier-General Richard Hannay could have been the original mould.)

Lawrence was in step with this tradition when he arrived in Constantinople in mid-December 1910, on his way to Carchemish. Work had started at the site—about sixty miles to the north-east of Aleppo—in 1878, but had yielded slender results and had been abandoned. Then in 1910, when the Berlin–Baghdad railway reached the Euphrates, there came a sudden revival of British interest in Carchemish. Sound archaeological reasons for this were conveniently to hand. The site had been identified as Hittite, a civilization about which little was known, but whose people had played an important role in the early history of the Levant. The British Museum notified the Turkish authorities of this new interest, Hogarth was put in charge of operations, and the dig was started again.

The British arrived as the German engineers were constructing a bridge over the Euphrates, and Hogarth's headquarters were half a mile from the Carchemish site. There can be no doubt that the dig had a dual purpose and that various members of the team kept an eye on the Germans and what they were doing. It may seem odd that it was possible for a British group to spy on Germans engaged in work for the Turkish government. Why did the Turks not expel the British archaeologists from their country? The main reason was that a situation close to anarchy was growing in several areas of the Ottoman Empire. The Central Government was preoccupied with the threat of war in the Balkans, where some states had united against Turkey, and remoter parts of the Empire were under no effective control. A secondary reason was the prestige the British enjoyed in the Middle East and the assurance and even arrogance with which they comported themselves. For example, Hogarth's successor at the dig, Leonard (later Sir Leonard) Woolley, a colleague of Lawrence's at Carchemish, appeared in a Turkish court in a case concerned with land ownership, and when the judges demurred about delivering a verdict he is said to have whipped out his revolver and menaced them with it. This sort of high-handedness seems to have gone all the way down the line: the watchman at the British Consulate at Aleppo used to amuse himself by firing at passers-by, secure in the knowledge that the Turkish police would not arrest him because he was in the service of the English, and that even if they did he was entitled to be tried in a British court. So Carchemish could be considered an ideal place for Lawrence to have been gently initiated into handling the 'nuts and bolts' of intelligence work. But his preparation was not yet complete. He enrolled in the school of the American Mission at Jebail, near Beirut, to improve his Arabic. 'For some reason', he later wrote to a Mrs Rieder, who taught languages at the Mission School, 'Mr Hogarth is very anxious to make me learn Arabic.' The reason was soon to emerge.

At the end of February Hogarth arrived in Jebail and joined Lawrence. They sailed from Beirut to Haifa, visited Mount Carmel, Nazareth, and the villages on the Yarmuk. At Deraa (later to play a vital part in Lawrence's life) they took the train along the Hejaz line—the pilgrims' route for Mecca—to Damascus, and thence went to Homs and Aleppo, arriving at Carchemish at the end of March. It was a roundabout journey and though the reasons for it remain vague it may reasonably be likened to a coach taking an athlete over his course to familiarize him with the terrain, suggesting how the race should be run, and giving the young man confidence in his ability to win.

The trip was highly successful. The excitement Lawrence had felt over his first visit to Syria in 1909 was reawakened. At the side of his master he fell for the lure which that country has held for many an Englishman and willingly let himself be schooled for the missions Hogarth was to plan for him.

Carchemish is on the west bank of the Euphrates, and from the top of the mound the whole of the plain of the river valley was visible. The archaeologists lived in a cabin made of clay. It was a primitive but not unpleasant life and Lawrence revelled in it. Stripped to his shorts, sunburnt, and with his Arabic improving rapidly, he soon became the best-known foreigner in the area. His handling of the two hundred or so Arab and Kurdish workmen

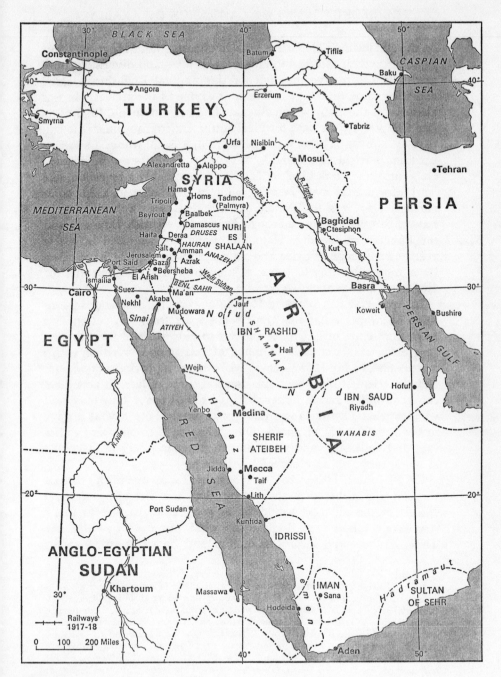

The Middle East in the First World War

on the site justified Hogarth's faith in choosing him. He spent hours listening to their talk and joining in their jokes and discussions until gradually the reserve they felt for this unusual Englishman eased and they came to accept him almost as one of themselves. He was already on the path which Buchan had set out in his 1906 essay (see Chapter 2), the path for ideal active imperialists, men who can pass as natives. There was one workman with whom Lawrence became particularly friendly, a young donkey-boy nicknamed Dahoum—'the Dark One', or 'Darky' (presumably a reversion, like 'curly' for a bald man, because actually Dahoum had a fair complexion). He was to become, as we shall see, a key-figure in Lawrence's private life. Through his friendship with Dahoum and the foreman of the dig, Hamoudi, Lawrence acquired in a few years a knowledge of Syria and its people which might have taken lesser men a lifetime to learn, a knowledge that was essential for Hogarth's long-range plan for him.

In April Hogarth returned to London, leaving Lawrence to continue his work. What this work was—apart from excavation—we learn from clues in Lawrence's letters to Hogarth and from the use Lawrence was later able to make of this period. Writing to his mother on 23 May 1911 he says, 'My camera is proving a good one: and the telephoto has been used several times of late. It acts (at a couple of miles) rather better than the naked eye'.* One may well wonder what Lawrence was doing with a telephoto lens at a stage in the development of photography when such things were rather rare and expensive, and what he was photographing at 'a couple of miles' range on an archaeological site.†

On 24 June 1911 he wrote to Hogarth: 'I may live in this district through the winter; it strikes me that the strongly-dialectical Arabic of the villagers would be as good as a disguise to me.'‡ Again one might ask: disguise for what purpose? By 1912 the Turks had become suspicious of him and he wrote to Hogarth:

---

* *Letters*, No. 30.

† The clearest indication of the use Lawrence made of some of the time spent in Syria in the years preceding the War comes in a letter to Hogarth dated 15 January 1915, from Cairo soon after Lawrence arrived there to join the Intelligence Department. He told him of Germans whom he had met in Syria being given appointments in the Turkish army. ('Musil . . . is head guide to the General Staff in Damascus . . . Moritz is out there, and Meisner, building railways.') And he knew in detail what was happening at Carchemish. ('The Germans have laid a light line through the S. Gate, and are taking stone from the Kalaat at Jerablus. The bridge is being pushed ahead'.) Clearly Lawrence must have had the services of agents and informers.

‡ *Letters*, No. 34.

'... The old Government has life in it yet ... it is beginning to keep watch on where I go at last.'*

Lawrence spent some of the summers, when the dig at Carchemish closed down, on long excursions, accompanied by Dahoum and Hamoudi. He also ferried camels across the Euphrates and spent some time in Port Said unloading colliers. He has recorded how, with Dahoum, he was arrested as a deserter from the Turkish army and imprisoned. Lawrence later told Liddell Hart that he escaped by bribing the guard. He also told the same story to one of his drivers, S. C. Rolls, during the period of the Revolt. As Rolls records it,† while they were at '... the ruined castle of Azrak ... Lawrence beckoned me ... and pointing to what looked like the crumbled mouth of an old well, bade me look into it. It appeared to be a sort of cellar, but all was black ... I looked at him enquiringly. He said "once I was kept a prisoner in that dungeon for months". ... He leaned down and pointed to the inside of the hole, at a place where the light just reached, and said, "Do you see those scratchings? Those are some of my attempts to escape." '

When Lawrence later looked back on this period he realized that Carchemish and his wanderings around Syria in those burning summers were the happiest years of his life. Perhaps this explains the anger he was later to show when French ambitions in Syria became clear, for only if it had such an emotional origin could it have provoked the hatred and distrust Lawrence expressed for the French. Even after war broke out and France was an ally of Britain, Lawrence's letters gave the impression that France was the enemy rather than Turkey.

He wrote to Hogarth on 18 March 1915: 'In the hands of France it [Alexandretta] will provide a sure base for naval attacks on Egypt, and remember—with her in Syria & compulsory service there, she will be able any time to fling 100,000 men against the canal in 12 days from declaration of war.'‡ (Many years later, when expressing his ideas for the organization of the RAF to meet the threat of World War II, Lawrence still considered France as the potential enemy rather than Germany.)

In 1913, when the dig closed down for the hot months, Lawrence brought Dahoum and Hamoudi back to England. In appreciation of their having looked after Lawrence when he was ill with fever, his father paid their expenses. Lawrence put the two Arabs in his

* Undated letter in the Ashmolean Museum, Oxford.
† *Steel Chariots in the Desert*. Jonathan Cape, London, 1937.
‡ *Letters*, No. 81.

4

bungalow in the garden of his parents' house, somewhat disconcerting the neighbourhood. In the autumn he returned to Carchemish, and the following January he and Leonard Woolley, on Hogarth's instructions, joined Captain S. F. Newcombe, of the British army, on a military intelligence trip through the Sinai Desert. The reason for this journey, which was secret at the time, is described in a letter from Newcombe to Sir Ronald Storrs (then Oriental Secretary at the British Agency in Cairo, and afterwards Governor of Jerusalem), written in 1953, when the need for secrecy no longer existed:

'The Egyptian-Turkish boundary, accepted by the Sultan of Turkey after the battle of Nasib, 1838 and agreed by the powers, England, France and Russia ... was a line drawn from Suez to Rafa. ... Therefore, S.E. of this line, including Nakhl, Mount Sinai, etc. were in Turkish area. ... Cromer* insisted on surveying the Rafa–Akaba frontier and erecting boundary posts visible from one to the next. Any passage across that line by Turkish troops meant war. That area S.E. of the Suez–Rafa line was administered henceforth (but not, I think, before? I forget) by Egyptian Army officers, a British officer from the Sudan being in command with Egyptians to assist. From about 1909–1910 various regular British officers and the Egyptian Survey Department surveyed that area N. of a line some twenty miles south of Nakhl and Suez: openly. After leaving the E[gyptian] A[rmy] to rejoin the British Army, I volunteered to survey for the 1912–1913 and 1913–1914 season of September–April, being bored with sitting still in England. The area Beersheba to Akaba had only been roughly mapped by Musil (Austria) and very roughly by K[itchener] of K[hartoum] in 1884: in fact he told me in November 1913, that his mapping was inaccurate and not worth attention, just as I was about to suggest the same news to him. Anyway, I pressed for permission to survey that ZIN area, to finish off the P[alestine] E[xploration] F[und] maps of . . . 1878 which stopped N. of the line Faga–Beersheba. Fitz-Maurice [an official at the British Embassy in Constantinople] got permission from the Young Turks in C.U.P.† and I was given Turkish authority and protection by gendarmes to survey N. of Akaba but not in the Akaba area. Woolley and Lawrence came from Carchemish where they were doing archaeology (Hittite) for the British Museum under D. G. Hogarth. They joined me at

---

* Evelyn Baring, 1st Earl of Cromer (1841–1917), British agent and Consul-General in Egypt, 1883–1907.
† The Committee of Union and Progress.

Beersheba in January 1914: see *The Wilderness of Zin* [the report Lawrence and Woolley produced to justify the overt purpose of the Sinai survey], and the leg-pull of its dedication to Capt. S. F. N. . . . Both Woolley and T. E. L. enthralled me at night by their archaeological and Biblical history, but to suggest that either of them were secretly working for M[ilitary] I[ntelligence] before that date is to me, ridiculous. T. E. was, of course, very observant, quick on the uptake, with an excellent memory: hence when he and Woolley came to Mil. Intelligence, Cairo, in December 1914 under me, he was able to put various items together better than most of us: due doubtless to his youthful interest in doing so as an archaeologist at Oxford.'*

Newcombe, of course, did not have all the facts, and so in the last sentence of his letter is off the mark. Lawrence was able to 'put things together' because of his training, and although he was not in Military Intelligence before January 1914, he was certainly in, for want of a better term, 'Hogarth's intelligence'. At any rate, Lawrence, Dahoum, and Woolley, under Newcombe, tramped the Sinai Desert for six weeks, mapping the tracks and watering places. Their cover was that under the highly respectable auspices of the Palestine Exploration Fund they were looking for 'the itinerary followed by the Israelites in the course of the famous forty years which they spent in the desert'. At Akaba the Turkish authorities refused to allow the party near the town, but Lawrence and Dahoum slipped by the sentries and carried out a quick survey. When the trip came to an end, Lawrence returned to Carchemish. Newcombe followed soon afterwards and Lawrence gave him such information as he had been able to collect at the site. Then, at Newcombe's instigation, Lawrence and Woolley set out to gather what military intelligence they could about a road that the Germans had built across the Taurus Mountains by which to send supplies for the construction of the Berlin–Baghdad railway. They were lucky enough to find a disgruntled Italian engineer who had been dismissed by the Germans and persuaded him to give them a set of plans for the mountain section of the railway.†

In June 1914 Lawrence went back to London. He and Woolley were being pressed by Lord Kitchener, then British Agent and Consul-General in Egypt, to write their report on Sinai. In a note

* Private letter.
† Leonard Woolley, *As I Seem to Remember*. Allen and Unwin, London, 1962, pp. 88–91.

on the typescript of Liddell Hart's *T. E. Lawrence: In Arabia and After*, Lawrence explained: 'Turkey was sore about the Sinai Survey, which it felt had been a military game. K[itchener] insisted on the Palestine Exploration Fund's bringing out its record of our archaeological researching, p.d.q. [pretty damn quick] as whitewash. Woolley and I had instructions to get it done instanter.'

When war broke out on 4 August 1914 Lawrence was in Britain. He immediately wrote to his friend Mrs Rieder, the language teacher at the American Mission School at Jebail, who was then in the United States, and got her to post him a Colt—he had left his pistol at Carchemish and could not get another in England, where they were hard to come by. In his letter he complained of boredom, and he wrote to other friends regretting that all his preparations appeared in vain because it seemed that Turkey would not enter the war: 'I'm sorry because I wanted to root them out of Syria.' Then on 29 October Turkey attacked Russia and Lawrence's years in Syria were soon to show they had been well spent.

There was, however, a little delay. He and Woolley approached Newcombe and asked his advice about getting a war job. Newcombe recommended them to a colleague in Military Intelligence, but nothing happened. Lawrence then turned to Hogarth, who got him a position, pending bigger things, in the intelligence section of Military Operations, General Staff, drawing the Sinai map. Early in December the posting he was awaiting arrived. Lawrence, Newcombe, George Lloyd,* Woolley and Aubrey Herbert MP, were to proceed to Cairo to reinforce the Military Intelligence Office there. Lawrence sailed from Marseilles on 9 December 1914. The most important years of his life were about to begin.

In Cairo Lawrence settled quickly into his new job. He wrote to Hogarth six days after his arrival saying that he and his colleagues were in the process of setting up an intelligence department from the beginning and 'it promises to be good fun'. Actually, Lawrence was already creating his own network. A few days after he arrived he made contact with his first wartime agent, Charles Boutagy, an eighteen-year-old Christian from Haifa. Boutagy had fled from Palestine on 5 December in an Italian ship, from which he had disembarked at Port Said, and after travelling by train to Cairo, applied to the office of the Sudan Agent to be allowed to enlist in the British army. Instead, he was interviewed at length by Colonel Gilbert Clayton, of Military Intelligence, who interrogated him

* Later Lord Lloyd of Dolobran (1879–1941). Successively High Commissioner in Egypt and Secretary of State for the Colonies.

about the Turkish positions in Haifa and then offered him a job as an interpreter. That same evening Lawrence called on Boutagy at his uncle's house where he had gone to stay. Lawrence introduced himself as a lieutenant attached to Intelligence and told Boutagy that his appointment as interpreter had been cancelled and instead he was to report to Lawrence at Intelligence the following day.

When they met, Lawrence asked Boutagy if he would be willing to go back to Haifa to act as a British intelligence agent—money would be no obstacle. Once a month, unless otherwise arranged, Boutagy would be contacted and he could pass on whatever information he had been able to gather about the Turks. Boutagy was willing to help, but explained that because he was officially a Turkish subject and of military age, he would be conscripted if he were to return to Haifa. He suggested that his father, a prominent citizen of Haifa, might be persuaded to take on the task, and with Lawrence's help a plan was devised. A woman friend travelling to Haifa smuggled a message to Boutagy's father arranging a meeting at night near an ice-plant on Haifa harbour. The son was to be conveyed there aboard an Allied warship and swim back to it after talking to his father. Five separate attempts failed through a series of ludicrous mishaps, the last of which resulted in Boutagy's father being arrested, tried, and eventually acquitted by the Turkish authorities. The sum total of these escapades, as far as Lawrence was concerned, was *nil*. However, Charles Boutagy went on to do other work, no doubt much of it of value. He travelled round the Eastern Mediterranean on Italian ships listening to gossip and making discreet enquiries; he boarded refugee ships to try to locate Turkish spies; he shadowed suspects in Alexandria; and he tried to recruit other agents for Lawrence. Boutagy has told us that he was trained for his missions by Lawrence personally, that he was certain that he was by no means his only agent and that Lawrence appeared to have recruited others before the war began. He is convinced that he was merely a member of a large network run by Lawrence himself. The information he was told to try to obtain was not always straightforward, but often of political or strategical importance: for instance, whether the Turks had given up the idea of an attack on Suez and had returned instead to a defence of the Dardanelles. Lawrence gave the impression that money was not important, provided that his agents produced results. Once when Boutagy asked Woolley, acting for Lawrence, for £5 for expenses, Woolley told him not to be a fool and pushed twenty-five sovereigns into his pocket. And judging from the apparent ease with which Lawrence arranged for allied warships to transport Boutagy to Haifa harbour, it seems obvious that Lawrence already had considerable influence in the right places.

The secret Lawrence, then, was not only a subaltern in the map section of Intelligence, or the scruffy officer whose appearance horrified the general staff—'the untidiest officer in Egypt' was Sir Ronald Storrs's description of him. The secret Lawrence was a tough, hard-working officer (Boutagy says that he seldom worked less than eighteen hours a day), interrogating prisoners and running a network of agents concerned with political and military espionage, and able to push his views, if only indirectly, at a very high level. For example, in a letter to Hogarth on the desirability of seizing Alexandretta, he wrote, 'The High Commissioner* is of the same opinion, and General Maxwell† also. K[itchener] has pressed it on us: Winston seems uncertain, and someone . . . perhaps Parker in the F.O. is blocking it entirely. I think that perhaps you can get a move on . . . can you get someone to suggest to Winston . . . then go to the F.O. if possible . . . tell the F.O. . . . that it is vitally important we hold it' . . . (later) 'Please try to push it through, for I think it is our only chance in the face of a French Syria.'‡

At this stage Lawrence was still dependent on Hogarth to push his views on policy through to ministers and the Cabinet. Later, as the importance of his work increased and his authority grew, he established direct lines of communication. But already he understood the techniques of political in-fighting and was in a position of considerable trust and influence.

* Sir Arthur Henry MacMahon (1862–1949). High Commissioner in Egypt, 1914–16, British Commissioner on the Middle East International Commission at the Peace Conference in 1919.
† General Sir John Grenfell Maxwell (1859–1929). Commanding Officer of the British forces in Egypt, 1914–19.
‡ *Letters*, Nos. 81 and 82.

4 A Special Mission

Lawrence is sent to Mesopotamia to try to rescue a British force trapped by the Turks at Kut. Although only a temporary captain, he overrides the wishes of the generals and incurs the lasting enmity of Indian army officers and the Indian government. His mission fails, but while in Basra he tries to find an Arab nationalist to act as leader of a revolt against the Turks.

Early in 1916 Lawrence joined a mission which must rank as one of the strangest in British military history. Briefly, though only twenty-eight and still nominally a junior intelligence officer with the Egyptian Expeditionary Force in Cairo, he was ordered to contact the commander-in-chief of a Turkish army which had surrounded a British expedition in Mesopotamia and offer him up to £1 million to release the British forces. Lawrence's authority came personally from the chief of the Imperial General Staff, Sir William Robertson. It not only overrode the generals trying to relieve the besieged army, but ignored the refusal of the Chief Political Officer for Mesopotamia, Sir Percy Cox, to associate himself with the project. This was an amazing mission for a young captain and it serves to show the degree of confidence placed in Lawrence by those in London.

The whole sorry mess had begun the previous year. General Townshend, a regular officer of the Indian army, who was in charge of a mixed British and Indian force, had driven the Turks up the Tigris to Ctesiphon, where he had come across some seasoned Anatolian troops who had put him to flight. He had retreated in disorder to Kut and there had entrenched himself, surrounded by Turkish troops under Khalil Pasha, who had as his adviser a German, Field-Marshal von der Goltz, a veteran commander who had reorganized the Turkish army. Ten thousand British soldiers were threatened with annihilation and a special expeditionary corps was formed to rescue them; throughout the winter of 1915–16 this corps made repeated, bloody and unsuccessful attempts to break through to Townshend. Under pressure to end this impasse, the War Office decided on a bold, unconventional stroke in the hope that such an effort might succeed where military tactics had failed. Kitchener, by now Secretary of State for War, first soldier of the Empire, and a man not averse to unorthodox action, liked the idea that Khalil Pasha might be bought off. On 29 March General Robertson sent the following telegram to the General Officer Commanding Force D, near Kut. It makes clear for the first time the importance of Lawrence's part in the operation:

CLEAR THE LINE 14895 CIPHER MOST SECRET AND FOR YOURSELF PERSONALLY. CAPTAIN LAWRENCE IS DUE AT BASRA ABOUT THE 30TH MARCH FROM EGYPT TO CONSULT WITH YOU AND IF POSSIBLE PURCHASE ONE OF THE TURKISH LEADERS OF THE MESOPOTAMIAN ARMY SUCH AS KHALIL OR NEGIB SO AS TO FACILITATE RELIEF TOWNSHEND. YOU ARE AUTHORISED TO EXPEND FOR THIS PURPOSE ANY SUM NOT EXCEEDING ONE MILLION POUNDS. AS NO SUITABLE NATIVE WAS IMMEDIATELY AVAILABLE LAWRENCE PROCEEDS ALONE BUT PERHAPS A SUITABLE GO BETWEEN CAN BE FOUND IN BASRA.*

For orthodox military and political leaders this was not only a startling but a shameful plan—Sir Percy Cox, for one, said it would be worse for British prestige than the surrender of the garrison. And as it was not specified whether this large sum was intended for Khalil Pasha's personal use, or for that of his uncle Enver Pasha, Minister of War and one of the Ottoman triumvirate then ruling the empire, or for the Turkish government, it was quite possible it would be used for prosecuting the war against the Allied Powers. In any case, the British generals in Mesopotamia appreciated that what they had failed to achieve by force, Lawrence was about to attempt by bribery, and they were understandably furious. But as Lawrence's orders came from the CIGS himself there was little they could do about the matter. It was a piquant situation for Lawrence, and no doubt he made the most of it. He left Cairo on 22 March, transhipped at Kuwait, stopped briefly at Basra, then reported at headquarters on board a steamer moored in the Tigris. He was not welcome. Two generals took him aside to explain, in his own words, 'that my mission (which they did not really know) was dishonourable to a soldier (which I was not)'. An accurate description of him would have been political intelligence officer turned HMG plenipotentiary-extraordinary. Lawrence not only ignored the officers: he gave them to understand that he considered them incompetent, and in a

* PRO, FO, 882/13.

report he submitted in Cairo he criticized everything from the system of berthing barges to the conduct of the whole campaign. The report had to be toned down, but word of it got back to Basra, and this was the beginning of a bitter feud between Lawrence and the officers of the Indian army and the Indian government which was to have repercussions on Lawrence's later career. At Kut, however, he was determined not to let the coolness of his reception interfere with his mission.

With Aubrey Herbert, who was also serving in Intelligence, Lawrence tried to carry out his orders to bribe Khalil. Villars says, 'Khalil was distant and derisive, and disdainfully refused the offer of a million and then two million pounds'.* It would appear from this that either Lawrence or Herbert doubled the offer on his own initiative.

Lawrence and Herbert were still there when Townshend surrendered unconditionally, his supplies and ammunition being virtually exhausted and his troops ill with malaria and dysentery. Again Lawrence usurped the role of the generals, and with Herbert met Khalil Pasha, on 29 April, to arrange details of the surrender. They tried to obtain assurances about the fate of the civil population in Kut, which had made the mistake of welcoming the British when they had driven the Turks away, only to find the British forced out in turn. Khalil, whose rise in the Turkish army had been marked by a particularly horrifying massacre of the Armenians at Malasgend, was amused at the Englishmen's concern. He reminded them that Townshend's surrender had been unconditional and would only say that he did not plan to be vindictive. (In fact, his reprisals were confined to the hanging of nine people: a Turkish deserter, a Jewish contractor, an Arab notable and his two sons, two Mukhtars, and two prominent sheikhs.)

Lawrence sent a secret report on his impressions of Khalil to the War Office. It is worth quoting most of it because it shows Lawrence's eye for detail, his knowledge of Turkish army procedure, and his grasp of where the Allies' best chance might be:

'KHALIL himself strong clean built, flat backed broad shouldered, active man, about 35, in accordance with appearances hard and energetic, supple in physique and characteristic. Large straight mouth, thin lips and large hard brown eyes. Without appearing exceptionally clever seems to have good memory, keen alert brain, good general grip affairs and above all personality and force of character. Polite and cordial, though slightly bored with details.

* *T. E. Lawrence*, Sidgwick and Jackson, London, 1958.

Somewhat restless and impatient, which traits combined with his determination and the freedom from fear of consequences which his relationship with ENVER* confers on him, might possibly impel him to rashness of action which would however probably be whole hearted and have strong driving power behind. He sets great store by personal bravery for which he himself is famed.

'He constantly changes headquarters mainly to keep in touch with situation along whole line. He is popular with all ranks. COL. KAZIM BEY, late on VON DER GOLTZ's staff is apparently C.G.S. to KHALIL. Captured diary records that he was to command during Khalil's recent temporary absence in March. KAZIM BEY is solid looking and is said to be highly educated. He probably supplied the brains and caution which are perhaps KHALIL's weak points, but in any disagreement KHALIL would have his way. COL. KIR SAAIS, Commander of the 52nd Division is a jovial, genial, popular man about 40. He was very friendly to our representatives, and from his conversation is probably an Old Turk and ITTILAFI. KHALIL had in his vicinity a staff of about 12 officers, 1 of whom was suspected to be German. Men and animals looked very fit and general impression was one of high moral [sic] and orderly and efficient. KHALIL refused to exchange Arabs with Indians saying that he would only shoot the latter [sic] if returned to him. He opined that 90% of Arabs were disloyal to the TURKS. In view of circumstances under which this information was gained it would not seem desirable to publish it in connection with KHALIL's name. Turkish officers had idea that Germany had broken military power of Russia. Also that there was friction between Entente Powers which they seem to have gathered from journal DES ARDENNES, a paper published in French under German auspices in BELGIUM. Some soreness exhibited over Turkish successes being attributed to German help.'†

Lawrence's main mission had failed, but to try to ransom Townshend's army was not the only reason he had come to Mesopotamia. Colonel Clayton and the other officers in the newly formed Arab Bureau‡ in Cairo had been working on a scheme to employ Arab

---

* Enver Pasha (1881–1922), leader of the Young Turks, who had incurred the hatred of the Old Turks by his ruthless and authoritarian treatment of them.
† PRO, FO, 882/18, May 1916.
‡ Set up on 1 January 1916 by Clayton, who was highly regarded in Arabia. The Bureau comprised 'a tiny intelligence and war staff for foreign affairs'. As 'a duly accorded branch of the Foreign Office' it merited high priority and the armed forces were warned that 'temporary naval or military rank held by officials of the Bureau *is in no way* indicative of their political status or duties'.

nationalism in the service of British war aims, and while Lawrence was in Basra he received a secret directive from Cairo (the relevant details of which are here published for the first time) saying that the time had arrived to put the plan for an Arab revolt into operation. Cairo had rounded up a number of likely-looking nationalist leaders and planned to send them off to Basra as a mission. Lawrence was told, 'As regards actually what you can do both now and when the Mission comes, I have no doubt that we or the War Office will be able to give you fuller instructions, but broadly speaking as far as I can see it will be a matter of seeing how far such Military Co-operation as the Mission can put at our disposal can be made use of and (when their proposals have received the approval of the G.O.C.) to do all you can to get the Arab and our own forces to co-operate'.* Later, with a cynicism—or realism, as it was regarded at the time—which indicates how British officialdom viewed these fledgling Arab nationalist movements, the directive went on, '. . . the most important thing of all (at all events when we are getting into touch and buying people and so on) will be cash.' Lawrence apparently followed these instructions to the letter. According to Suleiman Feidi, a member of the Ottoman parliament before the war, Lawrence asked him to collect a force and rebel against the Turks, promising him a virtually unlimited supply of gold to do this. Feidi declined the offer.

So in Mesopotamia Lawrence was having a dress rehearsal for the role he was later to play when the Arab Revolt got under way. He was also made privy to other aspects of British policy towards the nationalist movement besides those that concerned finance: ' . . . we do not intend to tie ourselves down to any details as to our future relations with such Arab government as it [sic] brought into existence in Irak until we have had an opportunity of seeing what the nature of that government is and how far it is in a position to carry out such assurances as it may give us. In a word for your own information, please note that we refuse to discuss with this party today any other consideration but a simple promise to do all we can to help Arab independence.'*

The same directive contains further evidence of Lawrence's real authority (as distinct from the military captaincy he held in Basra): 'General MacMunn is going out . . . to Basrah. We have had a talk with him and he has promised to give you all support possible. He knows all about you . . . if he won't help you, don't hesitate to wire to us.'*

* PRO, FO, 882/15, 26 March 1916.

Two of Lawrence's replies are illuminating. In the first, dated 8 April, he bluntly sets out his opinions of the Chief Political Officer for Mesopotamia: 'Cox is entirely ignorant of Arab Societies and of Turkish politics. . . . He does not understand our ideas but he is very open and will change his mind as required'.* This was amazing, because Sir Percy Cox had been known for a decade as 'the outstanding Englishman of the Gulf', and as 'Cox the Saint', for his cool and balanced approach to the complexities of Middle Eastern politics. Lawrence's second reply expresses his disillusionment at finding no sentiment for a revolt in Basra: 'I have been looking up pan-Arab party . . . it is about 12 strong. Formerly consisted of Sayed Taleb and some Jackals. The other BASRA people are either from NEJD, interested in Central Arabia only and to be classed with Arabia politically, or peasants who are interested in date palms, or Persians.' Then Lawrence quotes an extract from a letter written over a year earlier by another political agent—Captain William Shakespear. No doubt Lawrence did this as a hint to where he now considered the best hope for promoting a revolt could be: 'If the Sultan of Turkey were to disappear, the Khalifat by the common consent of Islam would fall to the family of the prophet, the present representative of which is [Hussein] the Sheriff of MECCA.'†

* PRO, FO, 882/15, 8 April 1916.
† PRO, FO, 882/15, 9 April 1916.

5 Revolt, Part 1: Paper Promises

The Sherif of Mecca raises his banner in revolt against the Turks. Lawrence, who has recommended that Britain should support the Sherif, and has written a paper outlining his views on the politics and strategy of the Revolt, is attached as liaison officer to Emir Feisal, the Sherif's son and military leader of the Arabs, to ensure that the Revolt runs in Britain's favour. To inspire the Arabs to fight, he promises them freedom and independence, knowing nevertheless that when the war is won Britain's imperial policy in the Middle East—a policy he has had a hand in formulating—will make these promises 'dead paper'. Worried by this deception, he tries to work out a compromise acceptable to his conscience, despite which, being above all a dedicated officer serving his country, he carries out his mission. He immerses himself in the ways of the Bedouin, wearing their clothes and adopting their customs—thus creating the basis of much of the romantic legend about himself— so as to be able to influence Feisal and 'handle' the Arabs; with the result that Feisal links himself to Lawrence and the British for the rest of the war.

In May 1916 Lawrence returned from Basra to Egypt by ship, spending the hot days in the Red Sea writing the explosive report on the Indian army as he had seen it in operation in Mesopotamia. He was hardly back in Cairo when Hussein, the Grand Sherif, pushed a rifle through the window of his house in Mecca, the city where the prophet Mohammed was born, and opened fire on the Turkish barracks, thus signalling the start of the Arab Revolt. The date was 10 June 1916.* This was the birth of the cause in which Lawrence was to immerse himself for the next five years. His part in the Revolt was to be the basis of a renown which has far outlived him. As seen by the American journalist, Lowell Thomas, Lawrence was the Robin Hood of the Desert, the latterday ghazi who led the tribes of Arabia in triumph to Damascus. This romantic

---

* Fighting had broken out five days earlier at Medina, the second holy city of Islam, where two of Hussein's four sons, Ali and Feisal, had deserted with 500 Turkish-trained Arab troops. They had sent a letter to the Turkish commanding officer saying that they were breaking off relations with the Turks on their father's orders and declaring a state of war.

version of Lawrence, the blue-eyed Englishman leading the Arab
Bedouin to victory against their Turkish oppressors, brought a much-
needed whiff of glamour to what had otherwise been a sickening
and sordid conflict. Lawrence added to this legend with his account
of the Revolt in *Seven Pillars of Wisdom,* in which he describes his
leadership in the guerrilla war carried on by the Arabs against the
Turks. But there was another side of himself that Lawrence did
not reveal, a side that some have guessed at but that has never
been fully exposed until now. Lawrence could not have written
about it, even if he had wanted to, because of the Official Secrets
Act to which his duties made him subject. The fact was that he was
there as political intelligence officer attached to Emir Feisal, son
of the Sherif of Mecca: his position was that of an *éminence grise,*
his task to control the tide of the Revolt so that it should run in
Britain's favour. This meant convincing the Arabs that Britain,
above all other countries, had Arab interests at heart and would bring
the Arabs what they most longed for: freedom. As Lawrence put it,
the Arab cause had won a province 'when the civilians in it had
been taught to die for the ideal of freedom'. His role was unenviable
and difficult, for he knew all the time that British policy, which he
had had a hand in formulating, was directly opposed to the sort of
freedom the Arabs wanted, to the type of post-war state they believed
they had been promised and were fighting for.

Lowell Thomas's picture of Lawrence, and in recent years the
film *Lawrence of Arabia,* show him as the champion of the Arabs in
their quest for freedom. They depict him as trying to bring to an
end the jealousies and rivalries of the Arab tribes and weld them
into a free and united nation. The reality, as Lawrence's own
reports now show, was that his main task from the beginning of
the Revolt was to bring the Arabs firmly under British control and
make certain that they remained jealous and divided. Evidence
for this is in a confidential paper he wrote in January 1916, headed
*The Politics of Mecca.** In this paper, written while he was still
nominally a second lieutenant attached to General Staff Intelligence
in Cairo, Lawrence sets out his views on an Arab revolt with neat
if chilling precision:

'... [Hussein's] activity seems beneficial to us, because it marches
with our immediate aims, the break up of the Islamic "bloc" and
the defeat and disruption of the Ottoman Empire, and because

* PRO, FO, 414/461.

*the states he would set up to succeed the Turks would be as harmless to ourselves as Turkey was** before she became a tool in German hands. The Arabs are even less stable than the Turks. *If properly handled they would remain in a state of political mosaic, a tissue of small jealous principalities incapable of cohesion,** and yet always ready to combine against an outside force. The alternative to this seems to be the control and colonisation by a European power other than ourselves which would inevitably come into conflict with the interests we already possess in the Near East.'

These views on the future of Arabia were incompatible with the promises of freedom and independence Britain needed to make to the Arabs to get them to rebel. Lawrence knew the truth of the matter and it irked his conscience. 'I could see that if we won the war the promises to the Arabs were dead paper. Had I been an honourable adviser I would have sent my men home, and not let them risk their lives for such stuff. Yet the Arab inspiration was our main tool in winning the Eastern War.'† So Lawrence 'risked the fraud, on my conviction that Arab help was necessary to our cheap and speedy victory in the East, and that better we win and break our word than lose'.‡ The tortuous double dealing and deceit that this role involved made Lawrence, like all agents playing a double game, doubtful at times where his loyalties lay. In *Seven Pillars* he claims that he worked out a personal compromise—'by leading these Arabs madly in the final victory I would establish them, with arms in their hands, in a position so assured (if not dominant) that expediency would counsel to the Great Powers a fair settlement of their claims. In other words I ... would ... be able to defeat not merely the Turks on the battlefield, but my own country and its allies in the council-chamber'.§ Lawrence's actions in Damascus, as we shall see, certainly appear to suggest that this was his aim. But there is also evidence that his real motives were not so much concern for promises made to the Arabs as his super-patriotic concern for Britain's position in the Middle East; his stubborn determination to see his plan for Syria—which he no doubt believed to be in the Arabs' best interests—triumph over that of his rivals in Whitehall; and his fanatical determination to make certain that the French were not allowed even a toehold in the area. The

* Authors' italics.
† *Seven Pillars*, Chapter XLVIII.
‡ Ibid, p. 24. Introductory Chapter, Penguin edition, 1962.
§ Ibid.

repercussions of Lawrence's actions to achieve all this are still being felt today, and it is in this aspect of his activities that his historical significance lies.

For nearly four hundred years the Ottoman domination of the Arab world had extended without a break from Algeria to the Persian Gulf and from Aleppo to the Indian Ocean. When the last of the absolute Turkish Sultans, Abdul Hamid, came to the throne in 1876, he found Britain, anxious to consolidate her coaling stations on the Arabian seaboard and guard her sea route to India, creeping steadily northwards from Aden* towards the head of the Persian Gulf. In Africa France had seized Algeria in 1830 and Tunisia in 1881. The following year Britain had occupied Egypt and then the Sudan, acknowledging the Sultan's nominal suzerainty as a sop to his prestige. In short, of all the North African coast once dominated by Turkey, the start of the twentieth century saw the Sultan in control only of Libya. Desperate to retain what was still left to him, Abdul Hamid began a reign of repression. All the instruments of government became corrupt, spies and informers were everywhere. The slightest sign of dissent was punished by death, deportation or exile, which, of course, only served to strengthen the resolve of the various Arab nationalist movements. These could be divided into those who were prepared to accept European help to get rid of the Turks and those who saw that co-operation with Britain or France might well lead merely to the exchange of one form of foreign domination for another.

Despite the strength of both movements, it is difficult to say what their attitude would have been at the outbreak of war had not the Turks forced the issue. The Turks were, after all, Muslims at war with Christians and, nationalist ambitions aside, it would have been more in keeping with their religious emotions for the Arabs to have sided with their brothers in Islam in their fight against the infidel. But at the beginning of the war Turkey saw the possibility of getting rid of various minority groups which had been causing her much trouble and undertook a deliberate policy of extermination.

In 1915 thousands of Armenians were massacred and many Chaldean Christians disappeared; famine, disease and repressive conditions killed off thousands of Greek Christians. Until this happened the Arabs had considered themselves reasonably safe;

* Occupied in 1839 and later formally possessed by the Crown; granted independence in 1967.

Lawrence the boy.

Lawrence, aged twenty-two, with his brothers Will, Arnold, Bob and Frank.

they represented an ethnic group too large for liquidation,* and because Abdul Hamid had tried to win them over by integrating them into all levels of Government, there were many Arab army officers and officials indispensable to the functioning of the State. The fate of the Armenians, Greeks, Kurds, and Chaldean Christians seemed to indicate to the Arabs that their turn might come next. When, early in 1915, the Turks found some documents which had been abandoned by a French Consular official, François Georges-Picot, and realized that the documents incriminated certain Syrian nationalists, they hit hard. Jemal Pasha, the Turkish Minister of Marine and GOC, Syria, hanged, imprisoned or deported those incriminated irrespective of rank or record of loyalty. A period of terror began and, convinced that the time had arrived for them to cast off their Turkish masters, the Arabs rose in revolt.

The timing was forced upon Hussein and the Allies by the arrival in the Hejaz of a Turco-German expedition under Major von Stotzingen. The object of this expedition was the building of a telegraph station in the Yemen to link Berlin with the German forces in East Africa; to foment revolts against the Allies in Eritrea, Somaliland and the Sudan; and to be an object lesson to the Arabs in the undiminished might of Turkey. The danger from this expedition was, in the words of Sir Ronald Storrs, 'much greater and more insidious than ever became generally known in England'.† Indeed, 'It is hard to over-estimate the importance of the Turco-German expedition, which might even have taken Aden by surprise'.‡ At the time, Hussein was worried that the mission might try to depose him, and he decided to bring forward the revolt he had planned for August 1916.§

The part Britain was to play in aiding and encouraging this revolt was influenced by deliberations conducted in London soon after Turkey entered the war. In June 1915 an inter-departmental committee under Sir Maurice de Bunsen‖ had examined 'British desiderata in Turkey-in-Asia'. The committee's report is worth examining because it set out early British territorial ambitions in

---

* The total population of the Ottoman Empire in 1908 was approximately 22 million, of whom 7½ million were Turks by race, 10½ million Arabs, and the remaining 4 million Greeks, Albanians, Armenians, Kurds or members of smaller ethnic groups.

† *Orientations*, Chapter VIII. Nicholson and Watson, London, 1943.

‡ Official History of the War: *Military Operations in Egypt and Palestine*, Vol. 1. HMSO, 1928, p. 230.

§ The Stotzingen mission collapsed when the Revolt broke out.

‖ Sir Maurice de Bunsen (1852–1932). After a distinguished career in the diplomatic service abroad, he had joined the staff of the Foreign Office in London.

the Middle East and was the preface to important wartime agreements reached with the Arabs, the French and the Zionists. The
de Bunsen Committee met against a background of claims by
France and Russia for choice cuts of the Ottoman Empire once
the Turks had been defeated. As the historian Aaron S. Klieman
points out, 'British policy-makers were confronted with the choice
of opposing the territorial claims of their Allies against Turkey
from the very outset, or, this proving impolitic, presenting counter-
proposals of their own'.*

The initial success of the Turkish attack in February 1915,
through the Sinai to the banks of the Suez Canal, had convinced
Kitchener that the post-war presence of Russia and France in the
Eastern Mediterranean would threaten Egypt, the Canal, and
ultimately India. Therefore a buffer state to protect Egypt was a
necessity. Lloyd George considered that Palestine would be suitable
for this role, especially as it offered port facilities at Haifa and rail
connections with Mesopotamia. While argument went on one
viewpoint began to emerge with some clarity—Britain was not
going to be left empty-handed in any division of Arab lands.
'If we were to leave the other nations to scramble for Turkey
without taking anything ourselves,' Asquith noted, 'we should
not be doing our duty.'† And Churchill was reported as being most
anxious that Britain 'should be able to appropriate some equivalent
share of the spoils'.‡

In May 1915 a new government, a coalition under Asquith,
came to power. The Allied attempt to invade Turkey by a landing
at Gallipoli had failed and the expedition was fighting for its life.
(It was evacuated in January 1916.) Strategy now shifted from what
was, after all, only a sideshow from a military point of view, back to
France and the real confrontation with Germany. In the vacuum
that this shift of interest created, the two main departments involved
in the Middle East—the India Office and the Foreign Office—now
felt free to pursue their own policies. The India Office, echoing the
feelings of both the civil and military authorities on India, were sorry
that Turkey had entered the war because they preferred the Turk
to the Arab, and were worried about the rise of Arab nationalism
and became furious when the Foreign Office encouraged it. The

* 'Britain's War Aims in the Middle East in 1915', *Journal of Contemporary
History*, Vol. 3, No. 3, London, 1968.

† PRO, CAB, 42/2, 3 March 1915. Papers of the War Council, Dardanelles
Committee and the War Committee.

‡ The Earl of Oxford and Asquith, *Memories and Reflections*, 1852–1927, 2 Vols.
Cassell, London, 1928.

Viceroy, Lord Hardinge, expressed these views when he wrote to
General Sir Reginald Wingate on 21 April 1915, deploring any
suggestion that Arabia should be handed over to the Arabs. 'Our
interests in the Persian Gulf . . . have of late been seriously
endangered by the Germans under Turkish protection. This is a
situation which it would be folly to allow to recur, and it is of no
use for the Arabs to say that this would not happen under their
rule, for it is always possible that it might, and Arabs have not a
great reputation for honesty.'* Eventually the views of the India
Office and the Foreign Office were to become so incompatible that,
according to Arnold Toynbee,† they virtually declared war on each
other and fought by proxy a minor battle to settle by force of arms
what they had been unable to resolve by memoranda.

In this atmosphere of uncertainty the Lawrence–Hogarth plan for
an Arab dominion within the Empire, pledging loyalty to it out of
respect for British law, order and civilization, had a noble air.
If only the perfidious French could be kept at bay and the right
Arab found to lead the revolt against the Turks, then Lawrence
could mould him for his role as Hogarth had moulded Lawrence. . . .
But where was this Arab to be found?

The most obvious candidate was Hussein, Sherif of Mecca.
Hussein was a dignified old man with beautiful eyes, a high forehead and a silky beard. Hogarth described him as full of 'hand-
patting and endearments, beautifully clean and the pink of courtesy',
but with a will of iron. He was the only Arab leader of high religious
standing, a direct descendant of Mohammed and guardian of the
Holy Places in Mecca and Medina. He had been in enforced residence
in Constantinople for seventeen years before his appointment as
Grand Sherif of Mecca and had come to know most of the leaders
of the Ottoman Empire. He was also the only Arab leader known to
Muslims outside Arabia, through his supervision of arrangements for
pilgrims, so he was acceptable to most Arab nationalists. If he agreed
to accept British support and to rise against the Turks this would
successfully counter the call of the Sultan of Turkey for a Jehad,
or holy war, against the Allies, with its risk of uprisings among the
millions of Muslim subjects in British, French and Russian possessions. For these reasons Lawrence considered Hussein the only
possible candidate, and early in 1916 he wrote a long memorandum
headed *The Conquest of Syria: if Complete.*‡ It is a remarkable document

---

* Lord Hardinge to General Sir Reginald Wingate, 21 April 1915, **Wingate**
Papers, Library of Oriental Studies, University of Durham.
† *Acquaintances*, pp. 183–4.   ‡ PRO, FO, 882/16.

in that it sets out the whole aim of the Arab Revolt—its politics, strategy, and tactics—as well as what Lawrence considered should be Britain's post-war aims. Published now for the first time, it includes Lawrence's views on British support for Hussein and the course a revolt should follow:

'This war should, if it resulted in anything at all, take away definitely and finally the religious supremacy of the Sultan [of Turkey]. England cannot make a new Khalifa [spiritual ruler] as she has made a new Sultan [of Egypt] any more than the Japanese could impose a new Pope on the R[oman] C[atholic] Church. Nor can the Sultan of Egypt make himself Khalifa: for his action would be suspect; from his relations with us; and the true Arab and even the Syrian has such a lively contempt and dislike for the loose-mouthed Egyptian as would entirely forbid him ever to recognize any spiritual overlordship assumed by one without the force to support him.

'The most probable claimant—barring the Sultan—to the Khalifate would be the Sherif of Mecca, who has been active in the last few years in Arabia and Syria, asserting himself as an arbiter of morals. He is held down by Turkish money—which we, via Egypt or India could replace with interest—and by a Turkish Army Corps. The only way to rid ourselves of this (hostilities in the Yemen being impossible) is by cutting the Hedjaz line. The soldiers are paid and supplied with arms, etc. along this line, and its existence is always a present threat of reinforcements. By cutting it we destroy the Hedjaz civil government . . . and we resolve the Hedjaz army into its elements—an assembly of peaceful Syrian peasants and incompetent alien officers. The Arab chiefs in the Hedjaz would then make their own play, and for our pilgrims' sake one can only hope, quickly. In any case, if we cut the Pilgrim Railway the Turkish Govt. would irrevocably lose the Haramein and that draws their teeth and renders them harmless. The Beduin tribes hate the railway which has reduced their annual tolls and way-leaves; and would help us cut it. This cutting can be done by occupying Deraa if Damascus is neutralised: at Amman, if Jerusalem can be passed, by blowing up a viaduct: and at Maan by an occupation.'

Here we have, well before the Revolt started, an outline of the tactics Lawrence was to persuade the Arabs to adopt. However, it was nearly a year before he became really involved. For after its initial success in capturing Mecca and securing much of the Hejaz the revolt bogged down in front of Medina. The Turks were besieged, but showed no sign of surrendering. They had plenty of ammunition, food and water and could be supplied indefinitely by the Hejaz railway, which the Arabs had been unable to cut effectively because they lacked the knowledge of demolition techniques. Hussein became anxious because he could not take Medina. His own supplies were getting short and some of his troops, bored by the lack of action, were deserting him. He appealed to the British to cut the Hejaz railway and to give him howitzers and mountain guns, but nothing happened. Hussein later maintained that the cutting of the Hejaz line was one of the main points he had agreed with the British before starting the Revolt and their failure to cut the line greatly harmed the Arab campaign. The British insisted that there had been no such agreement. What had really happened was that the Arab Bureau deliberately held back help to Hussein. As the *Arab Bulletin* of 9 July 1917 cynically noted: 'So long as [it] does not go too far there would be no harm in the Sherif suffering a mild check. He will be more modest and accommodating if he realizes more closely that he is dependent on our help for success.'*

It is clear from this that the British intended from the very beginning that the Revolt should be under firm British control and were determined to make Hussein realize it. They were forced, however, to step in when in October there were indications that the Turks planned to march out of Medina to capture Mecca, hang Hussein, and end the insurrection.

In October 1916 Ronald Storrs, Oriental Secretary to the British Agency in Egypt, and an official held in high trust by the Arabs, went down to Jedda to see what could be done to help the Revolt, in pursuance of his policy of getting the best nationalists to work for, rather than against, the British. Lawrence has described in *Seven Pillars* how he came to accompany Storrs:

'I had believed these misfortunes of the Revolt to be due mainly to faulty leadership, or rather to the lack of leadership, Arab and English. So I went down to Arabia to see and consider its great men. The first, the Sherif of Mecca,† we knew to be aged. I found Abdulla too clever, Ali too clean, Zeid‡ too cool. Then I rode up-country to Feisal,§ and found in him the leader with the necessary fire, and yet with reason to give effect to our science. His tribesmen seemed

* PRO, FO, 882/25, p. 83.
† King Hussein.
‡ These were respectively the King's second, first and fourth sons.
§ The King's third son.

sufficient instrument, and his hills to provide natural advantage. So I returned pleased and confident to Egypt, and told my chiefs how Mecca was defended not by the obstacle of Rabegh, but by the flank-threat of Feisal in Jebel Subh. . . . My chiefs were astonished at such favourable news, but promised help, and meanwhile sent me back, much against my will, into Arabia.'

The difficulty about this account is that it makes it appear that Lawrence went down to the Hejaz almost by accident, as the by-product of a period when he was intriguing his way from army intelligence into the Arab Bureau: 'I took this strategic opportunity to ask for ten days' leave, saying that Storrs was going down to Jidda on business with the Grand Sherif, and that I would like a holiday and joyride in the Red Sea with him.'*

Actually, as we have seen from his reports from Mesopotamia, his paper on *The Politics of Mecca*, and his memorandum on *The Conquest of Syria*, Lawrence had had a leading hand in pushing the idea of a revolt. He had been involved in the correspondence between Cairo and Hussein† and had become unhappy at Hussein's apparent lack of fire. There is no doubt that he went to the Hejaz as a political intelligence officer to assess for himself what should be done to revitalize the Revolt and, in fact, reported to the Arab Bureau on the situation the day after his arrival. Lawrence ruled out Hussein because, as he wrote in a report in 1917, 'once his mind is made up it would be a thankless task to try to make him change it'. (Lawrence, to his cost, proved this to be true when, in 1921, he tried to persuade Hussein to sign a treaty with the British.) He rejected the eldest son Ali because he was in poor physical condition, too pious and, more important, dominated by Hussein. Zeid, the youngest, was only nineteen, had a Turkish mother, and was no fanatic for Arab independence. This left Abdulla and Feisal. Abdulla, the second son, had a natural aptitude for tribal politics and was his father's right-hand man. He was fun-loving but shrewd and direct and interested in Arab independence. But he did not like Lawrence and suspected him of being less than frank. He says in his memoirs‡ that he did not want Lawrence to influence the Bedouin tribes and therefore asked him to confine his duties to railway demolition. Feisal, the third son, a tall, strikingly handsome man, was the most

* *Seven Pillars*, Chapter VII.

† PRO, FO, 882/19. Lawrence's orders concerning a draft letter to Hussein, 23 June 1916.

‡ *Memoirs of King Abdullah of Transjordan*, edited by Philip Graves. Jonathan Cape, London, 1950.

sophisticated and politically dependable. Because his followers
belonged to the more worldly coastal tribes he was able to allow
Lawrence a freedom of movement that Abdulla could never have
permitted among the more wary tribesmen of the interior. There
was also the consideration that Lawrence had an attraction for
Feisal, who found him interested in his difficulties, sympathetic
to his demands, and ready with respectful advice. Feisal thought
he could use Lawrence to further Arab independence in the Middle
East. Lawrence was certain he could use Feisal to divide the Islamic
bloc and to further British control in the Middle East. The aims
of each man were, of course, incompatible and could only result
in disaster.

We must pause here to consider Lawrence's motives. He was
about to become embroiled in the Revolt, supposedly against
his will: 'Clayton* told me to return to Arabia and Feisal. This
being much against my grain I urged my complete unfitness for the
job.'† Actually, Lawrence nearly did *not* get the job because of
falling foul of Sir Reginald Wingate, the Governor-General of the
Sudan and Sirdar of the Egyptian Army, who was responsible for
intelligence about Arabia. On 11 November 1916 London suggested
Lawrence or George Lloyd, who was also a member of the Arab
Bureau. Wingate recommended Lawrence, but then disagreed with
Lawrence's report that Christian troops should not be sent to the
Hejaz because this would give offence to the Arabs. Through some
departmental blunder the report was telegraphed direct to London
without first being shown to Wingate. Wingate commented, 'I
have no doubt that L. has done all this in perfectly good faith,
but he appears to me to be a visionary and his amateur soldiering
has evidently given him an exaggerated idea of the soundness of
his views on purely military matters'.‡ Clayton helped to soothe
Wingate and Lawrence was sent back to the Hejaz. He was about
to devote most of the next six years to an involvement with the
Arabs which—although he had been preparing for it since his first
visit to the Middle East—can be said to have had its official beginning
at this point. By his dress, habits, speech and actions he began the
legend of Lawrence, the champion of the Arabs, Prince of Mecca,
uncrowned King of Arabia. The basis of the legend is that Lawrence
was one of those Englishmen 'who have a *schwärmerei* for the Arabs',§

* Colonel G. H. Clayton, of the Arab Bureau in Cairo.
† *Seven Pillars*, Chapter XVII.
‡ Wingate to Colonel C. E. Wilson, 23 November 1916. Wingate Papers.
§ Hector Bolitho, *The Angry Neighbours*. Arthur Barker, London, 1957.

see in the clear clean air of the desert and the ways of the Bedouin a quality of life not attainable in Europe, and as a result receive from the Arabs in return an unquestioning devotion. The legend has been accepted wholeheartedly by friends of Lawrence, among them Robert Graves.

'He, a foreigner and an unbeliever, inspired and led the broadest national movement of the Arabs that had taken place since the great times of Mohammed and his early successors, and brought it to a triumphant conclusion. . . . If Napolean . . . had been in Lawrence's position at the close of the 1918 campaign he would have proclaimed himself a Mohammedan and consolidated the new Arabian Empire. Lawrence did nothing of the sort, though he had popularity and power enough perhaps to make himself Emperor even without an official change of faith . . . he came away and left the Arabs to employ the freedom that he had given them . . . '*

All that one can say about this is that there is evidence that Lawrence never intended the Arabs to have freedom as we understand the word today. He had no *schwärmerei* for the Arabs. He dressed and behaved as an Arab in order—in the typical colonial idiom—to be able to 'handle' them better. Evidence of his attitude to Arab aspirations towards freedom occurs in his report on *The Conquest of Syria*: 'If we wish to be at peace in S. Syria and hold S. Mesopotamia as well, and to control the Holy Cities, it is essential that the owner of Damascus should either be ourselves *or some non-Mohammedan power friendly to us*'.†

So Lawrence's plan for the conquest of Syria did not envisage Arab control of the capital; lest this evidence be considered inconclusive he goes on to say in the same report: 'The tribes of middle Mesopotamia would not be pleased at being left to Turkey (Pan-Arab feeling is very strong N. of Baghdad) *nor would they be an edifying sight if they were left to form their own government*'.† Later in the same report Lawrence states, 'Presumably if we were thus possessed of all Syria, it would be convenient for us to divide our spoils with France'.

In *The Politics of Mecca* he concludes: Hussein 'has a mind some day to taking the place of the Turkish Government in the Hejaz himself. If we can only arrange that this political change shall be a violent one, we will have abolished the threat of Islam, by dividing it against itself, in its very heart. There will then be a Khalifa in

* Robert Graves, *Lawrence and the Arabs*. Jonathan Cape, London, 1927.
† PRO, FO, 882/16. Authors' italics.

Lawrence in British army uniform with Arabian headdress.

Dahoum photographed by Lawrence.

Lawrence, in Dahoum's clothes, photographed by Dahoum.

Turkish infantry on the march, July 1916.

Turkey and a Khalifa in Arabia, in theological warfare, and Islam will be as little formidable as the Papacy when Popes lived in Avignon.'*

Evidence that Lawrence wore Arab dress and behaved as a Bedouin for reasons other than love or admiration for the Arabs is to be seen in his *Twenty-Seven Articles*, a manual for political officers on how to handle Arabs.† Written in August 1917, when he had been with Feisal for nine months, it shows clearly that he adopted an Arab pose to win the Arabs' confidence and to be better able to guide their ideas and their actions along lines most advantageous to Britain. The importance of this manual has hitherto been under-rated. 'Handling Hejaz Arabs,' says Lawrence, 'is an art, not a science.' In the preamble he writes '. . . we have a great chance there; the Sherif trusts us . . . If we are tactful we can at once retain his good will, and carry out our job.' But it is in his fourth article that Lawrence reveals the most illuminating side of his relationship with Feisal: 'Win and keep the confidence of your leader . . . never refuse or quash schemes he may put forward: but ensure that they are put forward in the first instance privately to you. Always approve them, and after praise *modify them* insensibly causing the suggestions to come from him, *until they are in accord with your own opinion*. When you attain this point, *hold him to it*, *keep a tight grip of his ideas*, and *push him* forward as firmly as possibly [*sic*], but *secretly* so that no one but himself (*and he not too clearly*) is aware of your pressure.'‡

Articles 18 and 19 reveal the real reason why Lawrence dressed as an Arab:

'If you can wear Arab kit when with the tribes you will acquire their trust and intimacy to a degree impossible in uniform. It is however dangerous and difficult. . . . You will be like an actor in a foreign theatre, playing a part day and night for months, without rest, and for an anxious stake. Complete success, which is when the Arabs forget your strangeness and speak naturally before you, counting you one of themselves, is perhaps only attainable in character; while half success (all that most of us will strive for— the other costs too much) is easier to win in British things, and you yourself will last longer, physically and mentally, in the comfort that they mean. . . . If you wear Arab things wear the best. Clothes

* PRO, FO, 414/461.
† PRO, FO, 882/7.
‡ Authors' italics throughout.

are significant among the tribes, and you must wear the appropriate, and appear at ease in them. Dress like a Sherif—if they agree to it.'

Lawrence continues this theme in Article 20:

'If you wear Arab things at all, go the whole way. Leave your English friends and customs on the coast, and fall back on Arab habits entirely. It is possible, starting thus level with them, for the European to beat the Arabs at their own game, for we have stronger motives for our action, and put more heart into it than they. If you can surpass them, you have taken an immense stride towards complete success, but the strain of living and thinking in a foreign and half-understood language, the savage food, strange clothes, and still stranger ways, with the complete loss of privacy and quiet, and the impossibility of ever relaxing your watchful imitation of the others for months on end, provide such an added stress to the ordinary difficulties of dealing with the Bedu, the climate, and the Turks, that this road should not be chosen without serious thought.'

In Article 27 he sums up his views on 'handling' Arabs:

'The beginning and ending of the secret of handling Arabs is unremitting study of them. Keep always on your guard: never say an inconsidered thing, . . . watch yourself and your companions all the time: hear all that passes, search out what is going on beneath the surface, read their characters, discover their tastes and their weaknesses . . . Bury yourself in Arab circles, have no interests and no ideas except the work in hand, so that your brain shall be saturated with one thing only, and you realise your part deeply enough to avoid the little slips that would undo the work of weeks. Your success will be proportioned to the amount of mental effort you devote to it.'

Lawrence, for his part, devoted everything he had to it, and his success was proportionate. Feisal linked himself firmly to Lawrence for the rest of the Revolt. He resisted the blandishments of Colonel Brémond, Lawrence's French counterpart, rejected tempting peace approaches from the Turks, and trusted Lawrence and the British— with only minor misgivings—until the end of the war. But by 1921 he was completely disillusioned: 'He was very bitter about what he considered was the way in which he had been treated by both

British and French and he made some wounding remarks about the British character in general.'* Lawrence, on his side, was later to write, 'Feisal was a brave, weak, ignorant spirit, trying to do work for which only a genius, a prophet or a great criminal was fitted. I served him out of pity, a motive which degraded us both.'†

* Alan Houghton Brodrick, *Near to Greatness: A Life of Earl Winterton.* Hutchinson, London, 1965, p. 20.
† *Seven Pillars*, Chapter CIII.

6 Revolt, Part 2: A Double Act

Sir Mark Sykes and Monsieur François Georges-Picot draw up an agreement dividing the choicest parts of the Ottoman Empire among Britain, France and Russia, leaving little worthwhile for the Arabs. Lawrence keeps the full import of this agreement from Feisal, knowing that if the Arabs discover what has happened they will stop fighting. The agreement is kept from them for nearly two years; then the Bolsheviks seize power in Russia and, as part of their policy, reveal all secret agreements to which Russia is a party, including the Sykes–Picot Agreement. The Turks, seeing a chance to end the Revolt, hasten to tell the Arabs that Britain has betrayed them and offer peace terms. The Arabs are tempted to accept the terms, but King Hussein questions the British, who deny that any such agreement exists and reaffirm their promise to free the Arab peoples. Lawrence and Hogarth work to undermine the Skyes–Picot Agreement—not because it betrays the Arabs, but because it lets the French into their plans for an Arab dominion.

While Lawrence was establishing himself with Feisal and working towards the post-war Arabia that he and Hogarth wanted, certain policies were being developed in the Foreign Office which, in their main outline, were contrary to everything Lawrence was planning. These policies, projected eventually as the Sykes–Picot Agreement— so called because of its originators—belong to a period which can be seen in retrospect to have been riddled with intrigue, double-dealing, inter-departmental warfare, and personal back-stabbing.

Negotiations for this agreement between Britain and France— described by the Arab historian, George Antonius, as 'a shocking document ... the product of greed at its worst ... a startling piece of double-dealing'—began in 1915 and were carried on into the following year. As we have seen, Britain had decided that she would be neglecting her duty if she failed to 'appropriate some equivalent share of the spoils' when Turkey was defeated. The de Bunsen Committee had given much attention to a scheme which involved the partitioning of the Ottoman Empire. One of the committee's members, a fervent advocate of this scheme, was Lieutenant-Colonel Sir Mark Sykes, MP, traveller, politician and expert on the Ottoman Empire. Sykes favoured partition because it would enable Britain, as he said, to 'stand square with our Allies, with instruments we can adhere to, boundaries we can see, and interests we can respect, and consequently shall be able to unite in a co-operative policy with permanent purpose and unanimity'.* These views made Sykes the ideal advocate for Britain during the formal negotiations for the agreement with the French and Russians during 1915-16. His opposite number, France's representative, was Monsieur François Georges-Picot, the former Chargé d'Affaires at the French Consulate-General in Beirut who, at the outbreak of war, had been forced to flee, leaving behind papers which incriminated many Arab nationalists. (See Chapter 5.)

Georges-Picot was a career diplomat of the old school, a member of a distinguished family, and a graduate of the select Ecole des Sciences Politiques and of the Ecole de Droit. He had been posted to Beirut after a brilliant début in the diplomatic service, but when he was sent to London in August 1915 for preliminary talks with Sykes, his knowledge of the Middle East was comparatively slight. The most likely reason for his appointment was that he was a firm believer in the Entente and very pro-British. He had many English friends, and in fact might have passed for an Englishman himself. He was tall and distinguished to look at, with a small moustache and a fondness for tweeds and hand-made shoes. Like Sykes, he was convinced that the Entente should be the corner-stone of French policy in the Middle East. Since the Crusades, France had felt that she had a historic destiny in Syria and Palestine. Britain, for her part, coveted Mesopotamia. Why quarrel over the spoils of war when there was enough for everyone?

Sykes, like Georges-Picot, was a Roman Catholic, and had spent some years at the Jesuit College in Monaco. He spoke fluent French, understood the French mentality and knew better than most members of the Foreign Office, the strength of French feeling about Syria. He came from an old Yorkshire family and his physique bore the marks of an outdoor upbringing. He was over six feet tall, loosely and powerfully built, with a dancing eye and a moustache like Kitchener's. He had a genial smile, a persuasive personality, and a gift of imaginative gesture which, while not always successful, was bound to be unusual.†

* PRO, CAB, 27/1, deliberations of de Bunsen Committee.

† He is credited with being the author of the following telegram sent from the War Office to Allenby just before Jerusalem fell:

IN THE EVENT OF JERUSALEM BEING OCCUPIED IT WOULD BE OF CONSIDERABLE POLITICAL IMPORTANCE IF YOU ON

Sykes's father was a noted traveller, and Sykes had spent a great deal of his boyhood with him in the Near and Far East. He continued these trips as an undergraduate at Cambridge, and on his travels got up to much the same sort of thing in Mesopotamia as Lawrence got up to later in Syria—mapping for the War Office and collecting any interesting items of intelligence that came his way. When war broke out, he became Assistant Secretary to the Committee of Imperial Defence and travelled widely in the Middle East. No one denied his brilliance—he had a quick, perceptive mind— but sometimes he lacked concentration and discernment. He had an exhibitionist streak and given enough encouragement, it was said, could put on a whole play, complete with sound effects of trains and cannon, and taking all the parts himself. He was a dangerous man in an office fight, as the following extract from one of his letters shows: 'I also had to clear up my own position which had been heavily attacked in my absence ... However such worms do not take much dealing with, a few rights and lefts, a breakfast with the P.M. and a successful speech in the House laid them low.'* His main disadvantage in matters of government was that his enthusiasm for the causes he championed sometimes blinded him to other issues. So although he knew better than his collaborator the problems which the Sykes–Picot agreement would bring to the Arabs, he was so dazzled by this new extension of the Entente that he failed at first to see the difficulties to which it must inevitably give rise.

He and Georges-Picot got on extremely well and from the beginning they committed themselves heavily to supporting their agreement, making repeated trips to the Middle East to ensure its application and guarding it from attack at home, where opposition to it had been expressed very strongly in various departments of the Foreign Office. Hogarth naturally suspected the French of some elaborate plot and wrote of Georges-Picot, 'I have never been able to get out of M[ark] S[ykes] what or whom P[icot] really represents. (I know it is the Catholics, but who else?) M.S. says, "Well, the French Government up to Tuesday last"; but admits that he can't vouch for much else, "but, why choke off the only Anglophile, in God's name?" '†

OFFICIALLY ENTERING THE CITY DISMOUNT AT THE CITY GATE AND ENTER ON FOOT. GERMAN EMPEROR RODE IN AND THE SAYING WENT ROUND 'A BETTER MAN THAN HE WALKED'. ADVANTAGE OF CONTRAST IN CONDUCT WILL BE OBVIOUS.

* Letter to Clayton, 22 July 1917. Sledmere–Sykes papers.
† Letter from Hogarth to Clayton, 11 July 1917. Hogarth Papers.

Lawrence thought the agreement had been devised to 'plaster over a split in policy by a formula vague enough for each to interpret in his divergent way'.* He did not like Georges-Picot and had little time for Sykes. (Georges-Picot, for his part, hated Lawrence and contemptuously dismissed him as a *franc-tireur*.)

Lawrence saw Sykes as an 'imaginative advocate of unconvincing world-movements . . . a bundle of prejudices, intuitions, half-sciences. He would take an aspect of the truth, detach it from its circumstances, inflate it, twist and model it, until its old likeness and its new unlikeness together drew a laugh; and laughs were his triumph. His instincts lay in parody: by choice he was a caricaturist rather than an artist, even in statesmanship.'†

Both Lawrence and George Antonius say that before Sykes's death, which occurred suddenly from influenza during the Peace Conference in 1919, he had come to realize that the agreement was a mistake. Antonius says that the strength of the Arabs' desire for independence and unity had begun to dawn on him and with it 'the injustice and folly of the partition envisaged in the Agreement'.‡ Lawrence says, 'He had returned [to Paris] from a period of political duty in Syria, after his awful realization of the true shape of his dreams to say gallantly, "I was wrong: here is the truth." '§

Georges-Picot, however, stuck to the agreement to the last, his belief in paternal colonialism of the French variety unshaken. As acting High Commissioner in Syria after the war, he advised his government that the only way to make it clear to the Arabs that the French were there to stay was to send 20,000 French soldiers to Syria and ask Britain to hand it over—which was more or less what the French eventually did.||

In retrospect, it is hard to understand why more people did not see the Sykes–Picot Agreement for what it really was: a straight-forward imperial carve-up of Ottoman territory as one of the rewards of victory. Under its main terms Britain was to get a band of territory running from the southern part of Syria across to Mesopotamia (now Iraq), where it spread to include Baghdad and Basra—as had been recommended at one stage by the de Bunsen Committee. (It is worth noting that at this period, when the British were promising to do all they could for Arab independence, the Committee, referring to the

---

* *Seven Pillars*, Chapter CI.   † Ibid, Chapter VI.
‡ *The Arab Awakening*. Hamish Hamilton, London, 1938.
§ *Seven Pillars*, Chapter VI.
|| Georges-Picot's career continued to prosper. He became ambassador to Brazil in 1927, retired in 1929, weighed down with honours, and died, a true servant of Imperial France, in 1953.

advantages of taking Mesopotamia, was writing: 'We could develop oil-fields and *establish Indian colonists* with reference solely to our own interests and convenience'.*)

The agreement gave France the greater part of Syria and the Mosul district in Mesopotamia, an idea the British did not object to at the time because it was in keeping with British–Indian strategy of not having a frontier too close to Russia. They changed their minds later, however, when they realized they had given away what could turn out to be some of the best oil-fields in the Middle East. Palestine was reserved for a special international regime of its own— which was to make the Zionists believe that an opportunity was at hand at last to realize their dream of a national home for the Jews. The point about the agreement was that it left hardly anything worthwhile for the Arabs, and if Hussein had got to hear of it there is little doubt that the Arab Revolt would rapidly have come to a halt, the Arabs believing, rightly, that there would be little sense in their helping to defeat the Turks if this merely meant exchanging one master for another. But the agreement was secret. Even MacMahon did not hear of it until Sykes, on a visit to the Middle East, called on him and told him about it. There was no reason to believe that it would ever have been shown to the Arabs—until it was too late— if the Bolsheviks had not come to power in Russia in November 1917 and, as part of a deliberate policy on secret agreements, revealed the Sykes–Picot agreement to the world.

The Turks saw in this an excellent chance to end the Arab Revolt, and the Turkish Commander-in-Chief in Syria, Jemal Pasha (known as the Butcher), hastened to send the news of the agreement to Feisal by secret letters. Jemal said that the British and the French planned to divide Arabia and rule it and that Hussein had fallen into a trap laid for him by the British. Later, Jemal's successor, also called Jemal Pasha (but known as the Lesser), sent emissaries offering the Arabs specific peace terms, which there is reason to believe the Arabs were tempted to accept.

Lawrence got to know all about the Turkish offers, down to the last detail, by the simple method of looking at the files in Feisal's secretariat when Feisal was not there.† This sort of action was not unusual; the British, when they thought it necessary, were not above intercepting telegrams between Hussein and Feisal, doctoring them to suit British policy, and then delivering the revised version.‡

---

* Authors' italics.   † PRO, FO, 371/3381. Hogarth to Foreign Office, no date,
   ‡ Wingate Papers, FO telegram 54402, Commandant Akaba to GHQ.
3 September, 1918.

(Above) *Dr D. G. Hogarth, Lawrence's mentor.*

(Below) *Hussein, Sherif of Mecca, leader of the Arab Revolt.*

(Right) *Lawrence in Arab dress.*

Lawrence, D. G. Hogarth, and Alan Dawnay, in Cairo.

Feisal, disturbed by what the Turks told him, passed their letters to Hussein, who had once assured him that 'A British promise is like gold. No matter how hard you rub it, it still shines.' Hussein replied reassuringly by telegram: 'The Allies are too great and high to have any confusion caused in the slightest thing of our agreements with them',* but just to be on the safe side, he sent the Turkish letters to Sir Reginald Wingate, the High Commissioner in Egypt, and asked for his comments.

Telegrams flew between Wingate and the Foreign Office, which eventually authorized him to reply to Hussein as follows: 'The Turkish policy is evidently to sow distrust between the powers of the entente and the Arabs . . . by suggesting to the Arabs that the Entente Powers desire Arab territory . . . H.M.G. reaffirm their former pledges to His Highness in regard to the freeing of Arab peoples. Liberation is the policy H.M.G. have pursued and intend to pursue with unswerving determination.'†

Jemal Pasha (the Lesser) retaliated by publishing the text of the Sykes–Picot agreement as released by the Russians. The Foreign Office appeared to be cornered, but eventually, on Wingate's advice,‡ and with the approval of Mr Balfour,§ the Foreign Secretary, authorized the British agent at Jedda to send Hussein a masterpiece of evasion, distortion, omission and lies which in effect denied that the Sykes–Picot agreement existed: Wingate's draft reads as follows:

'I have advised agent to say that "Bolsheviks found in Petrograd Foreign Office record of old conversations and provisional understanding (not formal treaty) between Britain, France and Russia early in the war to prevent difficulties between Powers in prosecuting the war with Turkey. Jemal . . . has omitted its stipulations regarding consent of native populations and safeguarding their interests, and has ignored fact that subsequent outbreak and success of Arab revolt and withdrawal of Russia had . . . created wholly different situation". Can I add that we regard agreement as dead for all practical purposes.'

All of this had placed Lawrence in a delicate and dangerous situation. He knew about the Sykes–Picot agreement and French

---

* PRO, FO, 686/37, 11 January 1918.
† PRO, FO, 686/75, FO telegram, 4 February 1918.
‡ PRO, CAB, 27/27, Wingate to FO, 16 June 1918.
§ Arthur James Balfour (1848–1930), later 1st Earl Balfour, Unionist Prime Minister, 1902–5; First Lord of the Admiralty, 1915–16; Foreign Secretary, 1916–19.

and British aims. He had known since early in 1915 that the French wanted Syria in any post-war carve-up. 'The French insist on Syria—which we are conceding to them',* he had written to Hogarth. Admittedly, he had always planned to prevent this if possible: 'If Idrisi [an Arab leader] is anything like as good as we hope, we can rush right up to Damascus, biff the French out of all hope of Syria. It's a big game, and at last one worth playing . . . . Won't the French be mad if we win through?'† The Arab Bureau had been kept informed of the Sykes–Picot developments and in May 1917, Sykes and Picot had gone down to the Hejaz to see Hussein in order to allay his growing fears that his Allies were intending to sell him out. These fears first arose when he learnt that Georges-Picot had been to Cairo to win over Syrian nationalist leaders to the idea of the French taking control of Syria. When this was confirmed to Hussein he sought assurances from Wingate, who suggested that Sykes might try to calm Hussein and pave the way for a visit from Georges-Picot himself.

Accordingly, Sykes went to Jedda, saw Hussein, and then returned with Georges-Picot for further interviews. They had a long audience on 19 May 1917 and another on 20 May. In the years that followed the war Hussein asserted emphatically that no mention of the Sykes–Picot agreement was ever made to him during these audiences and that the first inkling he had of it was when its existence was revealed by the Bolsheviks in November and December 1917, six months later.

Hussein's claim appears to be true, because in 1918 Wingate said in a telegram to the Foreign Office, 'You will recollect that King was never officially informed of Sykes–Picot Agreement'.‡ There is also a record, admittedly second-hand, of what occurred at these meetings between Sykes, Georges-Picot, and Hussein. Lawrence went to Jedda on 22 July 1917, and on 29 July Hussein, in the course of a long private conversation, gave Lawrence his views of the talks with Sykes and Georges-Picot. Lawrence wrote a secret report for the Arab Bureau§ based on what Hussein had told him:

'The main points were that he had altogether refused to permit any French annexation of Beyrout and the Lebanon. . . . He is extremely pleased to have trapped M. Picot into the admission that France will be satisfied in Syria with the position Great Britain desires

* *Letters*, No. 81.
† *Letters*, No. 82.
‡ PRO, CAB, 27/27. Telegram 948. 16 June 1918.
§ PRO, FO, 882/12.

in Iraq. That he says, means a temporary occupation of the country for strategical and political reasons. . . . In conclusion the Sherif remarked on the shortness and informality of conversations, the absence of written documents, and the fact that the only change in the situation caused by the meeting was the French renunciation of the ideas of annexation, permanent occupation, or suzerainty of any part of Syria. But we did not embody this in a formal treaty.'

Hussein said to Lawrence: 'I merely read out my acceptance of the formula: "as the British in Iraq"; proposed to me by M. Picot, since Sir Mark Sykes assured me that it would put a satisfactory conclusion to the discussion.'*

At this remove in time one can only feel sorry for old King Hussein; no written documents, no formal treaty, and on this occasion only Lawrence—who, of course, knew what the British and French were really up to—in whom to confide.

Hussein thought the French had agreed to a 'temporary occupation' of Syria. In fact, the Sykes–Picot agreement, signed and sealed, gave France most of Syria—including the Lebanon—with 'liberty to establish such direct or indirect administration or control as [it] may desire'. (In practice, this meant a colonial administration which lasted until 1945. And in Iraq Britain exercised an indirect control, firmly putting down Arab rebellions until a revolution in 1958 overthrew the pro-British elements in the government.) Hussein might have felt that he had reached a satisfactory conclusion with Sykes and Georges-Picot. But by November, Feisal had become suspicious. The newly-raised Arab Legion at Ismailia had not been sent to join him because the French had shared in its expense and under the Sykes–Picot agreement had to be consulted before it was committed. When the Legion did not arrive Feisal gave Joyce, the British liaison officer, a difficult time. Joyce reported that it seemed 'to lead him [Feisal] to the idea that we are withdrawing support and he has twice asked me lately if the French intervention is the cause of this'. Joyce pleaded with Clayton to inform Feisal of 'the true state of affairs, or authorise me to do so. Otherwise we are not being straight with him.'† All this suggests that even if, as Lawrence claims in *Seven Pillars*, 'I had early betrayed the [Sykes–Picot] treaty's existence to Feisal',‡ he had certainly not told him of its full import. Otherwise, why was Feisal alarmed to hear of details of

* Ibid.
† PRO, FO, 882/7 Joyce to Clayton, 4 November 1917.
‡ Chapter CI.

the treaty from the Turks? Why did Hussein imagine the French were going to be satisfied with 'a temporary occupation' of Syria? And why was Joyce pleading with Clayton to inform Feisal of 'the true state of affairs'?

If Lawrence had not told Feisal the precise terms of the agreement, it was because he and Hogarth and most other members of the Arab Bureau were violently against the agreement and had been working to undermine it—not mainly because of any sense of having betrayed the Arabs, but because the French had been allowed to creep into their plans for the Middle East. Hogarth had even gone from Cairo to London to lobby officials in high places. He wrote a caustic memorandum on the agreement, saying that it unfairly favoured France and ignored the wish of the majority of Arabs to be under British protection because 'we should exploit Arab lands less selfishly than another Power and be more willing to leave them one day to themselves'. This memorandum, as might be expected, made Sykes very angry. He and Hogarth were both writing to Clayton in Cairo, and their letters provide an interesting glimpse of Civil Service in-fighting. At the same time as Hogarth was writing '. . . so far I have found no one who both takes the S.P. Agreement seriously and approves it—except M.S. himself', Sykes was writing a different story: 'Hogarth arrived and played hell by writing an anti-French anti-Agreement memorandum. Pouring cold water on the Arab movement and going in for Gnome-Imperialism [Sykes's term for Government of India mentality] and a British Mecca. He got trounced by the Foreign Office for meddling in affairs without consulting proper authorities . . . thus departmentalism for once served my ends.'

Sykes went on to set out his policy as follows:

'The Entente first and last, and the Arab nation the child of the Entente. Get your Englishmen to stand up to the Arabs on this and never let them accept flattery of the "you very good man him very bad man" kind. I am going to slam into Paris to make the French play up to the Arab cause as their only hope. Colonialism is madness and I believe P[icot] and I can prove it to them. Lawrence's move is splendid and I want him knighted. Tell him now that he is a great man he must behave as such and be broad in his views. Ten years' tutelage under the Entente and the Arabs will be a nation. Complete independence means Persia, poverty and chaos. Let him consider this as he hopes for the people he is fighting for.'*

* Sir Mark Sykes to Clayton, 22 July 1917. Sledmere–Sykes papers.

Sykes had misjudged Lawrence, who was quite prepared for the
Arabs to have ten years' tutelage before independence. Indeed, his
scheme saw them indefinitely under British guidance being directed
towards dominion status. What Lawrence and Hogarth objected
to was the French having any say in the matter. Their view had not
changed greatly since Lawrence's statement more than two years
earlier—'we can biff the French out of all hope of Syria'.

Lawrence had his own secret plans for doing just that. His
reaction to Arab doubts about British intentions revealed by the
publication of the Sykes–Picot agreement was to urge them to fight
all the harder, a move some authorities say was his greatest contribution to the war. His reason was soon to emerge. In outright
opposition to official policy, he was working on a scheme to get
Feisal into Damascus before the Allies and establish him there,
by force, if necessary, as ruler of Syria. He hoped that his government,
presented with a *fait accompli*, would come to its senses, renounce
the Sykes–Picot agreement, and support Hussein, or preferably
his son Feisal, as ruler of Syria under British protection. At the
ruler's right hand would be, of course, Lawrence himself, and under
Lawrence's guidance the dream of an Arab dominion in the Empire
would become, at last, a reality.

7 Revolt, Part 3: The Road to Damascus

Lawrence clashes with his French counterpart in the Hejaz, Colonel Edouard Brémond, over the course the Arab Revolt should take, and defeats him. Free to develop an irregular campaign, he adopts the Bedouin way of life and perfects the guerrilla tactics for which he is remembered. He reports that during an expedition with Auda, a renowned fighting sheikh, he made a lone reconnaissance behind Turkish lines to Damascus, a journey that is still the cause of controversy. With Auda, Lawrence captures the Red Sea port of Akaba and, as a result, is fêted in Cairo. He continues his raids on the main Turkish supply line, the Damascus–Medina railway, blowing up locomotives and viaducts. During a spying expedition to Deraa he is captured and according to what he writes later, tortured and buggered by the Turks. He escapes and later the battle of Tafileh, in which the Arabs defeat a superior force of Turks, becomes the highlight of his military career. During Allenby's drive on Damascus, Lawrence and the Arabs play an important part, the Arabs enthused by a new British declaration that any territory they liberate themselves will become independent. When the city falls and four centuries of Turkish rule is at an end, Lawrence deposes the Arab governor, who he is certain is a traitor, and instals his own candidate, a move which outwits the Australian cavalry general, Chauvel. At a conference Allenby tells Feisal that he is to have nothing to do with the civil government of Damascus. Feisal protests and Lawrence is placed in an impossible position. After hard words with Allenby, Lawrence suddenly leaves Damascus for Britain.

Much has been written of Lawrence's fame as a military leader of the Arab Revolt. He has been compared with Napoleon; described as father of modern guerrilla warfare and as the master from whom Orde Wingate and Lord Wavell drew lessons of strategy and tactics; the man to whom, according to Sir Basil Liddell Hart, the widespread use of guerrilla warfare in World War II can be indirectly attributed. It is certainly true that Lawrence realized that a sophisticated army relying heavily on its communications for its supplies is vulnerable to tip-and-run attacks from guerrilla and subversive forces; and that he helped to wage a war of detachment so successfully that many Turks on the Arab front were defeated without ever having fired a shot. These guerrilla actions drew strength from the fact that they were 'an influence, an idea, a thing intangible, invulnerable, without front or back, drifting about like a gas'.* Yet given the success of these tactics—to say nothing of Lawrence's brilliance as a political officer—his lasting fame is still not entirely explained. After all, the war in the Middle East was, militarily speaking, a sideshow, and Lawrence's campaign a sideshow to the sideshow. Why, then, has he been remembered when greater military men have been forgotten?

It is to the nature of Lawrence's war that we must look to discover the source of his personal magnetism, and here it is apparent that he was taking part in a highly individual campaign. While on the Western Front the enemy appeared as a wave of figures being cut down coldly, mechanically, efficiently, in the desert the enemy was a man you could see, sometimes even smell; the fat Turkish official, one minute sipping coffee in the shade of the railway ticket office, the next bowing slowly out of his chair as the report of a rifle echoes across the biblical landscape. This was a war of centuries-old tribal tactics, wild men on camels against planes and machine guns, courage and endurance against order and discipline.

In a letter to his fellow officer Stirling, free from the restraint of official report writing and with no need to strive for literary effect, Lawrence captured the atmosphere perfectly:

'The last stunt was the hold up of a train. It had two locomotives, and we gutted one with an electric mine. This rather jumbled up the trucks, which were full of Turks, shooting at us. We had a Lewis, and flung bullets through the sides. So they hopped out and took cover behind the embankment, and shot at us between the wheels, at 50 yards. Then we tried a Stokes gun, and two beautiful shots dropped right in the middle of them. They couldn't stand that (12 died on the spot) and bolted away to the East across a 100 yard belt of open sand into some scrub. Unfortunately for them, the Lewis covered the open stretch. The whole job took ten minutes, and they lost 70 killed, 30 wounded, 80 prisoners, and about 25 got away. Of my hundred Howeitat and two British NCO's there was one (Arab) killed, and four (Arab) wounded.

'The Turks then nearly cut us off as we looted the train, and I lost some baggage, and nearly myself. My loot is a superfine red Baluch prayer-rug. I hope this sounds the fun it is. The only pity is the sweat to work them up and the wild scramble while it lasts.

* *Seven Pillars*, Chapter XXXIII.

It's the most amateurish, Buffalo-Billy sort of performance, and the only people who do it well are the Bedouin. Only you will think it heaven, because there aren't any returns, or orders, or superiors, or inferiors; no doctors, no accounts, no meals, and no drinks.'*

In short, Lawrence's war appears glamorous and adventurous and exciting because, as wars go, it was just that, and Lawrence made the best of it. For two years he lived and fought with the Arabs. He wore Arab clothes, went barefoot, ate Arab food, and suffered Arab fleas. He had malaria, dysentery and boils. It was a rough, tough life. Tom Beaumont, Lawrence's machine-gunner, has given the authors a vivid description of it:

'There was no thought of changing or of undressing at night. We slept in a hollow made in the sand with a blanket or two to cover us. It was often four months before we could get a change of clothing. We used aviation petrol to wash clothes. Shaving was with a Players-fifty tin of water to ten men. Lawrence was lucky here in that he didn't need to shave except perhaps once in three or four months. He was incredibly tough and made a point of doing anything the Arabs could do and doing it better. He could ride a camel faster than most of them. He could run alongside and swing into the saddle—about nine feet from the ground—while it was moving, and he could do it more easily than all the Arabs. The Arabs accepted him because of feats like this. He knew how to get along with them. They would go anywhere with him.'

This is the basis of the legend of the Prince of Mecca, the Robin Hood of the Desert. And yet Lawrence's first battle in the desert was not at the head of the Bedouin, or even against those traditional officers of the British and Indian armies he so heartily disliked. It was against a French officer, who, if he had had his way, would have cut short the legend of Lawrence of Arabia by changing the whole nature of the Arab Revolt. The officer was Colonel Edouard Brémond, head of a mission sent to Jedda in September 1916 to match the influence of the British with Feisal.

Brémond was a professional soldier at mid-point in an outstanding career (he became a general at forty-nine). He had been at the famous St Cyr military academy and had served in Morocco and Algeria. He was a scholar, a linguist who spoke perfect Arabic, and a man of culture and integrity. But he was abrupt, patronizing,

* Letter to W. F. Stirling, 25 September 1917, Bodleian Library.

jealous of his reputation, and filled with a distrust of the English that was not untypical of French colonials at that time. Brémond was all in favour of regularizing the Revolt, the pouring in of large numbers of French and British troops for a conventional confrontation with the Turks; a policy which, incidentally, had support in some British quarters because the Bedouin could not cope with Turkish regular soldiers.

Lawrence was bitterly against this. The Bedouin would desert immediately. if they saw foreigners, especially infidels, landing in their country. The war would have to be an irregular one, fought mainly by the Arabs themselves, but with the Allies furnishing arms, gold, food, and a few English officers. Brémond said later that Lawrence was against regularization because it would have ended his own romantic and independent role. He was scornful of Lawrence's military qualifications, describing him as 'completely ignorant of the art of command'—and attacked him personally, claiming that his behaviour made him a case for a psychiatrist. Lawrence said Brémond favoured regularization because the arrival of large numbers of French troops would mean promotion for him. Lawrence considered, no doubt correctly, that Brémond had no faith in the Revolt, and indeed that an explosion of Arab nationalism could only cause trouble in those French and British colonies where there was a large Muslim population—a view which approximated to that of many officers of the Indian government. Furthermore, Brémond spoke openly of a French Syria, and this so disturbed Lawrence that he could hardly contain his anger. In the end, Lawrence's views prevailed. He out-manoeuvred Brémond, who failed to get sufficient support from his government. Their meetings became barely polite and the bitterness between them was to last the rest of their lives.

Once Lawrence had succeeded in bending the policy of the Revolt to suit himself, he needed a successful action to demonstrate his wisdom in doing so. This was provided by his second battle, which is perhaps the main basis for his fame: the capture of the Red Sea port of Akaba in July 1917. While Lawrence was at Feisal's camp at Wejh, helping to organize the Arab forces, Auda, Sheikh of the Abu Tayeh clan of the Howeitat tribe, described by Lawrence in *Seven Pillars* as 'the greatest fighting man in Northern Arabia', joined the Revolt. Auda played a leading part in the attack on Akaba and some say that the plan was in fact his. Others insist that it was Lawrence's idea, still others that it was Feisal's. It is impossible at this distance in time to unravel the truth.

The plan, whoever its originator, was to cross the desert with a few tribesmen, move north-west, raise the local tribes in revolt, then strike at Akaba from the rear. It was a dangerous and unconventional move, but if it were to succeed the Turks would lose their last port in the north of the Red Sea, one they had been using as a base for mine-laying, and the Arab army would be in contact with the army of Egypt.

The expedition left Wejh on 9 May 1917 and headed north. It included—besides Lawrence—Auda; Sherif Nasir, one of the most ardent leaders of the Revolt; two Syrians, Nasib al Bekri and Zeki Drubi; and thirty camel-men armed with rifles. In his saddle bags Lawrence carried twenty thousand gold sovereigns to help to spread the Revolt. The little band crossed one of the hottest and most arid landscapes in the world, two hundred miles of thirst, dirt, hunger and exhaustion. When they reached Wadi Sirhan there was a respite while Auda, Nasir, and the Syrians persuaded the tribes to give their support to Feisal. Lawrence has said in *Seven Pillars* that this left him little to do, so he planned to 'go off by myself... on a long tour of the north country. I felt that one more sight of Syria would put straight the strategic ideas given me by the Crusaders and the first Arab conquest....'* Lawrence was away from the camp from 5 to 16 (or 18) June. This was the famous Damascus trip which has aroused so much controversy. In his report to the Arab Bureau on 10 July 1917† Lawrence said that he had been behind enemy lines to Damascus where he had met the Arab in charge of the Turkish forces, Ali Rida al Rikabi. (Actually, Rikabi, a retired general, was then mayor of Damascus.) He had interviewed sheikhs in several areas to discover their loyalties, carried out a reconnaissance, damaged the Hejaz railway line at several places, and wrecked a train.

This was a remarkable feat and contributed, with the capture of Akaba, to Lawrence's being appointed a military Companion of the Bath. It is known, in fact, that Sir Reginald Wingate recommended Lawrence for the Victoria Cross ('A magnificent achievement... one of the finest done during the whole war.'‡), but because the exploit did not fulfil certain requirements for this award—it had not been witnessed by an officer, for one—the recommendation was not acted upon.

Some of his biographers doubt that Lawrence ever made this

* Chapter XLVIII.
† *Letters*, No. 97.
‡ Wingate Papers. Wingate to Colonel C. E. Wilson, 15 July 1917.

journey to Damascus. Suleiman Mousa claims that he interviewed two Arabs who were with Lawrence during this period—Nasib al Bekri and Faiz al Ghussein—and others indirectly involved, and that Nasib al Bekri told him that at this time Lawrence was not absent from the camp even for a day. Suleiman Mousa says Faiz Al Ghussein considered it would have been impossible to cover the distance involved in the time, and asked, 'Was Lawrence a bird to have gone all these distances?' He argues that the journey would have been impossible because Lawrence could not have hidden his identity for twenty-four hours, particularly in a country where the people are naturally inquisitive. 'Every time an Englishman attached to the Arabs went on a mission, he went with a Sherif or an Arab the Sherif would trust. Who were Lawrence's companions on this expedition? Where did they stay from day to day? Where did they get their food? Why did Lawrence devote so little detail in *Seven Pillars* and *Revolt in the Desert* to what was considered a major exploit? The account does not ring true. It has many contradictions. I am convinced the trip to Damascus never took place.'*

Lawrence's diary tends to confirm his own account. Written on army message forms, rubbed and occasionally illegible where they have been folded and kept in his belt, they begin in much the same way as his report to the Arab Bureau. The reference to the Damascus trip, published here for the first time, begins, 'O my . . . I'm terrified [determined] to go off alone to Damascus . . . to get killed . . . for all sakes try and clear this show up before it goes further. We are calling them to fight for us on a lie and I can't stand it.' Later Lawrence has written, '[I] learnt that Hachim was NE of Ragga and Ibn Murshid in prison in Damascus and my plan thus failure . . . I was able to get satisfactory assurances . . . in el Gabbu [Gaboun] . . . has been entrusted by the Turks with the defence of Damascus.'†

The secrecy and apparent discrepancies in Lawrence's various accounts of the exploit can perhaps be explained on the grounds of security. Sir Reginald Wingate, in his recommendation for the VC, for example, mentioned that he felt it necessary to curtail the official communiqué and had 'confined the scope of his reconnaissance in public to the Maan–Akaba neighbourhood'. It seems inconceivable that Lawrence could have successfully fooled men of the knowledge and perception of Clayton and Wingate. The

* Interview with the authors.
† British Museum MS 49515. Omissions are due to illegibility.

evidence is deeply conflicting, but in the light of what is known about Lawrence's courage and endurance it seems not unreasonable to believe that he did undertake a solitary mission of some sort involving grave difficulties and dangers. And it is not out of keeping with his character that he may have deliberately added to the mystery of this journey by his own reticence. The issue must remain unresolved.

On or about 19 June 1917 the second part of the expedition's plan began: the attack on Akaba. The band had now grown to some 500 men and on 2 July they attacked the Turks holding the pass at Aba el Lissan which commanded the route to Akaba. After an inconclusive morning's fighting, Auda led his men against the Turks in a camel charge. Lawrence, driving his camel wildly at the enemy and firing his pistol as he rode, accidentally blew out his mount's brains and was thrown heavily and knocked out. When he recovered consciousness the battle was over. Three hundred Turks were dead and there were 160 prisoners—for the loss of two Arabs. With Aba el Lissan taken, Akaba was a plum. It surrendered on 6 July, exactly two months after Lawrence had set out from Wejh. On his return to Cairo, Lawrence found himself something of a hero. The capture of Akaba meant that the line of Turkish communications was now menaced for six hundred miles. Only Brémond tried to minimize the victory, but nevertheless later he prepared a citation recommending Lawrence for the Croix de Guerre, and when it was approved he himself presented the award to Lawrence.

In August 1917 Feisal and his forces and Lawrence were transferred from Wingate's command to General Allenby's. This transfer 'did something the implications of which could not have been foreseen—It moved Feisal [and Lawrence] from the restricted and defined field of military operations for the freedom of the Hejaz, to the far wider and more complicated territory of a world war and world politics'.*

Lawrence took full advantage of this new role and of the favourable atmosphere he found with Allenby. He asked for and was given a free hand for his future action and £200,000 in gold to distribute. How much did gold contribute to the success of the Revolt? There

* R. E. L. Wingate, *Wingate of the Sudan*. John Murray, London, 1955.

is reason to believe that this supply of sovereigns was a factor which, until now, has been much underrated. Suleiman Mousa says that Lawrence's fame and prestige in the eyes of the Bedouin began with gold. 'They decided that a man would have to be a very important representative of his government to have responsibility for such large sums of money.' And after Lawrence's death Sir Reginald Wingate wrote privately: 'There can be no question of his personal pluck, gallantry and resources, but the money with which I was able to supply him in such large quantities had much more to do with the success of the Arab operation than is realised.'* With gold or without, there is no doubt that by now, despite criticism from some Arabs of Hussein's willingness to use infidels, Lawrence was a popular hero with those Arabs who knew him. Some of the English officers who went with him to the Bedouin camps have described the enthusiasm of the greetings, the cries of his name as pronounced by the Arabs, 'Aurens, Aurens', repeated over and over again. But his popularity and the series of railway raids which he now carried out were, he felt, not enough for the new commander in chief, General Allenby, and in October, the same month in which the Germans paid the British the compliment of starting an Arab Bureau in Damascus, he proposed a raid on the Yarmuk viaduct inside the Turkish lines, with the aim of cutting the only means of communication between the north and the Turks on the Palestine front. The raid failed when a noise alerted a Turkish sentry just as Lawrence was about to place his explosives. But en route to the Yarmuk an incident of some significance had occurred. An Arab notable of Algerian birth, Abd el Kadir, disappeared from Lawrence's expedition. Brémond had told Lawrence that Abd el Kadir was a Turkish agent, but the fact that the warning came from Brémond was enough to make Lawrence take the Algerian along with him. He now became suspicious, and in view of what then occurred to him, his doubts hardened to certainty. Lawrence decided to make a reconnaissance of Deraa, the heart of the Turkish communications centre. Wearing ragged Arab clothes, he entered the town accompanied by an old peasant. He has vividly recorded (in *Seven Pillars* and in a letter to Charlotte Shaw) how he was captured and dragged before the Bey, then beaten, tortured and buggered before he could escape. (See Chapter 15.) The incident is mentioned at this point because Lawrence reported later that he believed that Abd el Kadir and his brother Mohamed Said betrayed both the Yarmuk mission

* Wingate Papers.

and his reconnaissance in Deraa and this belief greatly influenced Lawrence's actions after the fall of Damascus.

In January 1918 Lawrence took part in a battle which has been described as the highlight of his military career. This was the battle of Tafileh, when three Turkish infantry battalions (comprising about nine hundred officers and men), a cavalry company, and two Austrian mountain guns, attempted to re-take a village which was occupied by Hussein's youngest son, Zeid, with about three hundred men. According to Lawrence's report to the Arab Bureau, he suggested the tactics for the battle. A few troops supported by villagers (who would have been executed if the Turks had re-occupied the town) broke the Turks' advance, then fell back. Other light detachments, falling back successively, occupied the Turks, breaking the spirit of their advance until they ran into fire from Egyptian and Moroccan machine guns. A hundred men armed with light machine guns then turned the enemy's right flank and cut them to pieces with sustained fire. It was a classically perfect manoeuvre. The Turks lost four hundred dead, two hundred and fifty prisoners, twenty-seven machine guns, and two hundred pack animals. This was Lawrence's last solo effort and for it he was awarded the Distinguished Service Order. By July the war had moved a long way towards being 'regularized'. (Brémond was not around to see it. Discouraged, he had abandoned command of the French mission at the beginning of the year and had returned to France, gone, though only temporarily, from Lawrence's life.) Feisal's army now had attached to it three hundred Camel Corps men, thirty-five Egyptian sappers, thirty Gurkha machine gunners, one hundred and forty North Africans and forty Englishmen (to man five armoured cars equipped with artillery and machine guns). Lawrence wrote, 'Now the desert was not normal, indeed it was shamefully popular'.

On 19 September Allenby ready for the final push, struck at the weakened Turks. Using his two-to-one superiority with masterly tactical skill, he flung the full force of the British XXI Corps against the Turk's left wing, forcing it to fall back in disorder. Allenby's cavalry poured into the opening thus made and by sunset on the second day of the battle the British held three sides of a rectangle within which were trapped the entire Turkish Seventh and Eighth Armies. The only way of escape lay across the Jordan, but this was fast being closed by divisions of the XX Corps. In the hilly regions beyond the Jordan the Arab forces were moving on the Turkish II Corps, and on a signal from Feisal the whole countryside had risen to attack the demoralized Turks. It was a magnificent victory and one in which the Arabs had played no small part. All that remained was for the remnants of the Turkish army to be driven northwards; then Damascus could be taken, thus finally ending four hundred years of Ottoman domination.

It is easy to imagine the emotion that swept through the Arabs with news of the advance on Damascus. King Hussein saw it as the climax of his struggle and the realization of his ambitions. As we have seen, the visit of Sykes and Georges-Picot, because they failed to tell the King the import of the Franco-British agreement to dismember Syria, had left him firm in his belief that the future of Syria was in his hands. More than one British official had become worried about this misunderstanding. On 31 July 1917, in a secret note to Wingate, the British Agent in Jedda, Lieutenant-Colonel C. E. Wilson, had written: 'I do not know if His Majesty's Government has been informed of this fear of a misunderstanding as to what was or was not, agreed upon at the meeting between Sir Mark Sykes, Monsieur Picot and the Sherif . . . I am much afraid that, if the Sherif is under a genuine (or what he considers a genuine) misunderstanding a serious and difficult situation will almost surely arise because the Sherif will consider that His Majesty's Government have broken faith with him.'* During the same month Clayton had written to Sykes: 'Fuad el Khatib† has come to Cairo and from conversations with him it appears almost certain that the Sherif has not at all understood the situation, as explained to him, by you and Picot, regarding the future of Syria and Iraq. He seems under the fixed impression that both will fall to him unconditionally and has given this out publicly.'‡ Clayton suggested that an 'aide-memoire' on what was intended be given to the Sherif, but the Sherif later insisted that he never received any such memorandum.

Then in June 1918, still another declaration of British policy was issued. Seven Arab nationalist leaders in Cairo expressed concern that they might be subject to rule by Hussein, whom they regarded as Bedouin and unsophisticated. Probably because Turkish propaganda over the Sykes–Picot agreement and feeling over the Balfour Declaration (see Chapter 8) were 'working havoc with the Anglo-Arab

* PRO, FO, 882/12.
† Acting Foreign Secretary to Hussein.
‡ PRO, FO, 882/16.

alliance',* the British government felt obliged to make fresh promises to the Arabs. These promises were set out in a document known as the Declaration to the Seven (Syrian nationalist leaders), a copy of which went to Hussein and to Feisal. Its two main points were that Arab territories which were free and independent before the war would remain so and that in territories liberated by the Arabs themselves the British government would recognize the 'complete and sovereign independence of the inhabitants'; elsewhere governments would be based on the consent of the governed. We shall shortly see just how little these promises meant.

This Declaration threw matters into even greater confusion than before. Did it mean, for example, that the Sykes–Picot agreement was to be allowed gracefully to die? Were French interests to be ignored? Lawrence certainly thought so, and took heart at the thought that his plan for Feisal and for Syria stood a chance of success, provided he could reach Damascus first, install a strong Arab government, and present the Allies with a *fait accompli*. For their parts, Wingate and Allenby were uncertain what effect the Declaration would have. Five days before the first Allied troops entered Damascus the Foreign Office sent Wingate the following telegram:

IF GENERAL ALLENBY ADVANCES TO DAMASCUS IT WOULD BE MOST DESIRABLE IN CONFORMITY WITH ANGLO-FRENCH AGREEMENT OF 1916 HE SHOULD IF POSSIBLE WORK THROUGH AN ARAB ADMINISTRATION BY MEANS OF FRENCH LIAISON. WE HAVE TELEGRAPHED TO HIM IN THIS SENSE.†

Throughout the last stages of the campaign Allenby found himself pursued by dispatches like this exhorting him to stem Arab aspirations and remember the Sykes–Picot agreement. The political niceties of the situation made his position an unhappy one. He was a plain, blunt man, heavily built with an almost super-martial appearance, known to his troops as 'The Bull'. He loved fishing and gardening and the English countryside and once went through a course of horse-shoeing with a local blacksmith. He was an inventive and resourceful commander in the field, but he hated the intrigue in which political considerations sometimes involved him. So when asked by the Australian General, Harry Chauvel—who was to lead the cavalry advance on Damascus—what was to be done about the administration of the city once it was captured, Allenby replied,

* Antonius, p. 270.
† Allenby papers.

'You know what we did at Jerusalem. Do exactly the same. Send for the Turkish Wali [Civil Governor] and tell him to carry on, giving him what extra police he requires.'*

Chauvel then asked, 'What about these Arabs? There is a rumour that they are to have the administration of Syria.' Allenby replied, 'Yes, I believe so, but that will have to wait till I come and, if Feisal gives you any trouble, deal with him through Lawrence, who will be your liaison officer.'† Feisal was to give trouble, but Lawrence was not the man to deal with him, for the simple reason that Feisal's trouble-making was at Lawrence's instigation and received his support. Allenby was later to realize this and it was to lead to a bitter scene.

So with the Allies poised at the gates of Damascus, a three-cornered battle was about to develop between Lawrence, Chauvel, and Mohamed Said and Abd el Kadir—the Algerian brothers whom Lawrence believed had betrayed him at Deraa. At stake was control of Damascus and, through it, the realization of Arab aspirations. What happened is important in Lawrence's story because it makes clear at last the reason for his sudden departure from Damascus at a time when it would seem that he should have been enjoying his greatest triumph.

The story begins in the city itself at noon on 30 September 1918. The Turkish administrators, warned by the army that it would be only a matter of hours before the city fell, packed their papers and prepared to evacuate it after four centuries of Ottoman rule. Before the Wali departed he summoned the Algerian leader, Mohamed Said, and told him that the Turks were withdrawing. While the last Turks were still leaving the city, Mohamed Said hoisted the Hashemite flag, the colours of King Hussein, over Government House, formed a provisional council of government and declared Syria independent in the name of Hussein. He then sent telegrams to the main cities in Syria and the Lebanon informing them of the withdrawal of the Turkish forces and asking them to form Arab administrations in the name of the King.

By sunset the Allies were just outside the city, and the 14th Cavalry Brigade was within sight of the southern entrance. Beyond this brigade lay the Arab forces under Sherif Nasir. In *Seven Pillars* Lawrence claims for the Arabs the honour of entering the city first. He describes how during the night, 4,000 armed Arab tribesmen

---

* Chauvel's report for the Australian War Memorial, Canberra ACT, now among the Allenby Papers, St Antony's College, Oxford.
† Ibid.

went into Damascus.* General Chauvel does not agree with this.
He contends that the Arabs could not have slipped past the cavalry
brigade, that there was not enough time for them to have made a
detour, and that the first Arab forces to enter Damascus were those
which arrived with Lawrence the next morning, 1 October, by
which time 'an Australian Brigade [the 3rd Light Horse] and at
least one regiment of Indian cavalry had passed right through the
city'.† He confirmed this in a telegram to Allenby according to
which the advance Australian units entered Damascus on the night
of 30 September:

THE AUSTRALIAN MOUNTED DIVISION ENTERED OUTSKIRTS
OF DAMASCUS FROM THE NORTH-WEST LAST NIGHT. AT 6 A.M.
TODAY THE TOWN WAS OCCUPIED BY THE DESERT MOUNTED
CORPS AND THE ARAB ARMY.‡

Lawrence, who was none too fond of the cavalier attitude of the
Australians towards what he regarded as a high moment of history,
wrote in *Seven Pillars* that they 'ran the campaign as a point-to-point
with Damascus as the post'. Glory aside, the argument about who
actually entered the city first is not important politically because the
Arabs in Damascus had already acted to declare their independence.
Allenby was quick to point this out to the War Office. 'When my
troops entered the city ... an Arab administration was in being
and the Arab flag was flying from the Government buildings.'§

Although generally this was in keeping with the plan Lawrence
had envisaged, on one point matters had gone wrong; the government in Damascus was in the hands of Mohamed Said, the Algerian
whom Lawrence claimed had betrayed him at Deraa. This did not
suit Lawrence at all. He hastened to alter the position.

He had been delayed because at a conference on 25 September
Allenby, in approving Chauvel's plans for the capture of Damascus,
had assigned Feisal and his troops to a position east of the Jordan
under Major-General Sir George Barrow with Lawrence acting as
liaison officer. But by 30 September it was clear that the main thrust
into Damascus would be made by Chauvel and that Barrow's
division was becoming virtually a reserve. Lawrence, anxious to be
back at the centre of events, slipped away from Barrow before dawn
on 1 October without telling anyone.

---

* Chapter CXIX.
† Chauvel's report.
‡ Allenby Papers.
§ PRO, CAB, 27/34. Allenby to War Office, 6 October 1918.

'When dawn came we drove to the head of the ridge, which stood over the oasis of the city, afraid to look north for the ruins we expected; but, instead of ruins, the silent gardens stood blurred green with river mist, in whose setting shimmered the city, beautiful as ever, like a pearl in the morning sun. The uproar of the night had shrunk to a stiff, tall column of smoke, which rose in sullen blackness from the storeyard by Kadem, terminus of the Hedjaz line.

'We drove down the straight banked road through the watered fields, in which the peasants were just beginning their day's work. A galloping horseman checked at our head-cloths in the car, with a merry salutation, holding out a bunch of yellow grapes. "Good news: Damascus salutes you".'*

Chauvel learnt of Lawrence's absence from Barrow's camp when he went to see Barrow at about 7.30 a.m. Chauvel, a tough, country-born Australian, who rose to be 'the best leader of horse in modern times', and one of his country's greatest generals, was angry about this: 'I was anxious to get the civil administration of Damascus arranged for without delay and here was my only political adviser gone off without any instructions and without, so far as I knew, knowing what those instructions would be.' He decided to enter the city himself. He found Lawrence outside Government House, surrounded by a crowd of exuberant Arabs, one of whom Lawrence introduced as Shukri Pasha. Chauvel writes:

'Lawrence's excuse for his unceremonious departure from General Barrow was that he thought I would like him to come in at once and find out what the situation was and tell me. He then proceeded to tell me that Shukri was the Governor of Damascus. Shukri was quite obviously an Arab so I said, "I want to see the Turkish Wali. Will you send for him at once." Lawrence then informed me that the Wali had fled the day before ... and that Shukri had been elected Military Governor by a majority of the citizens. I took Lawrence's word for it and, on behalf of the Commander-in-Chief, agreed to Shukri's appointment, arranging with Lawrence to be liaison between us and telling him to let me know as soon as possible what police would be required.'†

Lawrence had won the first round; an Arab was governor of Damascus and Lawrence had put him there. What had happened to

* *Seven Pillars*, Chapter CXIX.
† Chauvel's report.

Emir Mohamed Said, the Algerian who had taken over from the
Turks? Lawrence claims that he deposed him. When the Arab
forces had entered the city at about 6 a.m. Mohamed Said had sought
out Sherif Nasir, Feisal's second in command, and asked him to take
over the government. Nasir, ill and exhausted, declined, and instead
gave Mohamed Said written authority to carry on: 'H. H. Emir Said
is authorized to take charge of the administration till the arrival of
our Lord Emir Feisal.'*

As soon as he learnt of this arrangement, Lawrence set about
undoing it. 'Emir Said and Abd el Kadir . . . were not nationalists
working with Feisal . . . they were working with the Ottoman Government and were in touch with France . . . When Lawrence expressed
a desire to depose them I agreed.'† Why was Lawrence so bitterly
opposed to Mohamed Said taking charge pending Feisal's arrival?
In a secret report to the Chief Political Officer GHQ Cairo, on
28 June 1919‡ Lawrence sets out his reasons and describes the action
he took.

'I want to begin at the beginning about this as to do so will probably put the question at rest for good. These brothers Mohamed Said
and Abd el Kadir were judged insane in 1911, but escaped detention
in asylums by free use of their wealth. Mohamed Said holds a
world's record for three successive fatal pistol accidents . . .

'The Ottoman Government decided that they might be useful,
and Abd el Kadir offered to run a counter-Sherifian Arab propaganda . . . against the British in Egypt. He was accordingly . . .
sent down to Damascus. Thence he made a sham escape to Feisal,
and went on to Mecca (in October 1917). He persuaded Hussein
that he was a man of first importance in Syria, and was commended
by him to Feisal. He returned to Akaba in the end of October 1917,
and was sent up by Feisal with Ali ibn Hussein and me, to try and
cut the Deraa bridges behind von Kress during Allenby's Jerusalem
push.

'Abd el Kadir was a fanatical Moslem, and had been much
annoyed by the Sherif's friendship with the British . . . [He] deserted
one night from Azrak . . . and rode into the Turks at Deraa. He told
them the results of his mission, and especially that Ali and I were
going for the Yarmuk bridge that week. The Turks ordered out

---

* *Memoirs of Emir Said*, published in Arabic in Damascus, p. 105.
    † Dr Ahmad Qadri, *My Memoirs of the Great Arab Revolt*, in Arabic, Damascus,
1956, p. 74.
    ‡ Privately owned.

cavalry to intercept us, but we made our attempt that very night, failed, and slipped back before the Turkish cordon was complete. Abd el Kadir then went to Damascus. I went into Deraa in disguise to spy out the defences, was caught, and identified by Hajim Bey, the governor by virtue of Abd el Kadir's description of me. (I learned all about his treachery from Hajim's conversation, and from my guards.) Hajim was an ardent paederast and took a fancy to me. So he kept me under guard till night, and then tried to have me. I was unwilling, and prevailed after some difficulty. Hajim sent me to the hospital, and I escaped before dawn, being not as hurt as he thought. He was so ashamed of the muddle he had made that he hushed the whole thing up, and never reported my capture and escape.

'I got back to Azrak very annoyed with Abd el Kadir, and rode down to Akaba ... When the Turkish débâcle came, Abd el Kadir ran away quickly to Damascus, and as soon as the Turks had gone took forcible control of the local Government, in virtue of the remains of his Algerian volunteers.

'When Nasir and I arrived Abd el Kadir and Mohamed Said were sitting in the Serail with their armed servants. Feisal had begged me to get rid of them, so I told them to go, and that Shukri el Ayubi would be military governor till Ali Riza returned. Abd el Kadir refused to go, and tried to stab me in the Council Chamber, Auda knocked him down, and Nuri Shaalan offered me the help of the Rualla [tribe] to put him out. Mohamed Said and Abd el Kadir then went away, breathing vengeance against me as a Christian. I thought they would be quiet, but that night they called a secret meeting of their Algerians and the Druses, and begged them to strike one blow for the faith before the British arrived. I heard of this, warned General Nuri Said, and borrowed the Rualla from Nuri Shaalan. With the latter I rushed Abd el Kadir's house, and took him, while Nuri Said cleared the Druses out of the streets. I meant to shoot the two brothers, so interned Abd el Kadir in the Town Hall till I should have caught Mohamed Said. Before I had done so Feisal arrived, and said that like a new sultan he would issue a general amnesty. So Abd el Kadir escaped again. He got some of his men to shoot at me that same day, but I won. (Later on Abd el Kadir broke out again, and went for Feisal's house, and was shot, but I believe by one of the sentries. This was after I left.)

'If ever two people deserved hanging or shooting in Syria, they were these two brothers, and I very much regret that Mohamed Said has been given so much rope. Feisal has asked several times for his internment. He is the only real pan-Islamist,* in Damascus, and in his insanity, is capable of any folly or crime against us.'

It appears from this that Lawrence's hatred of Mohamed Said stemmed from the belief that it was Mohamed Said (or if not Mohamed Said, Abd el Kadir) who betrayed him to the Bey at Deraa, and that the two brothers were in league with the Turks. But Chauvel says, 'I do not think he [Abd el Kadir] gave the Turks any information of any value to them. He was definitely anti-Turk, but he had no use for the Hedjaz Arabs either.'† The truth is more likely to be that Lawrence hated Mohamed Said and Abd el Kadir because he believed—and later events seem to confirm his view— that they were working for the French. The brothers in turn hated Lawrence because he was an infidel and they believed him to be a British spy. So when Abd el Kadir was shot, it was not unexpected that many people, particularly the French, believed Lawrence had had a hand in his death.

The official version of the shooting is that Feisal urged that Mohamed Said and Abd el Kadir be arrested and deported. 'On the morning of November 7 the Chief Administrator sent police to arrest them, but Abd el Kadir resisted and after firing at the police, mounted his horse and galloped up the street. The police fired on him and killed him.'‡

Suleiman Mousa's version,§ almost the same as the official one, is that Abd el Kadir was furious at being confined to his house and deliberately galloped his horse round the streets in Damascus as an act of defiance. An Arab police patrol called on him to stop and shot him when he refused to do so. Mohamed Said supports this version,‖ blaming the then military governor, Ali Riza Rikabi, for having given the order to arrest Abd el Kadir. What is certain is that the French used the incident for a whispering campaign against Lawrence at the Paris Peace Conference, and although Lawrence had left Damascus by the time Abd el Kadir was shot, put around the story that the shooting had been carried out on Lawrence's instructions.

On the morning of 1 October all this was in the future. Lawrence

---

* Mohamed Said was not a pan-Islamist. He later began campaigning to help the French to become installed in Damascus, hardly the action of a man devoted to the concept of Pan-Islam.

† Chauvel's report.

‡ PRO, CAB, 27/36. EC 2287, 8 November 1918.

§ *T. E. Lawrence, an Arab View.* Oxford University Press, London, 1966.

‖ *Memoirs of Emir Said.*

had persuaded General Chauvel to confirm Shukri's appointment as governor of Damascus pending Feisal's arrival; he had also suggested—and it seemed reasonable enough—that Chauvel should establish his headquarters at the British Consulate. The Australian commander immersed in a general's problems of prisoners, supplies, orders and reports, thereafter forgot all about Lawrence until Captain H. W. Young, senior supply officer with the Hejaz Forces, arrived to see him. What Young told Chauvel seriously disturbed him. 'It looked as if I had made a mistake in putting Shukri in as Governor. He had not been elected by a majority of the residents,* but only by a comparatively small faction, i.e., the Hedjaz supporters, and by installing him, I had virtually admitted the rule of King Hussein over Syria. . . . There was chaos in the city, the Bazaars were closed and looting was already going on. The Hedjaz supporters . . . were endeavouring to make the populace think that it was the Arabs who had driven out the Turk. That was quite evidently why I had been asked to keep my men out of the city and why I had not yet been asked for any police. The Hedjaz people were trying to cope with the situation with their newly-organised gendarmerie.'†

Young advised Chauvel not to take over the British Consulate, because by doing so he would define the British as allies of the Arabs and not the undisputed controllers of Damascus; instead Chauvel should take possession of Jamal Pasha's house, which was being reserved for Feisal. The point was not lost on Chauvel, who also decided, despite Lawrence's opposition, on a show of force and marched through Damascus the following day, 2 October, at the head of a large body of troops. 'The effect was electrical, the Bazaars were opened and the city went about its normal business; but I had to find a whole regiment of police, the [Arab] gendarmerie not proving to be of much value. I also took possession of Djemal's house, allotting the British Consulate to one of the divisional commanders.'‡

Chauvel was carrying out his orders to secure Damascus for the British. As a military man he had little interest in whether the politicians might later decide to divide Damascus or Syria with the French or anyone else. Lawrence was also trying to secure Damascus —and thus Syria—for the British, via the Arabs, but he had no intention of letting the French get so much as a toe in the door. So what must have seemed to Chauvel close to insubordination on

---

* As Lawrence had told Chauvel.
† Chauvel's report.
‡ Ibid.

Lawrence's part had a definite aim: 'The course I mapped for us was proving correct. Another twelve hours, and we should be safe, with the Arabs in so strong a place that their hand might hold through the long wrangle and appetite of politics about to break out about our luscious spoil.'*

The wrangle was to break out sooner than Lawrence expected. Allenby arrived in Damascus at 1 p.m. on 3 October and immediately sent for Chauvel. There had been complications with the French, he said, and he needed to see Feisal immediately. On being told that Feisal was not expected until 3 p.m., when, as arranged by Lawrence, he was to make a triumphal entry, Allenby's manner was curt. 'I cannot wait until 3 p.m. You must send a car out for him and request him to come in and see me at once. He can go out again for his triumphal entry.'†

Hastily Chauvel sent his ADC in his Rolls-Royce to request Feisal to call on Allenby at once. 'He came but not in the Rolls-Royce. He managed to dodge my emissaries somehow and arrived at the Hotel Victoria on horseback at a hard gallop followed by some forty or fifty Bedouin horsemen. As a triumphal entry, it fell a little flat as it was nearly an hour before the populace expected him.'

There are three recorded versions of what occurred at the conference which followed—Allenby's, Lawrence's, and Chauvel's. Put side by side, they might be about different events. Allenby is brief and selective:

'In the presence of our respective staffs I had an interview with Sherif Feisal and I informed him that I was prepared to recognise the Arab administration of occupied territory east of the Jordan from Damascus to Maan inclusive, as a military administration under my supreme control. I further informed him I should appoint two liaison officers between me and the Arab administration; one of whom would be British and the other French and that these two officers would communicate with me through my Chief Political Officer. As long as military operations were in progress I explained that I was in supreme command, and that all administration must be under my control. I communicated to Sherif Feisal the fact that the British and French Governments had agreed to recognise the belligerent status of the Arab forces fighting in Palestine and Syria as allies against the common enemy.'‡

* *Seven Pillars*, Chapter CXX.
† Chauvel's report.
‡ PRO, CAB, 27/34. Allenby to War Office, 6 October 1918.

(Above) *The Bey of Deraa* (centre), *with his officers, January 1918.* (Below) *Deraa railway station.*

(Left) *A tulip bomb explodes on the railway track near Deraa.*

(Right) *A wrecked locomotive on the Hejaz line, photographed in 1965, nearly fifty years after Lawrence destroyed it.*

(Below) *The capture of Damascus, October 1918.*

Feisal's headquarters in Damascus, with (right) a primitive gallows.
Lawrence arrives in Damascus in his Rolls Royce.

In a letter to Wingate on the same day Allenby added, 'I've told Feisal that he, personally, has nothing to do with the Civil Government. He is to rest, recruit and refit his army for further advance.'*

Lawrence, in *Seven Pillars* is, as usual, atmospheric and impressionistic:

'Then we were told that Feisal's special train had just arrived from Deraa. A message was hurriedly sent him by Young's mouth, and we waited till he came, upon a tide of cheering which beat up against our windows. It was fitting the two chiefs should meet for the first time in the heart of their victory; with myself still acting as the interpreter between them.

'Allenby gave me a telegram from the Foreign Office, recognising to the Arabs the status of belligerents; and told me to translate it to the Emir: but none of us knew what it meant in English, let alone in Arabic; and Feisal, smiling through the tears which the welcome of his people had forced from him, put it aside to thank the Commander-in-Chief for the trust which had made him and his movement. They were a strange contrast: Feisal, large-eyed, colourless and worn, like a fine dagger; Allenby, gigantic and red and merry, fit representative of the Power which had thrown a girdle of humour and strong dealing round the world.

'When Feisal had gone, I made to Allenby the last (and also I think the first) request I ever made him for myself—leave to go away. For a while he would not have it; but I reasoned, reminding him of his year-old promise, and pointing out how much easier the New Law would be if my spur were absent from the people. In the end he agreed; and then at once I knew how much I was sorry.'†

It is left to Chauvel, in his bleak, soldierly style, to capture the high drama of the occasion:

'A conference was held at once at which the following were present: General Sir Edmund Allenby, Major-General Sir Louis Bols, Chief of the General Staff, E.E.F. [Egyptian Expeditionary Force], Myself, Brigadier-General C. A. C. Godwin, my Chief of Staff, The Emir Feisal, Nuri Bey es Said, acting Chief of Staff to the Emir Feisal, the Sherif Nasir, 2nd in command Hejaz Forces, Lieut-Colonel P. C. Joyce, Lieut-Colonel T. E. Lawrence, Major W. F. Stirling, Captain H. W. Young and Lieut-Colonel K. Cornwallis,‡ of the Arab Bureau, Cairo.

* Wingate Papers.   † *Seven Pillars*, Chapter CXXII.
‡ Cornwallis wrote later that he was left outside the door.

'Lawrence acted as Interpreter. The Commander-in-Chief explained to Feisal:

(a) That France was to be the Protecting Power over Syria.*

(b) That he, Feisal, as representing his Father, King Hussein, was to have the Administration of Syria (less Palestine and the Lebanon Province) under French guidance and financial backing.

(c) That the Arab sphere would include the hinterland of Syria only and that he, Feisal, would not have anything to do with the Lebanon, which would be considered to stretch from the Northern boundary of Palestine (about Tyre) to the head of the Gulf of Alexandretta.

(d) That he was to have a French Liaison Officer at once, who would work for the present with Lawrence, who would be expected to give him every assistance.

'Feisal objected very strongly. He said that he knew nothing of France in the matter; that he was prepared to have British assistance; that he understood from the Adviser whom Allenby had sent him that the Arabs were to have the whole of Syria including the Lebanon but excluding Palestine; that a country without a port was no good to him; and that he declined to have a French Liaison Officer or to recognise French guidance in any way.

'The Chief turned to Lawrence and said: "But did you not tell him that the French were to have the Protectorate over Syria?" Lawrence said: "No Sir, I know nothing about it." The Chief then said: "But you knew definitely that he, Feisal, was to have nothing to do with the Lebanon?" Lawrence said: "No, Sir, I did not."

'After some further discussion, the Chief told Feisal that he, Sir Edmund Allenby, was Commander-in-Chief and that he, Feisal, was at the moment a Lieut.-General under his Command and that he would have to obey orders. That he must accept the situation until the whole matter was settled at the conclusion of the war. Feisal accepted this decision and left with his entourage, except Lawrence.

'After Feisal had gone, Lawrence told the Chief that he would not work with a French Liaison Officer and that he was due for leave and thought he had better take it now and go off to England. The Chief said: "Yes! I think you had!", and Lawrence left the room.

'I thought the Chief had been a little hard on Lawrence and told him so. He said, "Very well, send him down to my Headquarters and tell him I will write to Clive Wigram† about him, asking him

---

* Allenby makes no mention of having told Feisal this.
† Equerry and Assistant Private Secretary to King George V.

to arrange for an audience with the King. I will also give him a letter to the Foreign Office in order that he might explain the Arab point of view." General Allenby then left by car for Tiberias.'*

No matter which account is accepted as being true, there is still one outstanding conclusion; the Sykes–Picot agreement was by no means dead and the French were pushing hard for their 'rights' in Syria. For the Arabs this meant that, at the best, they would have only 'the "half-loaf" offered by the S–P agreement'.†

For Lawrence this meant that his efforts to 'biff the French out of all hope of Syria' were in danger of being frustrated and his soul-sapping endeavours since the start of the Revolt totally in vain. On a more personal level, Allenby had placed Lawrence in an almost impossible position with his rapid-fire questions about what Lawrence had or had not told Feisal. Lawrence knew, of course, that in Syria France was to be the protecting power and that Feisal was to have nothing to do with the Lebanon. Yet he had hoped by his own manoeuvring and with support from powerful quarters to change all this, and therefore he had not been frank with Feisal. In the confrontation, Allenby had—probably without realizing it—placed Lawrence in a position where he had either to admit this and lose his special position with Feisal, or to lie. Lawrence lied because he felt that although he had won a round at Damascus and had succeeded in helping the Arabs to gain a measure of control, the campaign was not yet over: the French were prevailing in Whitehall and might yet win at the conference table. Others shared Lawrence's feelings about the French: Clayton, Wingate and Hogarth would help him and the Foreign Office must be made to listen. In fact, Clayton had foreseen more than a year before what would happen: 'The French are evidently nervous about any Syrian "stunts" by Lawrence and will, I think, try and insist on a Frenchman . . . co-operating with him.' All the same, Clayton hopefully suggested, 'we can skate over it'.‡

That was in October 1917. A year later Wingate was still skating cautiously, as when he wrote to Allenby on 8 October: 'It will be interesting to hear how the French Liaison system is going to work in Syria. I wonder if the Home people are now as enamoured of the S.–P. agreement as before? I doubt it.' Even Allenby himself, although professionally correct in his behaviour, was not unsympathetic to Lawrence's antipathy to the French, and he smartly slapped down

* Chauvel's report.
† Wingate in letter to Allenby, 3 October 1918. Wingate Papers.
‡ Letter to Wingate, 12 October 1917. Wingate Papers.

an attempt to label Georges-Picot 'French High Commissioner in Arabia'. Lawrence, then, was not a lone voice; and there was still the master himself, Hogarth, in whom reposed his greatest faith. Hogarth had been at work in London even before Damascus fell. 'I have asked to meet the Middle East Committee and I had better see Curzon who seems to vet Sykes nowadays. Policy re Near East seems to emanate (if at all) from an informal sub-committee . . .'*

There were, in fact, powerful allies for Lawrence's cause; the fight to upset the Sykes–Picot agreement was to continue on other battlefields and with other methods, and it is in this area that we must look for the reason for Lawrence's abrupt departure from Damascus. True, he was mentally and physically exhausted. Beaumont, his machine gunner says, 'He was at the end of his tether. He was terribly thin, down to about 5 stone 4 lb. He had a bad hand and had not got over the toe injury [caused on his trip to Deraa]. He was waving his hands and getting excited and this wasn't like him.'† But it was not exhaustion that made Lawrence leave. Until now the accepted views for his sudden departure have been: first, that he was disillusioned by his government's failure to fulfil its promises to his beloved Arabs; second—and this is based on his own public statement—that the change from war to peace conditions would be easier for the Arabs if his influence were removed; and, third, that as he explained privately, he had become so afraid of his desire for power and prestige that he had to escape. An examination of Chauvel's little-known report, the discovery in Cabinet papers, hitherto unavailable, of what Lawrence did on arrival in London, and information in letters from Wingate to Allenby, lead to a conclusion contrary to all these views: Lawrence went back to London to lobby the Government. He realized that with the fall of Damascus the future of the Middle East would now be decided in London and he wanted to be there to have his say. There is an indication in *Seven Pillars* that shortly before reaching Damascus he recognized that his form of underground political manoeuvring had been carried as far as it could go and that he would prefer a more open—and honest—battlefield.

'. . . I was tired to death of these Arabs; petty incarnate Semites who attained heights and depths beyond our reach, though not beyond our sight. They realized our absolute in their unrestrained capacity for good and evil; and for two years I had profitably shammed to

* Hogarth to Clayton, 14 August 1918. Hogarth Papers.
† Interview with the authors.

be their companion! Today it came to me with finality that my patience as regards the false position I had been led into was finished. A week, two weeks, three, and I would insist upon relief. My nerve had broken; and I would be lucky if the ruin of it could be hidden so long.'*

Next, there is evidence that Lawrence went back to London on a definite mission. En route, he called on Wingate in Cairo on 14 October and had a long talk with him. Wingate wrote to Allenby about this visit: 'Lawrence . . . intends to talk plainly when he gets to London—they should welcome the views of such an expert as he is, though I expect our French Allies would find them not exactly palatable and I shall be surprised if H.M.G. go as far as he recommends.'† Nine days later he sent Allenby another letter: 'I hear the anti-French parties are becoming increasingly restive; let us hope Lawrence's arrival at home will have the desired effect.'‡ Within two weeks of arriving back in London, Lawrence had drawn up and submitted to the government a surprising plan which was described as 'dealing comprehensively with the Arab question'. The plan proposed the abandonment of the Sykes–Picot agreement and the division of Arabia (apart from the Hejaz) into three states—Lower Mesopotamia, under Abdulla; Upper Mesopotamia, under Zeid; and Syria, under Feisal. Both Mesopotamias would be in the British sphere of interest and Lower Mesopotamia, in effect, under British control. It was a plan which was open to much the same criticism as the Sykes–Picot agreement; it cut up the best parts of the Middle East, and by placing them under non-Arab control killed any idea of a large, independent Arab state. Lawrence expressed his views on this independence very bluntly: 'Self-determination has been a good deal talked about. I think it is a foolish idea in many ways. We might allow the people who have fought with us to determine themselves. People like the Mesopotamian Arabs, who have fought against us, deserve nothing from us in the way of self-determination.'§ His plan suited British interests better than the Sykes–Picot agreement, and if Lawrence could get it adopted he would still be able to triumph over the French. He went willingly to work.

Hogarth, meanwhile, was busy nobbling Sykes. 'Don't take Mark

* Chapter CVII.
† Wingate to Allenby, 15 October 1918. Wingate Papers.
‡ Wingate to Allenby, 24 October 1918. Ibid.
§ PRO, CAB, 27/24. Minutes of a Meeting of the War Cabinet's Eastern Committee. (This is a strange thing for Lawrence to have said because some of the best Arab officers in the Revolt were from Mesopotamia.)

at his own valuation,' he wrote to Clayton on 1 November 1918, 'His shares are unsaleable here. . . . He is the last man in the world, in my opinion, to organize or run any Political Service: and you can take what line you like about him without fear of being let down.'*

Hogarth went on to describe Lawrence's lobbying in London with admiration. 'Our whole attitude towards the French is hardening here. Robert Cecil† has been excellent of late. . . . T.E.L. has put the wind up everybody and done much good, which I don't want him to undo by being here too long and treading too often on corns . . . meanwhile S.P. is considered scrapped here, but not so by Paris.'‡

The French certainly did not consider that the Sykes–Picot agreement had been scrapped, and had been making a point of pushing it hard as the British rolled up the last Turkish resistance in Syria. Shukri Pasha, the Arab whom Lawrence had made Governor of Damascus pending Feisal's arrival, had left for Beirut in the Lebanon as soon as Feisal reached Damascus and there he ran up the Hejaz flag over Government House and proclaimed Hussein's rule.

The French took strong exception to this, particularly as they suspected that Lawrence had planned the whole thing. To mollify the French, Clayton was sent hurriedly to Damascus to 'give Feisal a talking to, as he is getting rather out of hand'. He told Feisal that he should forget about the Lebanon and devote his energies to 'forming a sound and reliable administration in Damascus . . . so that he may have something tangible to show at the Peace Conference'. But Feisal was in no mood to listen, for Allenby's troops had removed the Hejaz flag in Beirut and Feisal's men were threatening mutiny. The sudden departure of Lawrence had aroused suspicion among some of the Arab leaders and a mood of apprehension as to the Allies' real aims swept over the Middle East. Within sight of the Armistice Britain and France were threatened with an uprising in the lands they had just taken from the Turks. As a result, Allenby and Clayton got together and both sent secret telegrams to London urging a public declaration of policy by the British and French governments as the only way to avoid trouble.§

So the British and French Governments drew up a declaration and gave it the widest possible dissemination (street criers even read

* Hogarth Papers.
† Lord Robert Cecil (1864–1958). 1st Viscount Cecil of Chelwood, third son of the Marquis of Salisbury, the Victorian Prime Minister. A lawyer and distinguished politician and one of the chief architects of the League of Nations.
‡ Hogarth to Clayton, 1 November 1918. Hogarth Papers.
§ Allenby Papers, St Antony's College, Oxford.

it aloud to the citizens in illiterate areas). This new declaration was as lavish in its promises as earlier statements, but couched in more flowery terms. Basically, it announced the liberation of populations living under the Turkish yoke and the setting up of national governments chosen by the people themselves—a clear promise of self-determination. It said that Britain and France were in agreement in their desire to see such governments set up and would assist in their establishment and grant them recognition as soon as they became established.

Cabinet papers on the subject now released make it clear that the British had a private motive for this declaration. They believed that they could use it at the Peace Conference as a means of wriggling out of the Sykes–Picot agreement. (Lord Robert Cecil later admitted as much to his colleagues: 'The reason why I was prepared to give great concessions to the French in order to get that declaration was because I thought it was of such tremendous value to us to remedy the evil of the Sykes–Picot Agreement.'*)

It was politics at its devious best—or worst: the declaration was issued later than the Sykes–Picot agreement, therefore it supersedes it. The declaration also promises self-determination to the liberated population of the former Ottoman Empire but Britain could safely insist that they have this—'because most of the people would determine in our favour'.†

But whatever its motives, the declaration brought almost immediate calm to Syria. It was not until the Peace Conference six months later that the Arabs began to suspect they had been sold short and that the declaration was not worth the ink in which it had been written. In the intervening period Lawrence was very active, gathering allies to help to cripple the Sykes–Picot agreement and looking round anxiously for a trump card to play at Versailles. For this he turned to a surprising quarter—the Zionists.

* PRO, CAB, 27/24.
† Lord Curzon, PRO, CAB, 27/24.

8 Prelude to Peace

As Turkey's defeat draws nearer, the Zionists prepare to build the national home in Palestine promised them by the British government. But Palestine has also been promised to the Arabs, so a campaign is mounted, with Lawrence to the fore, to persuade the Arabs to accept the new situation. Lawrence sees Zionist ambitions in Palestine as a counter to the Sykes–Picot agreement and a way of 'biffing' the French out of the Middle East. Within days of arriving back from Damascus he appears before the Eastern Committee of the War Cabinet to submit his ideas. He is immediately attacked by the India Office and a departmental war breaks out. Lawrence urges Feisal to come to Europe for the forthcoming Peace Conference, but when Feisal arrives at Marseilles, he and Lawrence are snubbed by the French in the person of Lawrence's old enemy, Brémond. In London Lawrence re-introduces Feisal to the Zionist leader, Chaim Weizmann, to further his master plan for the Middle East, a plan in which he envisages the Jews playing a vital part and which will sink the French once and for all.

While the European powers had seen the war with Turkey as an opportunity to divide the Ottoman Empire, and by so doing extend their imperial ambitions in the Middle East, the Zionists rapidly realized that the future of Palestine was now open, and with it the possibility that they might be able to play a large part in that future. Until the war, Zionist efforts in the political field had been concentrated unsuccessfully on trying to persuade the rulers of Turkey to permit increased colonization of the Holy Land. At the outbreak of war the centre of Zionist activity was Berlin, but as the possibility began to emerge that it might be the Allies who in the end would control Jerusalem, it was not long before the more prudent Zionist leaders began to think it wise to cultivate Britain and France also.

The British Zionists were led by Dr Chaim Weizmann, a brilliant scientist and chemist with strong political sentiments. Weizmann, a stocky, bearded figure, combined immense charm with a ruthlessness in attack that made him a dangerous enemy. He contributed greatly to the British war effort by discovering that acetone, an acid vital to the manufacture of TNT, and at that time produced only in Germany, could be replaced by a vegetable substance. Weizmann was a great traditionalist and saw an historic opportunity opening for Zionism, so he began to lobby influential British politicians. Though meeting with strong opposition at first, in December 1914, the Zionists arranged with Herbert Samuel,* then under-secretary at the Home Office, to put their case before the Cabinet. Samuel did this in a secret and somewhat rhetorical memorandum which he called 'The Future of Palestine'.†

Samuel said the time was not ripe for an independent, autonomous Jewish state, but that the Zionists would welcome the annexation of Palestine by the British Empire and he put forward attractive reasons why Britain should agree to this: 'It would enable England to fulfil in yet another sphere her historic part as civiliser of the backward countries.' And: 'Palestine . . . bulks so large in the world's imagination, that no Empire is so great but its prestige would be raised by its possession.'

Behind this romantic approach there was a lot of hard-headed realism. Samuel, the first practising member of the Jewish community to sit in a British Cabinet, knew that the question of who was to control the country that bordered the Suez Canal was one to which the Government would have to give serious consideration. But he was too early. Asquith, then Prime Minister, read the memorandum, and noted in his diary, 'It reads almost like a new edition of *Tancred* brought up to date . . . I am not attracted by this proposed addition to our responsibilities, but it is a curious illustration of Dizzy's favourite maxim that "race is everything . . .".'‡

Samuel got word of the Prime Minister's views, tidied up the memorandum, cut the lyricism, and circulated it again. This time he set out five possible alternatives for Palestine: annexation by France; to remain Turkish; internationalization; to become an autonomous Jewish State; or a British protectorate where Jewish settlement would be encouraged. Samuel advocated the last. But Asquith remained unimpressed: 'I think I have already referred to Herbert Samuel's dithyrambic memorandum, urging that in the carving-up of the Turks' Asiatic dominion we should take Palestine, into which the scattered Jews would in time swarm back from all quarters of the globe, and in due course obtain Home Rule. Curiously

* Herbert Samuel (1870–1963), later Viscount Samuel, a leading Liberal politician. From 1920–25 he was High Commissioner in Palestine. He had a seat in the Cabinet as President of the Local Government Board.
† PRO, CAB, 37/123.
‡ *Memories and Reflections.* 2 vols. Cassell, London, 1928. Vol. ii, p. 59.

enough, the only other partisan of the proposal is Lloyd George, who I need not say does not care a damn for the Jews or their past or their future, but thinks it will be an outrage to let the Holy Places pass into the possession or under the protectorate of "agnostic, atheistic France".*

Although Asquith was unsympathetic, the matter did not lapse, and in the summer of 1916 Sir Mark Sykes opened negotiations with the Zionists. Early in the talks the Zionists' leaders became attuned to the British government's feelings that only a British Palestine would be a reliable buffer for Egypt and the Canal, and issued a formal assurance that if Britain would support them they in return would work for the establishment of a British protectorate in Palestine. On 2 November 1917, Mr Balfour, the Foreign Secretary, announced the famous and deeply ambiguous Declaration: 'His Majesty's Government view with favour the establishment in Palestine of a national home for the Jewish people and will use their best endeavours to facilitate the achievement of this object, it being clearly understood that nothing shall be done which may prejudice the civil or religious rights of existing non-Jewish communities in Palestine, or the rights and political status enjoyed by the Jews in any other country.'

Britain had now manoeuvred herself into a remarkable position. The Sykes–Picot agreement by which she was bound provided for an international administration for Palestine. As we have seen, for strategic reasons this did not suit Britain. So among the many reasons for the Balfour Declaration one was certainly that Britain hoped thus to ensure Zionist opposition to an international administration and support for a British Palestine.

How did the pledge to the Zionists square with what had already been promised to the Arabs in return for their support in the war against the Turks? Had Palestine, in fact, already been promised to the Arabs? This has been a matter of continuing controversy for more than half a century, of sneers ('Palestine: the twice-promised land'), and of committees of enquiry; but it has never been satisfactorily resolved. The correspondence in 1915–16 between Sir Henry McMahon, High Commissioner in Egypt, and King Hussein in Mecca constituted the first agreements between the Arabs and the British. Did these letters include Palestine in the area in which Britain promised to uphold Arab independence? George Antonius, the Arab historian, says they did. After examining the correspondence, Antonius wrote: '[Palestine] must, in default of any specific

* Ibid.

agreement to the contrary, necessarily remain within the area of Arab independence proposed by the Sharif and accepted by Great Britain.'*

The Zionists say that Britain never intended Palestine to be included in the general pledge given to the Sherif. This has also been the official British attitude and it was endorsed by the Palestine Royal Commission report in 1937. In 1939 the Lord Chancellor, Lord Maugham, said, 'All governments of the United Kingdom from 1915 onwards have held firmly to the opinion not only that Sir Henry McMahon intended by his correspondence with the Sherif of Mecca ... to leave ... Palestine outside the area of Arab independence, but also that the correspondence in question could not then and cannot now be read as having any other meaning.'† This view had been argued by various ministers, including Winston Churchill and Herbert Samuel and, most conclusive of all, by Sir Henry McMahon himself, who after keeping silent for twenty years wrote, in a letter to *The Times* in 1937: 'I feel . . . called upon to make some statement on the subject, but I will confine myself in doing so to the point now at issue . . . I feel it my duty to state, and I do so definitely and emphatically, that it was not intended by me in giving this pledge to King Hussein to include Palestine in the area in which Arab independence was promised.'‡

Dogmatic as this statement might appear, it is not the last word. Two British government documents only recently released indicate that Palestine had indeed been promised to the Arabs. The first is an Arab Bureau report prepared by Hogarth and dated November 1916, which sets out a summary of what had and had not been agreed between McMahon and Hussein. Unlike the McMahon correspondence, the Arab Bureau paper is specific. The relevant clause reads: 'What has been agreed to, therefore, on behalf of Great Britain is: (1) to recognise the independence of those portions of the Arab-speaking area in which we are free to act without detriment to the interests of France. Subject to these undefined reservations the said area is understood to be bounded north by about latitude 37°, east by the Persian frontier, south by the Persian Gulf and Indian Ocean, west by the Red Sea and the Mediterranean *up to about latitude* 33°,§ and beyond by an indefinite line drawn inland west of Damascus, Homs, Hama, and Aleppo: all that lies between

* *The Arab Awakening*, p. 179.
† *The Times*, 17 April 1964.
‡ Ibid. 23 July 1937.
§ Authors' italics.

this last line and the Mediterranean being, in any case, reserved absolutely for future arrangement with the French and the Arabs.'* Two exemptions are then given: Aden and Iraq. In the area as defined here (see map), Palestine is definitely in that part of Syria promised to the Arabs. This widely-circulated Arab Bureau document was never rescinded or corrected.

The second document, which remained secret for nearly fifty years, is a verbatim report of a meeting of the War Cabinet's Eastern Committee in London on 27 November 1918. Its details are published here for the first time. In the chair was the Olympian figure of Lord Curzon, Lord President of the Council. The committee had discussed Syria and was about to move on to Palestine. Curzon, as was his custom, gave a résumé of the government's actions. (It is important to remember that he was presenting not a personal view, but the official attitude as set out in a brief prepared for him by the Foreign Office and that in the discussion which followed no member of the committee questioned his statement.) He began: 'The Palestine position is this. If we deal with our commitments, there is first the general pledge to Hussein in October 1915, *under which Palestine was included in the areas to which Great Britain pledged itself that they should be Arab and independent in the future.*'† This could hardly be more conclusive: Britain *did*, knowingly, first promise Palestine to the Arabs as part of an independent Arab area.

Following the Balfour Declaration in November 1917 every effort had been made to allay Arab suspicions of Jewish aspirations, and because of his special position with Feisal, Lawrence had been foremost in the campaign to persuade the Arabs to accept the situation. His first report on the matter shows him confident of being able to influence Feisal. Writing to Clayton from Tafileh on 12 February 1918 he said: 'For the Jews, when I see Feisal next I'll talk to him and the Arab attitude shall be sympathetic, for the duration of the war at least. Only please remember that he is under the old man,‡ and cannot involve the Arab Kingdom by himself. If we get Madeba he will come to Jerusalem and all the Jews there will report him friendly. That will probably do all you need, without public commitment, which is rather beyond my province.'§

Hogarth had been hard-headed. In January 1918 he had gone

* PRO, FO, 371/6237.
† PRO, CAB, 27/24. Authors' italics.
‡ King Hussein.
§ PRO, FO, 882/7.

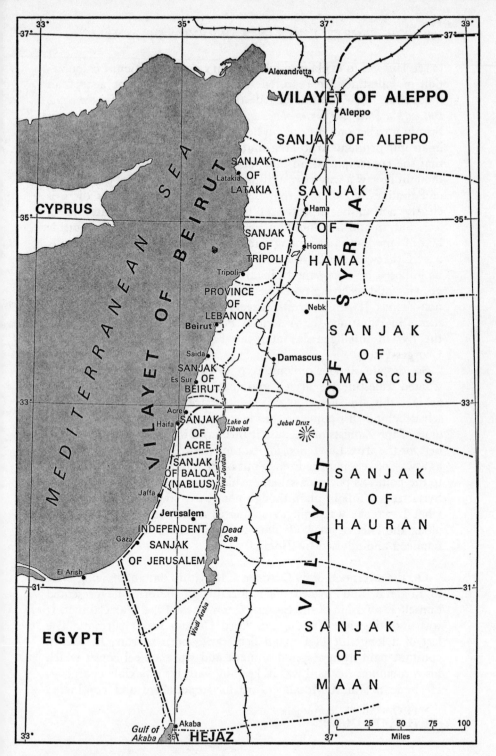

Ottoman Administrative Districts in Syria, 1914.

Heavy dotted line indicates border of Arab independent area, as defined in Arab Bureau paper

to see Hussein to explain to him Britain's policy on Zionist colonization of Palestine. He reported: 'The King would not accept an
independent Jewish State in Palestine, *nor was I instructed to warn him
that such a State was contemplated by Great Britain.*'* So not only was
Britain now set on reneging on her commitment to include Palestine
in an independent Arab area, but she was keeping it from Hussein
that she contemplated an independent Jewish state there. Hogarth
thought he saw a way out: 'Willing acceptance of Zionist penetration
of Palestine and of preferential treatment of the Zionists there is
clearly not to be expected of [the Arabs] in the country itself.
. . . But, should the Sherifian [*ie*, Hussein's family] element outside
become predominant among Arabs, a financial bargain is possible.
. . . Otherwise the British undertaking to the Zionists will have to
be imposed by *main-forte*.'† Hogarth said opposition to Zionism was
growing and receiving reinforcement from four main sources: strong
non-Zionist Jewish interests, largely represented by American elements in Palestine; the American Protestant Mission in Palestine;
the Syrian intelligentsia; and the French party represented by
Georges-Picot.

So, despite obvious difficulties, once Britain had decided that she
wanted Palestine for herself and that Zionism would help her to
achieve this aim, her chief officers in the Arab sphere threw themselves behind this policy, either because they sympathized with the
aims of the Zionists or because it furthered their beliefs in what was
best for the area. Lawrence, for example, saw the Balfour Declaration
as a way of keeping the French out of Palestine and, what was more
to the point, as part of a scheme which might also keep them out of
Syria. It was a bold plan, though not at this stage fully formulated:
what Lawrence was doing, startling as it may sound, was working
along the lines of an Arab state in Syria, under British protection,
financed and advised by Zionists!

On the afternoon of 29 October 1918 within days of arriving back
in England, and dressed uncomfortably in uniform, he presented
himself at a session of the Eastern Committee of the War Cabinet. It
was a distinguished gathering. Lord Curzon was chairman. The
last of a long line of Foreign Secretaries born to rule, he was in
constant pain from a spinal ailment and wore a steel corset which
his contemporaries said was in keeping with his inflexible character.
He had an almost Mosaic regard for imperialism and considered

* PRO, CAB, 27/36. Authors' italics.
† PRO, FO, 371/3381.

most means were justified if the end expanded British influence. 'I never spend five minutes inquiring if we are unpopular,' he said. 'The answer is written in red ink on the map of the globe.'

At his right sat Lord Robert Cecil, Assistant Secretary of State for Foreign Affairs, a scholarly, distinguished figure with an eagle-like profile and a high forehead, who took his Christian beliefs into public affairs with the conviction that there should be a covenant between the Church and State to help uplift national life. Farther down the table sat Edwin Montagu, Secretary of State for India, and a distinguished member of Britain's Jewish community. Although brought up in a strictly Orthodox family, Montagu refused to support the Zionist cause and said that national ties should count for more than bonds of race or religion. He had deep sympathy with India and had many Indian friends. Near to him was Sir Mark Sykes, who took the unusual position of supporting both Arab independence and Zionism and was disappointed that the Jews and the Arabs seemed unable to work together for the creation of a new Middle East.

Mr Balfour, the Foreign Secretary, looked in at the meeting from time to time, and annoyed Curzon by asking that the contents of reports be outlined to him because he liked to have the gist of the matter in mind before he read them. Present also was the Adjutant-General to the Forces, General Sir George Macdonogh, a taciturn soldier noted for his pithy comments; General Smuts, lean and hawk-like, at that time South African Minister of Defence and a member of the highest councils of Britain; and representatives of the Admiralty and Military Intelligence.

This was Lawrence's great moment. At the heart of power, he had a chance to consolidate his plans. Lord Curzon's stately introduction gave him confidence. Every member of the government, Curzon said, had watched with interest and admiration Lawrence's great work in Arabia and felt proud that an officer had done so much to promote the successful progress of the British and Arab arms. He understood Colonel Lawrence could give information regarding the views that were entertained by the Arab chiefs concerning the settlement of the conquered territories and Franco-Arab relations in particular.* Lawrence certainly could. Not only had he seen the trend towards a French take-over in Damascus, but he had stopped in Rome on his way back to London and had had a frank meeting with Georges-Picot, who had made it crystal clear

* PRO, CAB, 27/24.

to him that the French planned to run Syria their way and that under the Sykes–Picot agreement, whether Feisal liked it or not, he would have to accept French advisers.

Lawrence knew the feelings of most members of the Eastern Committee about the Sykes–Picot agreement (Curzon described it as 'hanging like a millstone round our necks'), so despite Sykes's presence Lawrence hit hard. He began by saying that Feisal was honest, straightforward and extremely pro-British, but his future attitude would depend on how far Britain backed French claims in the East. Feisal had originally come to know of the Sykes–Picot agreement from the Turks,* but he now felt that the Declaration to the Seven, which promised unlimited Arab sovereignty over territory actually captured by Arab arms, superseded that agreement. Lawrence first boldly admitted to having confirmed this view to one of Feisal's sheiks and then set out his own plan for the Middle East. It envisaged scrapping the Sykes–Picot agreement— apart from letting the French have Beirut and the Lebanon—and 'biffing' them out of everywhere else: Abdulla would rule Baghdad and Lower Mesopotamia, Zeid, Upper Mesopotamia, and Feisal, Syria. At this stage Lawrence made his main and most startling point. Feisal took the view, said Lawrence, that he was free to choose whoever he wanted as advisers and was anxious to obtain the assistance of British or American Zionist Jews for this purpose. The Zionists, Lawrence said, would be acceptable to the Arabs on terms. The committee asked Lawrence to write a memorandum on these lines,† and then passed to further business.

Lawrence had made his first big impact on the politicians and from this moment on was regarded as a main adviser, expected to assist in deciding Britain's demands and tactics for the forthcoming Peace Conference in Paris. It is worthwhile looking at further meetings of the committee because they give an illuminating view of how the government saw its obligations to its allies—French and American, as well as Arab—after the war had been won. (Lest we may be tempted to judge them too harshly, it is well to remember that these distinguished leaders were speaking together in camera to formulate a policy for what promised to be an unpleasant confrontation between victorious allies, the sort of encounter that is apt to make warfare itself appear less murky.) Curzon set the mood by complaining that Britain had committed herself to various policies, some of which appeared to be conflicting, yet

* Not, as Lawrence says in *Seven Pillars* (Chapter CI), from him.
† PRO, CAB, 27/36. Lawrence's report to the War Office, 4 November 1918.

it had to be remembered that on the way these policies were resolved
and the British case presented at the Peace Conference would depend
the future of the British Empire in the East. What now was to
be done about the Sykes–Picot agreement—'this deplorable Agreement to which ... the French seem disposed to adhere most
tenaciously'?* (Sykes was not present on this occasion.) Curzon
found two strains of opinion in the British camp: 'Some say "Back
the French at the expense of Faisal ... and do not be too much
concerned about the Arabs". On the other hand, there is another
party, of whom I think Colonel Lawrence is the spokesman, who
say, "The fact that you are involved with the French by agreements
out of which you want to extricate yourselves is no reason why you
should be at all unfair to the Arabs ... your policy is to back
Faisal rather than the French".' The committee, at this stage,
allowed itself to indulge in a little day-dreaming. Was there any
chance of the President of the United States, Woodrow Wilson,
getting Britain off the hook? Could he somehow be induced to say,
'Here we are inaugurating a new era of free and open diplomacy;
the various States of Europe have bound themselves by all sorts of
unscrupulous secret engagements in the earlier years of the war;
before we enter into any arrangements for the future let us sweep all
those off the board; let the Sykes–Picot Agreement go, let the
Agreement with the Italians go, and let us start with a clean slate'.
It was an ideal solution, but since there was no way of relying
on President Wilson to be accommodating, the committee came
to ground again. It was now that Curzon, as the Americans say,
laid it on the line. 'For the safety of our Eastern Empire I would
sooner come to a satisfactory arrangement with the Arabs than I
would with the French, but I would not carry the arrangement with
the Arabs to the point of quarrelling with the French.'† Lawrence
must have tensed himself when he heard this. Then with that Englishman's blend of superiority and self-interest which used to infuriate
foreign politicians, Curzon summed up: 'If that be our line of action
as regards Faisal, ought we not to play the policy of self-determination
for all that it is worth? ... I am inclined to value the argument of
self-determination, because I believe that most of the people would
determine in our favour ... We ought to play self-determination for all it is worth wherever we are involved in difficulties
with the French, the Arabs, or anybody else, and leave the case
to be settled by that final argument, knowing in the bottom of

* PRO, CAB, 27/24.
† Ibid.

our hearts that we are more likely to benefit from it than is anybody else.'*

We are faced here with the unusual definition that the committee apparently placed on 'self-determination', made no easier to understand by Mr Balfour's annoying habit of directing the short-hand writer to cease making notes at the more revelatory moments. Mr Balfour, however, is on record as saying that it would be unwise to become pedantic about self-determination because it was in-applicable to 'wholly barbarous, undeveloped and unorganized black tribes'; to which Lord Robert Cecil added the bewildering warning that while self-determination should be 'an indication . . . we should not attempt to leave it to the populations to say, because you would have the most awful rows if you did that . . .' Lawrence at any rate had an understandable point of view: 'Self-determination has been a good deal talked about. I think it is a foolish idea in many ways.'

On Mesopotamia the committee was on firmer ground. There would be no difficulty in establishing British control—it was merely a question of what sort of control. Lawrence's scheme for putting Zeid and Abdulla in as British nominees ran into bitter opposition from the India Office, and Sir Percy Cox, the British representative in Mesopotamia, no admirer of either Lawrence or the Hashemites, had earlier advised the Government to set up a High Commission system—what the committee referred to as 'a British administration behind a façade of native institutions'—and have nothing to do with Hussein or his family in any form. Colonel A. T. Wilson, the civil commissioner in Baghdad, was also outspoken about Lawrence's scheme: 'The policy suggested is totally impracticable and unsuited to conditions in Mesopotamia. . . . It would be easier to put a similar scheme into effect among the races of Europe than to make a success in Arabia of these proposals, which appear to me to ignore alike Mahomedan history and geographical divisions . . .'†

So by now the India Office and the French were both against the anti-Sykes–Picot section of the Foreign Office. The French were afraid that if the ex-Ottoman Arabs obtained independence it would have a disturbing effect on France's Muslim subjects in North Africa, and at the India Office there were similar fears about Muslims in India. The India Office's view proved too strong for Lawrence. There was no Sherifian settlement—at least for the time being—and his defeat in this matter was a hard blow. It was made even

* Ibid.
† PRO, CAB, 27/37. Political Baghdad to India Office, 20 November 1918.

more difficult to bear by the fact that in his memorandum he had written off all rivals to the Sherif, particularly Ibn Saud,* and had rashly predicted that if Ibn Saud attacked Mecca, then Hussein would deal with him—a view that was to prove disastrously wrong.

With his ideas for Mesopotamia scrapped, Lawrence's plan for the Middle East was now down to a recommendation that Feisal should be ruler of Syria. Could Palestine and the Zionists be used here as a bargaining counter with the French? The committee again found itself concerned by Britain's commitments under the Sykes–Picot agreement: 'In the Brown area (Palestine) there shall be established an international administration.' How could Britain, who wanted Palestine for herself, get out of such a well-defined agreement? Lord Robert Cecil tried: 'An international adminis-tration may mean anything, provided it is one internationally agreed upon';† but the committee did not feel that France would accept this tautological interpretation. But Lord Robert Cecil did speak for all the members when he went on to say: 'As for the proper thing, I do not think there can be the least doubt that, from the point of view of the inhabitants, we should almost certainly do it better than anybody else, and therefore it would be better for us to do it.' Lawrence thought he saw a chance to link the two problems. Britain wanted Palestine. She also wanted the French out of Syria. He told the committee that in his view there would be no difficulty in reconciling Zionists and Arabs in Palestine *and* Syria, which would go a long way towards excluding the French, provided the administration in Palestine remained in British hands—just the sort of opinion the committee longed to hear. In short, as Curzon put it, 'Faisal is in favour of the British in Palestine, and is also in favour of the British in Irak, and of a purely nominal Arab administration there. In so far, therefore, as Colonel Lawrence speaks for Faisal, if we can meet Faisal's views elsewhere in the West [ie, Syria], we know that Faisal is behind us.'‡

So, as far as the committee was concerned, these were the tactics to be adopted for the Peace Conference in Paris: cancellation of the Sykes–Picot agreement; to get Mesopotamia and Palestine for Britain, and reward Feisal by manoeuvering him on to a throne in Syria (which would have included what is now Jordan). But before the conference even began Britain was to receive a salutary indica-tion of just how strong French opposition was likely to be; a reaction

* Ibn Saud (1880–1953). Arab ruler, later King of Saudi Arabia.
† PRO, CAB, 27/24.
‡ Ibid.

which Lord Robert Cecil foresaw: 'Colonel Lawrence will not approve . . . but I am quite sure you will never get the French to give up the whole of Syria without the most tremendous convulsion. They would rather give up anything in the world than give up that claim to Syria; they are mad about it, and Cambon* himself is quite insane if you suggest it.'†

When the trouble did break, Lawrence, as might be expected, was where the diplomatic fighting was thickest. On 8 November he had sent a telegram, via Wingate in Cairo, to King Hussein in which he proposed that Feisal should represent the King at the Peace Conference, and suggested that if Hussein agreed, he should telegraph to Britain, France, America and Italy telling them of his decision. (Wingate, who apparently failed to realize how far Lawrence had risen in the world, delayed delivering the telegram while he enquired from the Foreign Office whether this was official policy or Lawrence's own initiative, and was reprimanded for his pains.) Feisal set sail on 22 November 1918 in the British cruiser *Gloucester*, which was due at Marseilles on 26 November. At this point the French stepped in. In a stiffly worded note to the British Ambassador they complained that they had not been consulted in the matter. Feisal could not speak at the Peace Conference in the name of any of the Arab populations because the wishes of these populations could not be consulted. The French government was surprised that he should be sent to France on British advice. This could only be due to a misunderstanding and France proposed to act as follows: it would treat Feisal as a distinguished foreigner, but would tell him that he had no official title and that until some agreement had been reached with Britain he could in no circumstances be admitted to any meeting of the Peace Conference as a representative of the Arabs.

Even couched, as it was, in diplomatic language, the note was hard-hitting enough to send the Foreign Office into retreat. The Ambassador in Paris was instructed to tell everything to Lawrence, who was en route for Marseilles, and to leave it to his discretion how best to explain this setback to Feisal. A possibility that the *Gloucester* might bring Feisal direct to London was rejected because the French, in the mood they were in, might have considered this had been done to encourage Feisal to adopt an anti-French attitude.

---

* Jules Martin Cambon (1845–1935), secretary-general of the Ministry of Foreign Affairs and later a member of the French delegation at the Peace Conference.
† PRO, CAB, 27/24.

The French, of course, already believed this and rightly blamed Lawrence as the chief instigator of the plan. Accordingly they worked out a programme for Feisal's reception which was coldly calculated to show both Feisal and Lawrence exactly how they were rated in French eyes. Lawrence's old enemy, Colonel Brémond, was instructed by M. Jean Gout, under-secretary for Asia, to 'treat Emir Feisal as if he were a general ... but without any diplomatic standing. Tell him he has been badly advised ... arrange matters in such a way as not to bring him to Paris without further instructions ... take him round to see anything you like.' As for Lawrence: 'Show him that he is on the wrong path. If he comes here as a British Colonel in British uniform ... we shall welcome him. But we shall not accept him if he comes as an Arab and remains disguised as such.'* This was a calculated insult, and although Feisal decided to follow the programme, Lawrence quickly returned to London.

Feisal's feelings at this introduction to European diplomacy in action can well be imagined, but he appears to have weathered the situation with dignity, and eventually went to Paris where, on 7 December, he met the President of France. Three days later Brémond handed Feisal over to Lawrence at Calais. Lawrence, reversing their roles at Marseilles, politely asked Brémond if he would be Britain's guest during Feisal's visit. The point went home and Brémond, acknowledging the thrust, declined with equal politeness.† Lawrence and Feisal crossed the Channel and then Lawrence officially welcomed Feisal to Britain.

Feisal stayed until 9 January 1919, when he returned to France. During his visit to London he was received by King George V and, with Lawrence, called on Mr Balfour for a few frank words. Balfour later told the Eastern Committee of the War Cabinet about their meeting. The verbatim report makes fascinating reading in its mixture of confusion and sophistry and bears out Zeine's conclusion‡ that politically Britain did not take the Arabs or her promises to them seriously.

MR BALFOUR: With regard to Beirut, Feisal came to see me the other day. He was most vehemently anti-French; I have never heard anything like it. But he seemed to think we had behaved

---

* Edouard Brémond, *Le Hedjaz dans la Guerre Mondiale*. Payot, Paris, 1931.

† This was their last crossing of swords. Brémond became a general in 1923, and was the author of several books on Arabs and the Middle East, including that already cited. He died in 1948.

‡ *The Struggle for Arab Independence*. Khayats, Beirut, 1960.

rather badly. He referred to some assurance which we had made
to his father, the King of Hejaz, which he seemed to think we had
violated in connection with Beirut. Do you know what it was?

SIR LOUIS MALLET:* The general statement of Arab independence.

LORD CURZON: There has been no specific statement about Beirut.

GENERAL SMUTS: It is the general statement, that the areas set free
by the Arabs should be independent. As a matter of fact,
they were in Beirut before we arrived, and they constituted
a government in front of us.

MR BALFOUR: That is the point. Is there any substance in it?

GENERAL SMUTS: No, I do not think so.

LORD CURZON: Do you object to giving Beirut to the French along
with the Lebanon?

GENERAL SMUTS: They go naturally together.

LORD CURZON: We cannot separate them.

MR BALFOUR: The Lebanon, I suppose, we must give them. So long
as the Lebanon remains independent we cannot withdraw it
from French tutelage.

But something more important than a meeting with a temporizing
and slightly bewildered Mr Balfour happened to Feisal in London.
With Lawrence, he got together with Chaim Weizmann, the
Zionist leader, at the Carlton Hotel and worked out a *modus vivendi*
for Arabs and Jews in the Middle East. Lawrence had met
Weizmann in Palestine at the fall of Jerusalem and had formed a
great admiration for him. Now, with the full approval of the
British government, he brought Feisal and Weizmann together and
put to the Zionist leader a new plan for the Middle East which he,
Lawrence, had devised and in which he wanted the Zionists to
play a major part.

Anthony Nutting says that Lawrence 'had always looked upon the
Semitic race of Jews and Arabs as an indivisible whole. At the same
time both he and Feisal no doubt felt that such avowed support for
Zionism at this time would be good politics, in that it would still
further commend the Arab cause to the American and British
delegations [to the Peace Conference] by showing that an independent Arab state would not conflict with Jewish interests and claims
as set forth in the Balfour Declaration.'†

* Sir Louis Mallet (1864–1936), a diplomat by career, though at this time
under-secretary of state for India and also a member of the British delegation to
the Peace Conference.

† *Lawrence of Arabia: the Man and the Motive.* Hollis and Carter, London, 1961,
pp. 187–8.

But there was more to the meeting of Feisal and Weizmann than this. In the last days of the war the Zionists had been negotiating a deal with Feisal, and the Carlton Hotel meeting was the outcome of these negotiations, not the beginning. Weizmann had gone to see Feisal near Akaba on 4 June 1918 and had decided to tell him, so he wrote, that 'if he wants to build up a strong and prosperous Arab Kingdom it is we Jews who will be able to help him, and we only. We can give him the necessary assistance in money and organising power. We shall be his neighbours and we do not represent any danger to him, as we are not and never shall be a great power.'* After this visit the Zionists tried for over a year to get down to terms with Feisal, who had been desperately short of money to run the territories the Arabs and the Allies had liberated. The Zionists estimated that his outgoings were about £200,000 a month and that his income would be nil until the 1919 harvest was gathered and could be taxed. Accordingly, they offered him a loan and the services of a financial adviser in return for his assistance over Palestine.† Exactly what this assistance was to comprise was to be hammered out between Weizmann, Feisal and Lawrence.

The first London meeting at the Carlton Hotel between Feisal and Weizmann—with Lawrence interpreting—was on 11 December, the day after Feisal arrived; none of Feisal's aides or officials knew about it or the subsequent agreement between them, and Weizmann, although he revealed the existence of the agreement in 1936, never mentioned these discussions. Briefly, according to Weizmann, Feisal expressed his indignation about the Sykes–Picot agreement, which he considered fatal equally to Arabs and Jews. The Arabs had set up a Government in Damascus, but it was extremely weak, with no money and no men and no ammunition for the army. His great hope was that America would destroy the agreement. To this, Weizmann replied that he had known of the agreement (meaning presumably the negotiations preceding its announcement) since 1915, had protested about it, and had asked American Zionists to act against it whenever possible. Weizmann said the Zionists' programme was that the Peace Conference and Feisal should recognize the national and historical rights of the Jews to Palestine; that Britain should be the trustee power; that Jews should have an adequate share in the government; and that the country should be developed so as to create room for four or five million Jews without encroaching on the

* Letter from Weizmann to Balfour, 30 May 1918, Lothian manuscripts, Scottish Record Office, Edinburgh.
† PRO, CAB, 27/35.

ownership rights of the Arab peasantry. In return, the Jews would be prepared to render Feisal every assistance in brains and money so as to help to revive his country. Feisal is then recorded as having remarked that he did not think that there was any scarcity of land in Palestine... 'besides there was plenty of land in his district'. Weizmann wrote: 'He assured us on his word of honour that he would do everything to support Jewish demands, and would declare at the Peace Conference that Zionism and the Arab movement were fellow movements, and that complete harmony prevailed between them.'*

This discussion anticipated an agreement whereby everyone got what he wanted in Palestine. The British got trusteeship; the Zionists the right of entry, land to settle (even beyond Palestine, if necessary), and a say in government; Feisal got from the Jews money for development, financial advice, and Zionist support at the Peace Conference. But on 3 January, when it came to signing the actual document, difficulties arose. According to what Lawrence later told Arnold Toynbee (the historian, who was a member of the British Peace delegation) Weizmann had included the phrases 'Jewish State' and 'Jewish Government' in the draft document. When Lawrence read this out, Feisal insisted that the words be altered to 'Palestine' and 'Palestine Government'. Toynbee set this out in an official Foreign Office report† and added, 'Dr Weizmann has accepted the principle that the State is not to be Jewish to the detriment of the Arabic-speaking inhabitants, but this will have to be looked after by the mandatory power.' Then Feisal, showing his inherent caution, insisted on writing in Arabic a reservation at the foot of the last page of the agreement. Lawrence wrote a quick translation: 'If the Arabs are established, as I have asked in my manifesto of January 4‡ addressed to the British Secretary of State for Foreign Affairs, I will carry out what is written in this agreement. If changes are made, I cannot be answerable for failing to carry out this agreement.' The translation was attached to the agreement as page 5 and Feisal and Weizmann both signed it. There are differences between Lawrence's translation and that made later by Antonius, whose version begins: 'Provided the Arabs obtain their independence as demanded in my Memorandum . . .' and is more positive: 'I shall not then be bound by a single word of

---

* The Weizmann Archives, Rehovoth, Israel.

† FO, 159 375/2/2.

‡ This was a mistake; Feisal was apparently referring to a memorandum he wrote on 1 January 1919.

the present Agreement which shall be deemed void and of no account or validity . . .' Lawrence has been accused of misleading Weizmann as to the strength of Feisal's reservation, and the differences in the two translations seems to bear this out. Lawrence has also been accused of failing to inform Feisal of the extent of the Zionists' aspirations. This is likely, because in the following October Feisal gave the *Jewish Chronicle** an interview in which he said he understood that all Weizmann wanted was regulated immigration, equal rights, and a say in the government. When the *Jewish Chronicle* representative said that Jewry understood the Balfour Declaration to mean that they had the right to set up a National Home which would eventually become a Jewish State, Feisal said the Arabs would 'fight to the last ditch against Palestine being other than part of the Kingdom and for the supremacy of Arabs in the land.'

It is probable that Lawrence preferred to let both Feisal and Weizmann imagine that each had got what he wanted. It must be remembered that the British government was anxious to get an agreement between the Zionists and Feisal signed and delivered before the Peace Conference, which was to open on 18 January, and had instructed Lawrence to use his influence with Feisal to try to bring this about. For his own purposes Lawrence was also anxious to arrange such an agreement, preferably on the lines of the 11 December discussions at the Carlton Hotel between Feisal and Weizmann. However, notably absent from the agreement that was eventually signed is any mention of Zionist finance for Feisal, which was discussed at this meeting. There is reason to believe that this was on the advice of Lawrence, who was anxious not to reveal his hand until he saw how the struggle of the Peace Conference would develop. For Lawrence believed he had discovered a way round the Sykes–Picot agreement—already, as we shall see, partly invalidated by Clemenceau—a way of pushing the French out of Syria, establishing Feisal as ruler and, at last, making it a Brown Dominion within the Empire. It involved what can only be described as a calculating use of Zionist aspirations. Lawrence described this plan in a letter to Alan Dawnay, who as a Staff Officer in Palestine had been one of his closest collaborators in the Arab campaign. It was written in London on 28 September 1919, nine months after the Weizmann agreement had been signed, and delivered by Lawrence personally, because 'this is material of an explosive nature'. The relevant part of this letter, published here for the first time, reads:

* 3 October 1919.

9

'The French will be on their best behaviour for months, and give Feisal his money unconditionally. Then they will try to turn the screw. He'll say he doesn't want their money, because by then the Zionists will have a centre in Jerusalem, and for concessions they will finance him (this is all in writing, and fixed, but don't put it in the Press for God's sake and the French). Zionists are not a Government, and not British, and their action does not infringe the Sykes–Picot agreement. They are also Semites and Palestinian, and the Arab Govt. is not afraid of them (can cut all their throats, or better pull all their teeth out, when it wishes). They will finance the whole East, I hope, Syria and Mesopotamia alike. High Jews are unwilling to put much cash into Palestine only, since that country offers nothing but a sentimental return. They want 6%.'*

This is what Lawrence was working for, and is the explanation of his readiness to help a union between the Zionists and the Arabs. It was a bold if cynical plan: the Arabs would provide the land, international Jewry the money at 6 per cent. It is interesting to speculate on the shape of the Middle East today had such a scheme succeeded.

* Bodleian Library.

9 The Battle at Paris

Lawrence attends the Peace Conference in Paris as a member of the British delegation, which uses him 'to influence Feisal in the right direction'. The French press their case for Syria and the British steadily yield. Hogarth returns in disgust to Oxford, 'sick at heart at all this fiasco'. While Feisal waits in Syria for an answer to his demands, Lawrence flies to Cairo to collect from the Arab Bureau the papers he needs for Seven Pillars of Wisdom, *which he has just started writing. His enemies intrigue against him in his absence, but prominent in the factors that finally defeat him is Britain's hunger for oil, which is stronger than allies or promises. He submits a last-ditch plan to make Arabia Britain's first Brown Dominion, but Curzon rejects it.*

The Peace Conference opened at the Quai d'Orsay in Paris on 18 January 1919, with a splendour and sparkle that hid the knives and knuckledusters. James T. Shotwell, a former professor of history at Columbia University and a member of the American delegation, wrote: 'The dining room of the Majestic* is at least twice the size of that of the Crillon. . . . The scene at dinner was the most remarkable I have ever witnessed. . . . Next to the Canadian table was a large dinner party discussing the fate of Arabia and the East with two American guests. . . . Between them sat that young successor of Mohammed, Col. Lawrence, the twenty-eight year-old conqueror of Damascus, with his boyish face and almost constant smile—the most winning figure, so everyone says, at the whole Peace Conference. . . .'

But behind this façade of crystal and fine wine the political double-dealing had already started.

The fate of Germany was, of course, the main subject; the problem —how to make the German nation pay for the cost in lives and material that the war had caused and how to ensure she should never again become a threat to the peace of the world. The Middle

* The hotel in which the British delegation to the conference had its head-quarters.

East was a sideshow, but one where the intrigue was subtler, the knives sharper, and the possible rewards richer. It had begun with a row with the French as to whether Feisal could attend or not; someone leaked to the French newspapers a memorandum by Feisal pleading for Arab independence and there was an outcry at 'the untenable pretensions of this country [Hejaz] whose history is short but whose appetite is great'. Feisal felt out of his depth in an alien world. He was forced to rely on Lawrence to look after his interests and was especially grateful when Lawrence managed to get him not one but two seats at the Conference. What Feisal did not know was that Lawrence was at the Conference primarily to assist in looking after British interests, despite which he was often under heavy attack from members of his own delegation, who had their own views on the best way to advance those interests. Feisal thought Lawrence spoke for the British government, not realizing that Lawrence usually spoke only for some section of the government, and sometimes, indeed, only for himself. The India Office, for example, continued to attack him. It reported to the Secretary of State for India, Edwin Montagu, that it had 'no confidence in Lawrence's opinions on the Mesopotamian question'. This followed an interview between Feisal and one of the India Office's own men in Mesopotamian Military Intelligence, Major J. C. More. In a report to the India Office More said that he found Feisal a very ambitious man, nervous of Ibn Saud and 'very bitter against the Government of India for encouraging him'. Montagu passed the whole file to the Foreign Office for comment and received a highly significant, if rather tart, reply from Sir Louis Mallet: 'There is no doubt of the ambition of Feisal. Colonel Lawrence, however, holds the view that we shall find the Arab national movement easier to control if we retain his [Feisal's] confidence.'* This remark highlights the dichotomy of Lawrence's role at the Peace Conference. His task, as he himself set it out, and as Mallett echoed it, was to retain Feisal's confidence in order to make the Arab national movement easier to control—in fact, a continuation of his role since the start of the Revolt. But what if the manner in which the British Government wanted the Arab national movement to be controlled should differ from the manner in which Lawrence considered it should be controlled? What if the plans of Lawrence's enemies in, say, the India Office appeared to offer a more attractive course of action than those of Lawrence? He could only continue to plan secretly and hope that his views would eventually triumph.

* FO, 159 (375/2/2).

But in the meantime it was essential to maintain, by no matter what means, the absolute confidence of Feisal. In other words, Lawrence's situation meant that he could never be completely frank with Feisal and at times had to deceive him, because, as during the Revolt, he could not risk Feisal's turning away from him. At least one Arab saw through Lawrence. Awni Abdul Hadi, a member of Feisal's delegation at the Conference and later Jordan's Foreign Minister, wrote of Lawrence that he worked for the good of his country, and it was in this spirit that he worked with Feisal in London and Paris: 'His prime object was to make Feisal cling to the British and come to believe they were his only real friends. . . .'* So while Feisal believed that through Lawrence he could get what he wanted *for* the Arabs, Curzon and others believed that through Lawrence the British could get what they wanted *from* the Arabs. ('Let us by all means make use of Colonel Lawrence to influence Feisal in the right direction. . . .'†) The demands were totally different and the strain of this double role began to tell on Lawrence.

Then it fell out, to his chagrin, that just when he needed to show the strength of the Hashemites as the only Arab leaders capable of controlling the Middle East, they let him down. Ibn Saud, itching to check Hussein's pretensions to the title of King of Arabia and to suppress the decadence which his Muslim puritans believed the Hashemites fostered in Mecca, had for some time been making warlike moves against the Hejaz. Two expeditions against Ibn Saud failed, so in May 1919 Abdulla set off with 4,000 infantry and 10,000 cavalry to crush him. This news was received both in Whitehall and Paris with some consternation. In Whitehall the situation was complicated by the ludicrous antagonism that had sprung up between the India Office—which had financed and armed Ibn Saud—and the Foreign Office, which had financed and armed Abdulla. 'The sinews of war . . . were the subsidies that the two British departments in Whitehall had been paying to their respective Arab henchmen out of the British taxpayers' money. It would have been cheaper . . . and more manly of the civil servants in the two belligerent departments, if these had fought each other direct.'‡ At any rate, the Wahabis fell on Abdulla after a forced night march and slaughtered his army while it slept. His force was wiped out and Abdulla himself escaped only with difficulty. Ibn Saud was preparing to march on

---

* Private letter quoted in *T. E. Lawrence, an Arab View*, by Suleiman Mousa, p. 227.
† PRO, FO, 371/4183.
‡ Arnold Toynbee, *Acquaintances*, p. 184.

Mecca when an ultimatum arrived from the Foreign Office: Ibn Saud was to withdraw; if he did not, aircraft would be sent against him. The India Office prudently advised him to retreat and the invasion was over.*

This defeat was a blow to Lawrence because he had told the War Cabinet that if Ibn Saud attacked the Hejaz Hussein would deal with him. And it added to the distress Feisal was feeling as he saw the British steadily yielding to the French at the Peace Conference. Both took fresh heart, however when, at President Wilson's insistence, it was decided to send a commission of enquiry to Syria to find out the wishes of the people. The Americans appointed two members, Dr Henry C. King, President of Oberlin College, Ohio, and Mr Charles R. Crane, a member of President Wilson's diplomatic mission to Russia in 1917; and the British two—Sir Henry McMahon and D. G. Hogarth; but there were no French appointments. Hogarth hung about for two months waiting for something to happen, and then, since the French continued to procrastinate, gave up and went back to Oxford. In a letter to Clayton he summed up the bitterness he and Lawrence were beginning to feel as the French slowly achieved their aims over Syria:

'I have given H.M.G. till May 31st to get us off or, at least, definitely constituted, French and all. Failing that I must resign and go back to Oxford, sick at heart at all this fiasco and the melancholy consummation of four years' work. To think that we are to hand over Feisal and Syria to Senegalese troops and take Palestine with our hands and feet tied! I won't blame the Arabs of either land if they get out their rifles. I hate the idea of ever setting foot in an Arab land again.'†

Lawrence held out to the end. The Conference postponed a decision on Feisal's demands and Feisal went back to Syria to hope and wait. He placed great faith in the commission of enquiry, but this slowly faded as the French deliberately wrecked the scheme. The British, keen at first, rapidly became uninterested when it was suggested that the commission should extend its activities to Mesopotamia and Palestine. Only President Wilson stood firm and in the end the two American members, King and Crane, went on their own. Their report made blunt reading: there could be mandates for Syria, Palestine and Iraq, but for a limited term only;

---

* Ibn Saud finally took the Hejaz and the holy cities in 1924–5, and they have been part of Saudi Arabia ever since.
† Hogarth Papers.

and independence was to be granted as soon as possible. The United States should have the mandate for Syria, and Britain the mandate for Iraq; the idea of making Palestine into a Jewish commonwealth should be abandoned.

This was unpalatable advice, and the report was ignored, even in Washington. The suggestion that the Zionists should forget about Palestine must have seemed quite unrealistic. Zionist aims were too close to realization for them to be abandoned and the Zionist lobby at the Peace Conference was powerful and active. Hogarth gave an idea of its activities in a letter to Clayton:

'Weizmann is agitating for some certainty about Palestine and through Frankfurter* and the Paris Zionist Association he has put up an exceedingly moderate programme. I dined with him and Frankfurter two nights ago and found both singing very low, and talking of thirty, forty, fifty years' delay of a political state. . . . He [Weizmann] talks of half a million Jews in Poland with loins girt and staff in their hand ready to start, but admits that not above 10,000 a year can be introduced in practice. He tried to frighten Wilson with Bolshevism, but I gather without much success; and he is to try it on A. J. B[alfour] tomorrow. I am personally backing him wholeheartedly so long as he is moderate, but I fear that things have gone too far in Palestine for us to take over . . . with that Jew Council in evidence, without trouble. Still—there stands H.M.G.'s declaration about the National Home. It must mean something, and this is about the least it could mean.'†

Weizmann had no doubt what the Balfour Declaration meant. To him the Zionist platform was clear: 'A Jewish Palestine under British auspices.'‡ He tried to impress on Balfour the desirability of this, stressing the 'treacherous nature of the Arab', whom he described as 'superficially clever and quick-witted [who] worships one thing and one thing only—power and success'. He saw little hope of majority rule working in Palestine because 'the democratic principle . . . reckons with the relative numerical strength; and the brutal numbers operate against us, for there are five Arabs to one Jew. . . . This system does not take into account the fact that there is a fundamental qualitative difference between Jew and Arab. . . .

* Mr Justice Frankfurter (1882–1965). From 1939 a member of the United States Supreme Court; during and after World War I, a leader of the American Zionists.
† Hogarth Papers.
‡ Weizmann to Balfour, 30 May 1918. Lothian manuscripts, Scottish Record Office, Edinburgh.

The present system tends ... to level down the Jew politically to the status of a native ... the fellah is at least four centuries behind the times, and the effendi ... is dishonest, uneducated, greedy and as unpatriotic as he is inefficient ... the somewhat shifty and doubtful sympathies of the Arabs represent in the long run distinctly less than the conscious and considered policy of the majority of the Jewish people, which sees in a British Palestine the realization of its hopes and aspirations.'* While the Zionists waited to see what would happen about Palestine, and Feisal waited in Damascus with the hope that the commission of enquiry would support him against the French, Lawrence took the opportunity afforded by the break to go back to Cairo to collect his papers—which he needed for *Seven Pillars*—from the Arab Bureau. He was offered a lift in an RAF plane that was being ferried to Egypt, but the journey proved long and disastrous. The plane crashed on landing at Centocelle in Italy and he broke his collarbone and three ribs; an injury that was to worry him for the rest of his life. In August 1919 he was back in London, where he was shortly to survive a firm attempt to get rid of him. The atmosphere while he had been away had become distinctly more pro-French, and so the Foreign Office sent a private and urgent telegram to Balfour in Paris saying that Lawrence was planning to return there to meet Feisal and 'this is likely to cause us serious embarrassment with the French'.† The Foreign Office suggested that if Balfour regarded Lawrence as a member of his Delegation, then he should be refused permission to return to Paris. Meanwhile, enquiries were being made to see whether Lawrence was still in the army and therefore subject to military orders: 'He claims to have been demobilized but no trace of this can be found.'‡

The British delegation rushed to Lawrence's defence. Lawrence was under its orders and attached to its political section. Furthermore, 'If there is a settlement, the *only* way of reaching it—without bloodshed—is through Feisal . . . and if it would be a mistake to keep him from here, I consider it would be an equal mistake to keep Lawrence from Feisal. . . .' In a second note this was emphasized: 'He and he only can get Feisal to make reasonable concessions.'§

With his rear thus secured, Lawrence was ready to make a final

---

* Ibid.
† PRO, FO, 608/92. Telegram from Foreign Office to Balfour, 17 July 1919.
‡ Ibid.
§ PRO, FO, 608/92. Telegram and minutes—FO to Balfour, 17 July 1919–8 August 1919.

attempt to try to put Feisal into Syria and beat the French once and for all.

Apart from the strength of French sentiment for Syria—a sentiment, so Clemenceau, the French premier, told Lawrence, that had existed since the Crusades—the factors that were eventually to defeat Lawrence were the cry in Britain for demobilization, the need for the troops in Syria to go to real trouble spots like Ireland, Egypt and Mesopotamia, and Britain's thirst for oil. The war had made her realize the strategic importance of a cheap supply of oil under her absolute control. One of the reasons for Germany's oil-fired Navy being immobilized in port after Jutland was a shortage of fuel, and in Germany factory production was hindered by a lack of lubricants and civilian transport almost came to a halt. In Britain the buses continued to run and in America even private motoring was unaffected.

It was clear that in any future conflict oil would be an essential weapon. Yet, because of Kitchener's mania for buffer states, Mosul with its rich oil resources had been placed, through the Sykes–Picot agreement, in the French zone. Lloyd George, desperate to get Mosul back, had done a deal with Clemenceau when they met in London in December 1918: as a result, Mosul went to Britain in return for a French share of the oil rights, British support on the left bank of the Rhine, and agreement that there should be 'no dualism' in Syria—that is, no division between Beirut and Damascus. All the intrigues of the Peace Conference failed to move the French from this stand on 'no dualism', so Feisal and Syria were abandoned, among other reasons, for oil. This move had the concurrence of the oil lobby, but for a different reason. The oil men saw that concessions and royalties would be easier to negotiate with a series of rival Arab states lacking any sense of unity than with a large independent Arab state in the Middle East. (Private jottings by Llewellyn Smith, a member of the British delegation at Paris, give some idea of the oil lobby's intrigues. They mention 'bribing the French by a minority concession in Mesopotamian oil to help a pipe-line to Alexandretta. But all depends on permanent British control of Shell . . . also British rights in Algeria have to be settled.'*)

By September 1919 the two governments had hammered out an agreement on Syria and Feisal was invited to return to give his assent to what was in effect a *fait accompli*. The main points were that Britain

* Lothian manuscripts, Scottish Record Office, Edinburgh.

was to get the oil fields of Mosul and mandates—fixed at San Remo in April 1920—in Palestine, Iraq and Trans-Jordan; and France was to get the Lebanon, the substitution of French troops for British in western and northern Syria, and a tacit admission by Britain of the French aim to establish eventually a mandate over the whole of Syria.

Feisal reached London on 19 September, and when he heard the terms of the agreement he protested bitterly. In a final effort to have his own views accepted, Lawrence sent a memorandum to the Foreign Office on 15 September in which he went part of the way towards accepting the Lloyd George–Clemenceau agreement, but suggested ways of deterring the French from using force to get their mandate: 'Hostilities between the Arabs and the French will cut off all the inland food supply to the coast. The French should be informed that we will provide neither transport nor food for either side in such contingency.' Lawrence then went on to stress the advantages to the French of being patient, and in doing so revealed his low estimation of the Arabs' ability to govern themselves: 'If the French are wise and neglect the Arabs for about twelve months, they will then be implored by them to help them. If they are impatient now, they only unite the Arabs against them.'*

On 27 September Lawrence wrote privately to Lord Curzon and expressed his willingness 'to make Feisal accept the Paris arrangement of last week reasonably. . . .' This offer is remarkable both because it shows that he was still prepared to use his influence with Feisal to help the British government and because, read in conjunction with a letter he sent to Dawnay the next day, it shows also what Lawrence really had in mind. In the letter to Dawnay (see Chapter 8), Lawrence begins: 'Enclosed was from me to Curzon yesterday. Feisal jibbed at the agreement of last week (he was mishandled, because really it favours him and gives him a winning hand) and Ll. G. asked me to save the situation. I said, "Only on my own terms" which here in—and I think the Govt. will have to accept them because I'm the only person to rescue them from the knots they have tied.'

The letter to Curzon suggests a series of safeguards for Feisal in Syria and points out that because the French had accepted the formula, 'French in Syria as British in Mesopotamia', Britain should 'tend continually "left" ' as a remedy and safeguard against French colonial ambitions. 'My own ambition,' Lawrence wrote, 'is that the Arabs should be our first brown dominion, and not our

* *Letters*, No. 115.

last brown colony'—quite a progressive sentiment for its day, but far from what the Arabs themselves had in mind.

In the letter to Dawnay we see what Lawrence was really working for: 'The cardinal point is the putting Cornwallis* into Damascus [as British adviser]. That is a condominium, and all goes well thereafter.' He then goes on to tell Dawnay that Syria is not so important after all:

'The future is ours, as long as the Arabs of Mesopotamia back us, for the population of Syria is never to be more than 5,000,000 (no metals no fuel ∴ no industry; and little arable land) and Mesopotamia has thrice the acreage of Egypt (Egypt 13,000,000 ∴ Mesopotamia = 39,000,000) and besides agriculture it has more petrol than any place on earth (cheap fuel = industry) and about it, in Persia and the Kurdish hills, are copper, lead and iron. These 40,000,000 will be there in the third generation from now, or thereabouts, if they multiply like the Egyptians, and being Arabs they are not Asiatics, but Semites and their interests lie in the Mediterranean (they have never concerned Asia at any period). All the effort of this 40,000,000 will be towards the Mediterranean, and if you colour Mesopotamia green on a map you will see it is like a huge pistol pointed at Alexandretta Bay or Tripoli. They will get there eventually.

'Please emphasize the worthlessness of Basra. It is a back door only, and points only towards India. Nobody wants to go to India, and specially there is a colour-feeling between Arab and Indian . . .'

There follows the paragraph about Zionist finance for Feisal and 'the whole East' (see page 120). Lawrence then goes on:

'Point out, if you can that the British Empire has been increased by this [ie, 1914–18] war in Africa, and in Australasia: and in Asia we have taken on Persia, Mesopotamia, Arabia, and half of Syria. We will go crash with all these new houses, unless we can find tenants for some of them. Therefore we need Zionist and Arab co-operation.

'Australia won't like brown citizens of the Empire—but it's coming anyhow. They are 5,000,000 and the Browns about 300,000,000.

* An Egyptian civil servant and liaison officer between the Foreign Office and Feisal's delegation during the Peace Conference. He had served in the Arab Bureau and edited the *Arab Bulletin*.

'The French will hold an uneasy position for a few years on the Syrian coast, like the decadence of the Crusading Kingdom of Jerusalem, or Egypt before the Moroccan bargain—and then:

'No more of me & thee.'

This astounding last-ditch stand by Lawrence brought his opponents out in force. The letter was circulated for comment and Major Hubert Young, of the Eastern Department of the Foreign Office, replied within twenty-four hours—in terms that left no doubt as to how he regarded Lawrence: 'I understand that there is no intention of employing Colonel Lawrence as an official inter-mediary between Feisal and the Foreign Office . . . and [he] will undertake to make no promises to Feisal which the latter might imagine to be an official undertaking on the part of HMG. He will use his personal influence to secure Feisal's goodwill as far as possible, but only as a personal friend. I regard it as of first importance that this should be clearly laid down from the beginning. Colonel Lawrence's well-known antipathy to the French, and the suspicion with which they regard him, render it highly undesirable that he should be employed in any official capacity in the forthcoming negotiations [to get Feisal to accept the Anglo-French 'settlement' of the Middle East] if they are to have for their object a permanent British-French-Arab understanding.'* Young went on to suggest a plan of his own, stressing that French agreement to everything was vital, and ended by saying, 'If this proves unworkable, both British and French to step out of Arab Syria altogether, and leave Feisal to be financed as he pleases, preferably by the Zionists.'

This did not please Lord Curzon, the Foreign Secretary, who added a note to Young's comments: 'I strongly deprecate the idea of Feisal being run by the Zionists which I consider would be fatal. What would be the result? With Zionists already in the ascendancy in Palestine and financing, administering, arming and controlling Syria, they would become one of the most formidable factors in the East. This would be the "New Jerusalem" with a vengeance. Dr Weizmann let the cat out of the bag to me in conversation and I offered him no sort of sympathy or encouragement.'† But, overall, Curzon favoured Young, and he dismissed Lawrence's plan by writing: 'I prefer Major Young's general conclusion and many of his arguments.'

The British soon realized that Feisal was in no mood to accept the

* PRO, FO, 371/4183.
† Ibid.

Anglo-French agreement. They knew this because, apart from anything else, they were intercepting his telegrams to Hussein as they
passed through Cairo, deciphering them, and sending copies back to
the Foreign Office.* So they packed him off to Paris to come to terms
with the French by himself. Feisal, faced with French military action
if he refused, initialled the agreement, but said that final ratification
would have to await consultation with his countrymen. He was to
make desperate attempts to fight on alone, but within a year the
French army seized Damascus and the Arab dream of an independent
nation in Syria was over.

It is not difficult to imagine the bitterness that Lawrence must
have felt in seeing—as Hogarth had put it when he left Paris in
disgust—'all this fiasco and the melancholy consummation of four
years' work'. It was, for Lawrence, a humiliating defeat and one
from which he was never really to recover.

* Revealed in a 'very secret' memorandum from G. J. Kidston, of the Eastern
section of the Foreign Office, on discussions with the Director of Military Intelligence, PRO, FO, 371/4183.

10 The Colonial Office

Despite a vociferous Press campaign mounted by Lawrence over the Middle East, Britain stands by while a French army ejects Feisal from Syria—'a black spot in the annals of British support for the Arabs'. Disheartened and depressed by his failure, Lawrence retires to Oxford, where he throws himself into the writing of Seven Pillars of Wisdom. While his spirits are at their lowest, his reputation is being spread through Britain and the Commonwealth by an American journalist and lecturer, Lowell Thomas. Lawrence emerges from Oxford and plunges into a controversy over Mesopotamia where a revolt against the British has broken out. Although he now holds no official position, he is in the middle of a campaign to get the RAF the job of controlling the country. Churchill persuades Lawrence to join him at the Colonial Office as adviser on Arab affairs and together they prepare to 'settle' the Middle East question. Their proposals are announced after the Cairo and Jerusalem Conferences of 1921—but the main decisions have already been taken in London. Feisal is 'elected' King of Iraq, the chief opposition candidate having been kidnapped by the British. Abdullah is made ruler of Trans-Jordan, after promising that he will put a stop to anti-French and anti-Zionist activities. Lawrence now becomes a plenipotentiary and is ordered to persuade King Hussein to sign a treaty ratifying all that the Allies have done in the Middle East. Hussein refuses to sign. Lawrence has a short spell in Trans-Jordan reorganizing the administration there, then, claiming that all promises to the Arabs have been fulfilled, he leaves the Colonial Office to try to put Arabia behind him.

As the Anglo-French arrangements for Syria, Mesopotamia and Palestine were finally hammered out at the Peace Conference, and what President Wilson described as 'the whole disgusting scramble for the Middle East' drew to a close, Lawrence changed his tactics. From a frontal assault on his enemies in Whitehall he now switched to a public relations campaign, pouring out letters and articles to newspapers, sometimes under his own name, but often anonymously.

From the Civil Service point of view this recruitment of the Press to assist in a departmental feud was unforgivable, especially as Lawrence made no secret of it. 'Lawrence claims that he has written *all* the recent articles in the Press here on the Syrian question,' one

Foreign Office official complained. The tenor of Whitehall's reactions to Lawrence's campaign can best be judged from the Foreign Office file* following the publication in *The Times* on 11 September 1919 of Lawrence's famous letter, headed 'The Syrian Question', which began: 'Your Syrian correspondent has just referred to British promises to the French and the Arabs. When on Prince Feisal's staff I had access to the documents in question, and as possibly the only informed freelance† European, I may help to clear them up.' The letter goes on to list the promises Britain had made to the Arabs and the French and adds, surprisingly: 'I can see no inconsistencies or incompatibilities in these four documents, and I know nobody who does.' The letter continues:

'It may then be asked what all the fuss between the British, the French, and the Arabs is about. It is mainly because the [Sykes–Picot] agreement of 1916 is unworkable, and in particular no longer suits the British and French Governments.

'As, however, it is, in a sense, the "charter" of the Arabs, giving them Damascus, Homs, Hama, Aleppo, and Mosul for their own, with such advisers as they themselves judge they need, the necessary revision of this agreement is a delicate matter, and can hardly be done satisfactorily by England and France, without giving weight and expression also to the opinion of the third interest—the Arabs—which it created.'

This letter was duly circulated in the Foreign Office. First to comment on it was Major Young, no admirer of Lawrence's plans:
'Colonel Lawrence's letter is a carefully calculated indiscretion, written with the object of presenting the Arab case ... He hits us as hard as the French, and if the letter had been written by an Arab no possible exception could be taken to it. It is quite clear that ... his motive is solely to justify himself in the eyes of the people who helped to overthrow the Turks through his influence, and as a result of the confidence placed in him personally. . . .'

The file then went to another Foreign Office official, who was horrified: 'From the official point of view Col. Lawrence's publication of this letter is quite unpardonable. His claim to be a free lance is definitely disposed of by Mr Balfour's insistence that he is an official member of his Delegation in Paris.'

* PRO, FO, 371/4182.
† This claim to be a freelance was disputed by the Foreign Office.

And then Lord Curzon, the Foreign Secretary, had his say: 'I really don't see that any harm is done. But then *pace* Mr Balfour I have never regarded Col. Lawrence as a member of the British Delegation.'

In the end, all Lawrence's manoeuvres proved of little use. Feisal, abandoned by the British, made his peace with Clemenceau and returned to Damascus to try to convince his people he had taken the only course open to him, while still hoping that what Lawrence had prophesied would come to pass: that the French would wait a while, then cut Feisal's subsidy, hoping to force him into complete sub-servience; at which point Feisal would tell them that he did not want their money, the Zionists would step in with offers of finance and advice, and the French—short of taking military action—would be thwarted. But things did not work out this way. In March 1920, eighteen months after the Arabs had been liberated from the Turks, there was no sign that they were ever to get real independence. Feisal might argue that the plan for the dismemberment of Syria agreed between Britain and France (eventually ratified at San Remo in April 1920) was not final, but the nationalists did not believe him and began pressing for action. When the San Remo decisions became known there was an outburst of bitter anger; for the whole of the Arab rectangle lying between the Mediterranean and the Persian frontier—including Palestine—was to be placed under mandates, allotted to suit the imperialist ambitions of Britain and France. The Arabs saw this as a gross betrayal. Many took to arms again and began raiding French establishments, and the French, using these raids as an excuse, issued an ultimatum and marched on Damascus. Feisal continued to hope for a miracle. Failing to foresee America's withdrawal from European affairs and the beginnings of the period of isolation, he still had faith in President Wilson's declaration that no country would be governed against the wishes of its inhabitants. Nor could he believe that the British would stand by and see him crushed by the French, especially as Curzon had advised him to avoid a clash at all costs. So he accepted the conditions of the French ultimatum and waited confidently for the Americans or the British to call on France to halt. No such thing happened. Those Arabs who resisted were cut to pieces; the French occupied Damascus and 'invited' Feisal to leave the country.

When he did so on 28 July 1920, an embarrassed delegation of British officials waited on him as he passed through Palestine. The eyes of Sir Ronald Storrs, sharp if sorrowing behind his pince-nez, noted the pathos of the moment: 'We mounted him a guard of honour a hundred strong. He carried himself with dignity and the noble resignation of Islam ... though tears stood in his eyes as he was wounded to the soul. The Egyptian Sultanate did not "recognize" him, and at Quantara station he awaited his train sitting on his luggage.'*

Elizabeth Monroe rightly described the sacrifice of Feisal as 'a black spot in the annals of British support of the Arabs'. The reason for the British attitude was simple self-interest. Coincidentally, trouble had broken out in Egypt and Iraq, and Britain could hardly complain about the French use of military force in Syria when she herself was using military force to suppress the dissident Iraqis.

The humiliation of Feisal brought a sense of defeat and despair to Lawrence. In November 1919, Geoffrey Dawson, an ardent member of the Round Table, who had just left the editorship of *The Times*, had contrived to have Lawrence elected a Fellow of All Souls. He had now moved to Oxford and was dividing his time between his parents' home in Polstead Road and college. He was deeply depressed and, according to his mother, would sometimes sit between breakfast and lunch 'in the same position, without moving, and with the same expression on his face'.† In a letter to Wingate, Lawrence wrote, with a stoicism which sounds a trifle strained: 'I found myself out of tune with the ideas now prevailing on Eastern affairs and cut myself violently adrift from them. So now I just wander about quietly thinking, I am afraid, more about music than anything else. In many ways I am almost sorry, but the balance after all is in being quit of things, and as soon as I can get the nomad out of me and be quite peaceful, I shall not want to hear about the East again.'‡

Quit of things? He was certainly not quit of repercussions of the Revolt, for while he had been fighting a tenacious rearguard action for his plan for the Middle East, the American author and journalist, Lowell Thomas, was turning Lieutenant-Colonel T. E. Lawrence, Foreign Office political intelligence officer, into the Prince of Mecca, and the Deliverer of Damascus. The newly elected Fellow of All Souls, the saddened recluse of Oxford, became, as Lawrence of Arabia, the centre of a great fashion. Lowell Thomas, who had met Lawrence in 1917, opened a series of lectures at Covent Garden Opera House in August 1919, called 'With Allenby in Palestine and the Conquest

* *Orientations*, pp. 505–6.
† *The Letters of T. E. Lawrence*, p. 294.
‡ Repeated by Sir Reginald Wingate to Colonel Newcombe in a letter, 6 January 1920.

of Holy Arabia'. He later altered this to 'With Allenby in Palestine and Lawrence in Arabia'. The lectures, illustrated by lantern slides and film, were an outstanding success and were later transferred to the Albert Hall. Curiosity about Lawrence, once confined to Whitehall and well-informed readers of *The Times*, spread to all levels of society, and Arabia exerted its customary grip on British emotions. King George V participated in this new national enthusiasm by asking for a private performance of the show. The newspapers bid against each other for articles about Lawrence. Even *The Times*, in writing about Lawrence's All Souls fellowship, transmitted some of the legend: 'So great did his prestige become that the Arabs dowered him with supernatural powers, and King Hussein conferred upon him the unprecedented honour of creating him a Prince of Mecca.'* Lowell Thomas later toured Australia and New Zealand, and there his show was equally well received. It has been estimated that he made one million dollars out of the Lawrence lectures; if this is so it makes his lecture tour one of the most successful ventures of its kind in history. It is impossible to be certain of Lawrence's reaction to this unexpected exposure to the limelight. He went to hear one of the lectures incognito and told Thomas later that he was glad the lights were out. In a letter Lawrence said: 'Mr Lowell Thomas made me a kind of matinee idol'.†

It is easy to imagine Lawrence's distress at the gap between the popular conception of himself and the reality. To add to his discomfort there were several personal problems: he was intensely frustrated by his defeat at the Peace Conference; he was finding it difficult to adjust himself from the excitement of war to the routine of peace; he was in the middle of writing *Seven Pillars* and, apart from the physical strain that this involved, the emotional effort he put forth in re-examining and reassessing his motives, political and personal, must have been intense. Liddell Hart, who saw Lawrence during this period, says that the writing of *Seven Pillars* 'brought him perilously close to the border line'.

Amusing but sometimes vicious stories about his eccentric behaviour began to circulate. He was said to have bitten Lord Curzon at the Paris Peace Conference because Curzon had angered him; to have attached his Croix de Guerre to the collar of Hogarth's dog and to have led it through the streets of Oxford; and to have refused the Companionship of the Bath just as King George V was about to place the order round his neck. T. F. Breen, a former press attaché

---

* *The Times*, 7 November 1919.
† *Letters*, No. 122.

at the British Embassy in Berlin, was told this story by his old chief, Sir Horace Rumbold. 'In 1919 Sir Horace called on King George and was shown in just as Colonel Lawrence left. Sir Horace noticed at once that His Majesty was very much upset, flushed and distrait. After drumming on the desk with his fingers, the King turned to Sir Horace, apologised, and said that he had just had a stormy interview with Lawrence of Arabia, which had ended very abruptly.'

Lawrence, it seemed, had complained of the 'betrayal' of the Arabs, and alleged that he had made promises to them on the strength of a Foreign Office telegram purporting to be signed by the King. 'Lawrence then got very excited, spurned the decoration, used very bad language and walked out. "Luckily," the King added, "I have served in the Navy, when bad language did not upset me unduly. Only today I felt I had been played the Confidence Trick by an ex-Service officer of high reputation".'

Lawrence's own version of what happened occurs in a note by Robert Graves. The King had expressed a wish to meet Lawrence, who went to Buckingham Palace taking with him his rifle as a gift. The King thought the meeting would be a good opportunity formally to invest Lawrence with the CB and the DSO awarded to him during the war. Lawrence, however, told the King that he did not think it would be right for him to accept any award until the pledges given to the Arabs during the war were honoured. The King, thinking perhaps that Lawrence wanted something more important than the CB, mentioned an OM, but Lawrence again demurred. At this, according to Graves, the King sighed resignedly and said, 'Well, there's one vacant: I suppose it will have to go to [Marshal] Foch.'*

The official record states that on 20 October 1918, Lawrence had an audience of the King at which he was 'excused from accepting the insignia' of the CB and the DSO. But the awards had already been gazetted and when, three years later—in 1921—Lawrence was appointed as a plenipotentiary to negotiate a treaty with King Hussein, the official announcement referred to him as 'Companion of Our Most Honourable Order of the Bath, Companion of Our Distinguished Service Order'.

King George appears to have accepted Lawrence's refusal with good grace. Mr (later Sir) Owen Morshead, keeper of the Royal Library at Windsor Castle, wrote in 1930: 'I happened to mention to the King yesterday that I was hoping to have the pleasure of

* *Letters to his Biographers*, p. 107.

seeing Lawrence here on a private visit shortly and HM said that he would very much like to see him again.'*

Lawrence now plunged into controversy again. While he was becoming a 'matinee idol' the revolt in Iraq, formerly Mesopotamia, got worse, and the cost in lives and money of maintaining order grew daily. The government minimized the extent of the uprising as long as it could, but when the truth became known there was a general outcry. It was led, from the academic groves of All Souls, by Lieutenant-Colonel T. E. Lawrence. In articles in *The Sunday Times* and *The Observer*, he demanded to know: 'How long will we permit millions of pounds, thousands of Imperial troops and tens of thousands of Arabs to be sacrificed on behalf of a form of Colonial administration which can benefit nobody but its administrators?'† Lawrence also went for his old enemies in the India Office about the burning of the villages: 'It is odd we do not use poison gas on these occasions . . . By gas attacks the whole population of offending districts could be wiped out neatly; and as a method of government it would be no more immoral than the present system.' He was, of course, being ironic, but the grim truth was that something on these lines had actually been considered. As the cost of garrisoning Mesopotamia grew, the Government began to look round for some other way of maintaining order. A memorandum dated 19 February 1920 to the Chief of Air Staff, Sir Hugh Trenchard, from the office of the Secretary of State for War and Air, Winston Churchill, published here for the first time, shows how the Government was thinking:

SECRET

S. of S. tells me [the Assistant Secretary] today that the General Staff profess themselves unable to garrison Mesopotamia. The original estimate provided £21½ million for the purpose, which is considered to be more than the country is worth. S. of S. has had to cut this sum down,‡ with the result that the General Staff now propose a complete evacuation. He wishes to know whether you are prepared to take on Mesopotamia . . . It would . . . entail the provision of some kind of asphyxiating bombs calculated to cause

---

* O. F. Morshead to J. G. Wilson, 4 April 1930.

† It should not be imagined that Lawrence had changed his views and envisaged full independence for Iraq. What he had in mind was an Arab government with British advisers and the British government behind it, run on the lines of 'Cromer's Egypt'.

‡ A note in the margin says £5 million.

disablement of some kind but not death . . . for use in preliminary operations against turbulent tribes.*

Ten days later Churchill put the matter to Trenchard formally. He asked him to prepare a scheme for the RAF to take over control of Mesopotamia and an opinion as to whether the internal security of the country could be thus maintained. Lawrence got wind of what was happening and wrote to one of Trenchard's assistants offering advice. The assistant immediately showed the letter to Trenchard, who wrote to Lawrence on 17 March 1920 asking him to dinner for a talk. As a result, Lawrence had several dinners with Trenchard and a series of meetings with Trenchard's officers at which he put his views for a settlement in Mesopotamia. Lawrence's main points were that the air officer commanding Mesopotamia should also act as chief political officer; that the man for the job was Air Vice-Marshal Sir John Salmond; that Cornwallis (see page 129) or Ronald Storrs should be second in command; that Salmond's headquarters should be in Cairo and that of his second in command in Baghdad: and, most important of all, that Lawrence hoped 'for a native state with English advisers only'.†

The significance of all this lies not so much in the scheme itself as in Lawrence's part in it. He had no official position now and was merely a former Foreign Office official living in academic seclusion at Oxford. Yet not only was he helping devise a plan for controlling Mesopotamia, but also recommending the man to be in charge, helping to define his duties, and putting forward the names of former colleagues for the post of assistant. Furthermore, he was trying to find out what opposition the scheme was likely to encounter in the Cabinet by talking to friends in the War Office and the India Office and publicly expressing his views on what sort of Mesopotamian state *he* hoped for. This was the sort of fixing and arranging at which Lawrence excelled. He put his weight behind Trenchard's plan—and it is clear that it was with Trenchard that the plan originated—because it appeared that it would enable him to add most of his own political aims for the country as part of a package deal.

Early in 1921 Lawrence was offered a chance not only of assuring the success of the RAF scheme, but of helping to impose some kind of order on the whole of the British area of the Middle East. The Prime Minister, Lloyd George, had seen the need for fresh and radical thinking, and he took the Middle East out of the joint—but

* Trenchard Papers.
† Ibid.

rival—hands of Curzon at the Foreign Office and Edwin Montagu
at the India Office and put it under the Colonial Office, of which
Churchill was now in charge. Churchill gathered around him a
group of bright young men determined to tidy up an area which he
said presented 'a most melancholy and alarming picture'. After
several approaches he persuaded Lawrence to join his new Middle
East Department as adviser on Arab Affairs.

Lawrence flung himself whole-heartedly into this assignment. He
and Churchill got on extremely well and together began to formulate
a solution to the problems which the Peace Conference had left
untouched. Their plans were announced at the Cairo Conference
which took place in March 1921, though the use of the word 'conference' to describe the meeting is not really appropriate. Most of
the serious decisions had been taken by the Middle East Department
in London before the start of the Conference, the main purpose of
which was to decide the best way of putting these decisions into effect.
Lawrence admitted this: 'The decisions of the Cairo Conference
were prepared by us in London, over dinner tables at the Ship
restaurant in Whitehall',* and Liddell Hart wrote: 'Everything
staged before they went out for Cairo Conference. T. E. had settled
not only questions the Conference would consider, but decisions
they would reach. "Talk of leaving things to man on spot—we left
nothing".'†

Lawrence's first job was to make some sort of amends to Feisal,
and in secrecy and with some hesitation Feisal was offered the throne
of Iraq. He had arrived in London in December 1920, as an envoy
of Hussein, to have an audience with the King. Lord Winterton,‡
acting for the Middle East Department, invited him to a dinner at
which Lawrence was present, and he and Winterton spent hours
persuading the disillusioned Feisal to accept the Kingdom of Iraq.
As Winterton describes it: 'He was very bitter about what he considered was the way in which he had been treated by both British
and French and he made some wounding remarks about British
character in general.'§

The British hesitation about offering Iraq to Feisal sprang from
uncertainty as to the attitude of the Iraqis themselves—did they
want him? And if he agreed to accept the throne there would still

* *T. E. Lawrence by his Friends*, p. 230.
† *T. E. Lawrence to his Biographers*, p. 143.
‡ Lord Winterton (1883–1962). Conservative politician and later, through long
service, 'father' of the House of Commons. At this period he was concerned with
affairs in the Middle East Department of the Foreign Office.
§ *Near to Greatness: A Life of Earl Winterton*.

be the problem of getting him accepted. Although he was eventually elected King, the work of making certain of this began well before his candidature was announced at the Cairo Conference. A memorandum drawn up by the Middle East Department before the Conference reads: 'We consider that Feisal should be the ruler, and that the first step is to ascertain from Sir P. Cox [recently reappointed High Commissioner in Iraq] *that he can ensure the Council of State selecting him* . . .* As soon as the Council have notified their choice, Feisal should be invited to proceed forthwith to Mesopotamia.'†

It is worth following the steps by which Feisal was established on the throne of Mesopotamia as an example of British imperial diplomacy in action. Soon after the Cairo Conference opened Churchill sent a 'Personal and Secret' telegram to Lloyd George saying that the prospects in Mesopotamia were promising and adding, 'I think we shall reach unanimous conclusion among all authorities that Feisal offers hope of best and cheapest solution'. Lloyd George was worried about French reaction to the British making Feisal ruler in Mesopotamia, and he told Churchill: 'We think it essential that real initiative in any demand for Feisal should come from Mesopotamia.'‡

This made Churchill impatient. He told the Prime Minister that a procedure for having Feisal adopted as King had already been devised by Sir Percy Cox, Gertrude Bell (Cox's Oriental Secretary in Mesopotamia), and Lawrence. 'We are quite as fully conscious as you are of desire for securing a spontaneous movement for Feisal in Mesopotamia as a prelude to his being countenanced by us. Unless we have a mind of our own on the subject it is by no means certain that this will occur.'§

The situation was complicated, added Churchill, by the fact that there were other claimants to the throne, but he rapidly demolished their pretensions. 'Ibn Saud would plunge the whole country into religious pandemonium . . . Sayid Taleb . . . man of bad character and untrustworthy—Naqib is tottering on . . . brink of the grave.' Eager, perhaps, to have another 'biff' at the French, Lawrence became so certain that he and Churchill would get their way that a few days later he cabled from Cairo to Feisal in London:

THINGS HAVE GONE EXACTLY AS HOPED. PLEASE START FOR MECCA AT ONCE BY QUICKEST POSSIBLE ROUTE . . . I WILL MEET YOU ON THE WAY AND EXPLAIN DETAILS. SAY

* Authors' italics.
† PRO, AIR, 8/37.
‡ PRO, FO, 686/85.
§ Ibid.

ONLY THAT YOU ARE GOING TO SEE YOUR FATHER AND ON NO ACCOUNT PUT ANYTHING IN PRESS.*

When Lord Curzon, the Foreign Secretary, heard of this he was horrified. He had the unenviable task of persuading the French that Britain had had nothing to do with pushing Feisal's candidature as King of Mesopotamia. Since the French were not fools, he anticipated considerable difficulty in convincing them and hoped that Churchill would realize that 'the task would be doubly hard if, after meeting the Emir at Port Said, Col. Lawrence, known to be an official of the Colonial Office and to have been with Mr Churchill . . . were to accompany the Emir even as far as Jeddah on his return to Mecca, from which place he is presently to start with a view to setting himself up as candidate for the throne of Iraq'.†

So Lawrence did not go to meet Feisal, who proceeded to Baghdad and was duly elected King with one of those suspiciously large majorities—96·8 per cent. The only serious opposition candidate, Sayid Taleb, was successfully neutralized after Churchill had dropped a hint at the Cairo Conference: ' . . . all members of the [Mesopotamian] Government should use their best endeavours to promote the policy to be adopted.' The British Army in Mesopotamia saw its duty clearly: as Sayid Taleb left Sir Percy's house after having had tea with Lady Cox and Gertrude Bell, he was whisked into an armoured car and eventually sent for a long holiday in Ceylon.‡ Sayid Taleb might not have been a man of high principles— he might even have been, as some Arab sources suggest, 'a minor brigand'—but his kidnapping to clear the way for Feisal's election must be regarded as a characteristic climax to the Churchill– Lawrence intrigue and must have appeared to many Mesopotamians as a curious example of the democratic self-determination they had been promised.§

The memorandum which the Middle East Department drew up before the Cairo Conference not only recommended Feisal as King of Mesopotamia, but also examined the situation in Palestine, confirmed the terms of the Balfour Declaration, and considered the problem of the country's borders. It proposed that Palestine should end at the River Jordan, and although the area on the eastern side of the river was therefore not included, some way would have to be found of keeping it for Britain under the Palestine Mandate.

---

* Ibid.   † Ibid.
‡ H. St John Philby, *Arabian Days*. London, Robert Hale, 1948.
§ Feisal ruled until his death in 1933. His family remained on the throne until 1958, when his grandson, Feisal II, was murdered by revolutionaries.

The Conference had barely started when Abdullah, Hussein's third son, brought this problem into sharp relief by marching into Amman, Trans-Jordan's principal city, having announced that he planned to liberate Syria and restore Feisal as its ruler. The French prepared for an attack and urged Britain to turn Abdullah out. Thus Britain found herself back in the old cleft stick. She needed a stable, friendly leader in Jordan as security for Palestine, and no Arab leader presented himself other than Abdullah. But the French view was that Britain, by supporting Abdullah, was, as Churchill had said at the Cairo Conference, 'building a monster which would eventually devour us'. Churchill also saw another danger: that Trans-Jordan might be used as a base for anti-Zionist disturbances. Lawrence offered a solution: in four or five years, he said, under the influence of a just policy, opposition to Zionism would have decreased. In the meantime Trans-Jordan could be used as a safety valve by the appointment of a ruler—Abdullah—on whom he could bring pressure to check anti-Zionism. (Here we have Lawrence back in his old role as an *éminence grise*, only this time in the service of Abdullah instead of Feisal.) The ideal ruler, Lawrence said, would be a person who was not too powerful and who would have to rely upon His Majesty's Government for the retention of his office.

If all this smacks of horse-trading politics at its worst, it must be remembered that the Conference was out to settle the Middle East situation, no matter what the obstacles. Churchill, summing up the deal that Britain could offer, said that provided Abdullah could be made amenable to British policy by arrival at a general understanding with his family—which would include the appointment of his brother to the throne of Iraq, a subsidy to his father, King Hussein, and a guarantee to restrain Ibn Saud—it might be possible to enable him to set up a stable government in Trans-Jordan, on the understanding that he should use his influence to prevent anti-French and anti-Zionist propaganda there.

All that now remained was to get Abdullah to agree to these conditions. A meeting was arranged at Government House in Jerusalem on 28 March 1921. Lawrence met Abdullah at Salt across the Jordan the day before and prepared him for Churchill's proposals by implying that the main purpose of the meeting 'was to urge the necessity of helping Britain to install Feisal on the throne of Iraq'. As Abdullah recorded it: 'He said to me, "You are well known for sacrificing your personal ambitions for your country, so stay here. If you succeed, you will achieve the unity of Syria in six months. God willing, we will visit you in Damascus to offer our congratulations".'* According to Abdullah, Lawrence also pointed out to him what might happen if he did not co-operate; 'You may lose everything, as it is possible that Ibn Saud may reach Mecca in three days, and England has done what she can.'

The formal meeting in Jerusalem took three sessions, but all went smoothly. Churchill, Sir Herbert Samuel and Lawrence persuaded Abdullah without difficulty to accept all their proposals. It was fast, brilliant, and cynical diplomacy, complete with promises, threats, and a pay-off. The following digest of what took place is based on the official record.

Churchill suggested that Trans-Jordan should be an Arab province under an Arab governor responsible to the High Commissioner for Palestine. Abdullah countered this with an offer of his own: an Arab Emir over Palestine *and* Trans-Jordan on the lines of Feisal's position in Iraq; if this could be done, the difficulties between Arabs and Jews would be overcome. Churchill said Britain was already too far committed to a different system in Palestine. At this point Abdullah wanted to know what British policy really aimed at—did Britain mean to establish a Jewish kingdom in Palestine and turn out the non-Jewish population? If so, it would be better to tell the Arabs at once and not keep them in suspense. The Allies appeared to think that men could be cut down and transplanted in the same way as trees. Sir Herbert Samuel, who had been appointed the first High Commissioner for Palestine and Trans-Jordan in 1920, interrupted to say that there was no intention either to cut down or to transplant, but only to plant new trees. He then made a series of predictions (most of which were to prove wrong). There was, he said, no question of setting up a Jewish government in Palestine. The present administration would, he hoped, continue for many years. All religions would be equally respected. No land would be taken from any Arab, nor would the Moslem religion be hindered in any way. The Palestine Mandate embodied the terms of the Balfour Declaration in which two distinct promises had been made— one to the Jews and the other to the Arabs. His Majesty's Government were resolutely determined to fulfil both these promises. He was confident that in thirty or forty years it would be found that exactly the same policy was being pursued. No British High Commissioner, and certainly not himself, would ever countenance harm or injustice being done to the non-Jewish population. The bargaining continued, but Abdullah showed no sign of agreeing to anything. Just before the luncheon break, therefore, Churchill made the alternatives very

* *Political Dictates*, published in Arabic in Amman, 1939, p. 24.

plain; he was taking a great responsibility as the new Minister in charge of the Middle East in advising his colleagues to join hands with the Sherifan family. He had been told that His Majesty's Government would be better advised to split the Arabs up into distinct and separated local governments. He wished to impress upon the Emir that a very grave choice had to be made within the next few days by His Majesty's Government, namely, whether they should divide or unite the Arab peoples with whom they had to deal.

Under these threats, Abdullah yielded. He said he still thought his own solution was the best, but he was quite prepared to consider new proposals. Churchill suggested a short-term solution: Abdullah himself should remain in Trans-Jordan for a period of six months to prepare the way for the appointment, with his consent, of an Arab governor under the High Commissioner. Abdullah would receive money and troops and in return would guarantee that there would be no anti-French or anti-Zionist activity in the country. This six months' formula was just a charade and both Churchill and Abdullah knew Abdullah would be there indefinitely. Abdullah accepted it, asking only that he be regarded as a British officer and trusted accordingly.*

The final chapter to this sorry episode occurs in a letter from Churchill to Sir Herbert Samuel on 2 April 1921. On his way back to England Churchill was tidying up the arrangements over Trans-Jordan:

'Emir Abdullah has promised to work with us and for us to do his best to restrain the people from anti-French action . . . He must be given a very free hand, as he has a most difficult task to perform. Not only has he been checked in mid-career in his campaign against the French, but he has been asked to execute a complete *volte-face* . . . I wish you to make an immediate advance . . . up to £5,000 to Abdullah for his personal expenses, quite apart from administrative or military expenditure, in Trans-Jordania. This had better be arranged through Lawrence, as he will know better what Abdullah's needs are and how the payments can most conveniently be made.'†

Feisal on the throne in Iraq, Abdullah in Trans-Jordan; what still remained to be done? The buying off of Ibn Saud. Britain had

* Abdullah reigned until 1951, when he was shot dead while entering the Mosque of El Aqsa in Jerusalem in the company of his grandson, the present King Hussein. The assassin was a follower of the ex-Mufti of Jerusalem, Haj Amin el Husseini, who had accused Abdullah of having betrayed the Arabs over Palestine.   † PRO, AIR, 8/37.

kept Ibn Saud quiet for over a year by encouraging him to attack
the Shammar, the rulers of Northern Nejd, instead of Hussein. (One
wonders how the Shammar felt about being used as a punch-bag to
suit British foreign policy.) But now, as Lawrence pointed out,
Britain needed the friendship of the Shammar to protect a projected
air and road route from Palestine to Iraq, so another way of pacifying
Ibn Saud had to be found. It was not difficult. The conference
decided to recommend 'that a subsidy of £100,000 a year be paid
monthly in arrears to Bin [sic] Saud . . . and that a British representative be sent to him to explain to him the new conditions, and impress
on him that on their fulfilment depends the payment of each
monthly instalment'.* And there was still another principal to be
considered, King Hussein, Sherif of Mecca, the man who had
raised the Arab Revolt.

'King Hussein . . . concerns us as guardian of the Holy Places
and because of his attitude towards the decision of the Allies as
regards Arab areas. Unless he accepts these decisions in their newly-
modified form he will be a cause of unrest in the mandated territories
and a nuisance in the Hedjaz. The Moslem world believes we
created him, and will blame us if with the disappearance of the
Turks from Arabia the pilgrimage conditions [to Mecca and
Medina] become worse . . . we recommend that enough subsidy be
paid to King Hussein to enable him to put his house in order; and
on the grounds of principle we recommend that he be paid the same
rate as Bin [sic] Saud, namely £100,000 a year. To pay one more
than the other causes jealousy and unfavourable comment.'†

This was *realpolitik*, but before Hussein was to get his subsidy
there were various conditions which British—and French—interests
required him to fulfil, the main one being to ratify the Treaty of
Versailles, 'including acceptance of the mandatory principle and the
disposal of the Arab countries'. (This was the one which interested
the French. France wanted Britain to get—in writing—Hussein's
acceptance of the French position in Syria.) No one imagined that
it would be an easy task to get the Old Man of Mecca to signify his
agreement to the way the Arab countries had been 'disposed', but
no one, especially Lawrence, who was to undertake the mission,
realized just how difficult it was going to be.

Before the Cairo Conference wound itself to an end Churchill,

* PRO, AIR, 8/37.
† Ibid.

Lawrence, Trenchard, and Gertrude Bell rode on camels to the Pyramids and were photographed for history. Churchill fell off his camel and insisted on remounting, while Lawrence shook with laughter. On the official train to Jerusalem some Arabs blocked the line with their bodies. Lawrence spoke to them, then told Churchill that they wanted to see him. Churchill stood at the window of the train and two Arab leaders presented him with a petition dealing with Jewish policy in Palestine. 'Winston accepted it gravely and, as he placed it in his pocket, the crowd roared approval. Suddenly they began dancing like children, cheering madly, and as the train gathered speed they continued to dance alongside, cheering and waving us farewell.'*

It was a touching incident, and not untypical. One wonders whether the historians have not perhaps got it all wrong and that it was the Arabs who had a soft spot for the British rather than the other way round.

In London Lawrence and other members of the Middle East section started preparing a treaty for King Hussein to sign, and on 8 July Lawrence sailed for Jedda with full plenipotentiary powers to negotiate with Hussein. The two men had their first meeting on 30 July, and during the next two months, in the heat of the Arabian summer, they had a series of abortive discussions in which Hussein's obstinacy over Palestine ('Britain must withdraw from Palestine and leave the question to the nation') drove Lawrence to such a fury that he was unable to disguise his annoyance. An examination of the telegrams exchanged between him and the Foreign Office during this period† shows his sense of bitter frustration and both his and the Foreign Office's determination to get Hussein to sign even if it meant using such tactics as suppressing his telegrams and withholding his subsidy.

At first Lawrence was reasonably optimistic: 'Have had several meetings with King . . . He has announced his abandonment of position founded on MacMahon letters‡ but raises absurd new ideas daily. Old man is conceited to a degree, greedy and stupid, but very friendly and protests devotion to our interests.'§

A charming little exchange of telegrams between Lawrence and Sir Percy Cox in Baghdad followed. Lawrence learnt that Hussein had cabled to Feisal, and, worried in case this might upset the

---

* W. H. Thomson, *Guard from the Yard*. Jarrolds, London, 1938.
† PRO, FO, 686/93.
‡ See Chapter 8.
§ PRO, FO, 686/93.

arrangements for settling Feisal into his kingdom, Lawrence decided to use Zeid, Hussein's youngest son, as a pawn. He sent a priority message to Cox:

KING HUSSEIN HAS WIRED TO FEISAL IN CYPHER TONIGHT. I HOPE YOU WILL SUPPRESS IT AND DELIVER HIM FOLLOWING, BEGINS 'NEGOTIATIONS WITH LAWRENCE ARE GOING ON WELL AND CONCLUSIONS WILL BE SUBMITTED TO YOU—ZEID'.

This unusual request alarmed Cox. He held up Hussein's telegram, but he telegraphed to Lawrence:

CAN YOU NOT SEND ME ZEID'S AUTHORITY TO SUPPRESS.

Lawrence ignored this for four days and then he said:

HUSSEINS TELEGRAM MAY NOW BE DELIVERED WITH MESSAGE FROM ME THAT KING IS GRADUALLY COMING AROUND TO OUR POINT OF VIEW AND HAS BEEN PROVISIONALLY PAID A MONTH'S SUBSIDY IN CONSEQUENCE. THE NEGOTIATIONS HAVE BEEN DIFFICULT.

Lawrence's actions approached the dishonourable, unless, of course, he was acting with Zeid's knowledge and consent in a sort of family conspiracy to protect Hussein from himself. But Emir Zeid is still alive and now lives in London. He emphatically denied, on being shown a copy of the telegram that Lawrence wanted to send in his name, that he had ever authorized such a proceeding. At any rate, negotiations continued, with the King apparently growing nearer the end of his tether. Lawrence reported contemptuously to London: 'Have had more conversations with the King . . . I gave him my candid opinion of his character and capacity. There was a scene, remarkable to me that not only the Foreign Secretary but the King also burst into tears . . . The King is weaker than I thought, and could, I think, be bullied into nearly complete surrender . . . If he is beaten over this business he will come easier next time.' On his own responsibility Lawrence gave the King a loan of 80,000 rupees*—'he was in urgent need of it, and so proportionately grateful'—but was alarmed to find later that Hussein had bought ten aeroplanes, six of which came from Italy. This was a facer both for Lawrence and the Colonial Office, but Lawrence explained that the money came from Hussein's own pocket and added—somewhat unconvincingly—that 'perhaps it is not understood . . . what rubbish the Italian aeroplanes here are . . . and how disgusted King Hussein will

* At that time the equivalent of approximately £8,000.

shortly be with his very expensive purchases. I think it is an admirable lesson for him.'*

After five weeks London was becoming impatient, and Lawrence felt constrained to stress the difficulties. 'He [Hussein] feels himself immune in Mecca from reprisals: and would like to be a martyr, and . . . we can only incline him our way by appealing to his good nature, by stopping his subsidy, by blockading his port, or by loosing Bin [sic] Saud upon him.'†

Lawrence had time for only one more attempt. On 24 June 1921, General Henri Gouraud, the French Commander-in-Chief in Syria, and later Chief Commissioner there, and the man who had driven Feisal from Damascus, had been ambushed between Dama and Kuneitra and an attempt made to assassinate him. The French had made capital out of this, claiming that Arabs from Trans-Jordan were responsible. They demanded that Abdullah should hand over a number of nationalists whom they listed by name. The British pressed Abdullah to comply and, feeling that they were no longer giving him the support he needed, Abdullah chose this moment to announce that he wanted to go to London, as a dignified method of retiring from his post.

The effect of all this was that Curzon, worried about what Abdullah's resignation might lead to, ordered Lawrence to forget about Hussein and to go to Trans-Jordan as soon as possible to try to settle matters. After Lawrence had left, the Colonial Office began to try other tactics with the old King: 'Inform Hussein that Prince of Wales will visit him at Jeddah and will convey an invitation to him to visit England as guest of HMG . . . provided that King Hussein signs treaty in time arrangements to be made. King Hussein will receive £5,000 monthly, first payment being made one month after date of signature of treaty.'‡ It was no use. Hussein refused to budge.

In Trans-Jordan Lawrence was more successful. Pending the finding of a permanent officer, he had been deputed to the post of Chief British Representative at Amman, where he checked and reported on internal security plans, tidied up the administration, defied the French ('We cannot afford to chuck away our hopes of building something to soothe our neighbours' feelings'),§ persuaded Abdullah to stay on, and convinced Sir Herbert Samuel that this was

* PRO, FO, 686/93.
† Ibid.
‡ Ibid.
§ Letter to Colonel S. F. Newcombe, 8 December 1921.

the right decision. He also lost no time in recommending that St John Philby* be installed as local representative of the High Commissioner for Palestine in place of the system of having several district officers who had tended to run their areas on Indian lines. When Philby arrived, Lawrence spent a few days showing him round, before leaving for London early in December. Philby recorded in his diary: 'The departure of Lawrence leaves me in full charge, and at the same time a gap which will not be easy to fill . . . that he has affected a great change in the situation since he came here two months ago admits of no doubt . . . the administration which he had encouraged to function is working smoothly; Abdullah has apparently become resigned to being a puppet figurehead. In short, there are great possibilities in the situation as it appears to me now.'† There was, however, also the matter of Lawrence's official accounts, never one of his strong points. As Philby records it: 'All he handed over to me on his departure was a few confidential documents . . . and a small sheet of paper containing his accounts of the expenditure of about £100,000 during his short term of office. One item of £10,000 was simply written off as "lost or mislaid"; and by a curious coincidence, sometime thereafter a steel safe containing ten thousand gold sovereigns did come to light buried in the sand dunes of Akaba.' It appears that what actually happened is that Lawrence buried the safe for security reasons under a concrete cover on the quay at Akaba and then forgot about it; he left the key in a drawer of his desk where some time later it was found, the safe located and the money (in reality £7,500) recovered.

Even yet his protracted struggle with Hussein was not over; for before he left Amman, Lawrence again became involved in trying to get the King to sign the treaty. Hussein had empowered Abdullah to negotiate for him and on 9 December, just before Lawrence left Trans-Jordan for England, the two of them reached an agreement which they both signed. This agreement was then sent to Hussein for ratification, but the old King, obstinate to the end, refused to put his signature to it. Negotiations went on throughout 1922 and 1923, but Hussein still held out. He continued to reign, bitterly regretting having raised the Arab Revolt, until Ibn Saud and the Wahabis overran Mecca in 1924, when he abdicated and went into exile, first at Akaba and then, when Ibn Saud protested to Britain about this, in Cyprus. Britain awarded him the Grand Cross of the Order

* St John Philby (1885–1960), explorer and Arabist, friend and adviser to Ibn Saud.

† *Forty Years in the Wilderness*. Robert Hale, London, 1957, p. 108.

THE COLONIAL OFFICE 151

of the Bath, and Ronald Storrs, by then Governor in Cyprus, carried out the investiture. In 1930 at the age of seventy-five Hussein had a stroke, and the British government allowed him to go to Amman to end his days near his sons. He died the following year.

There was no doubt that Hussein was a stubborn old man, irascible and difficult to deal with. But there is also little doubt that Britain treated him shabbily, flattering and inflating him when it suited her and abandoning him when he refused to come to heel. Lawrence had no time for him and appears at one stage to have considered that Ibn Saud in Mecca might be preferable to Hussein. In an annotation to a Foreign Office telegram of 18 April 1919, while Hussein and Ibn Saud were making war-like noises at each other, Lawrence wrote: 'If he [ie, Ibn Saud] abandons the Wahabi creed, we will not do too badly. If he remains Wahabi, we will send the Moslem part of the Indian Army to recover Mecca, and break the Wahabi movement . . . I offered at Xmas 1918 to do it with ten tanks.'*

Lawrence was now ready to say goodbye to the Colonial Office. Churchill made several attempts to persuade him to stay on, dangling before him the promise of a glittering career. But Lawrence was not interested. He regarded the Middle East settlement he had helped Churchill make as redemption in full by Britain of her promises to the Arabs: 'So we were quit of the war-time Eastern adventure, with clean hands.'†

It was a hollow vindication. Britain made many promises to the Arabs. If one takes only the last, the Anglo-French declaration made just before the Armistice, as the one which the British considered binding, then was it fulfilled? It promised the setting up of national governments chosen by the people themselves: in short, a clear pledge of self-determination. But whatever else the Churchill–Lawrence settlement in the Middle East might be said to have achieved, self-determination was certainly not part of it; so it is hard to see how Lawrence's statement can be justified.

The settlement did bring a semblance of order, but time has shown that this only postponed the reckoning. As we have seen, Feisal's family survived in Iraq until 1958 when Feisal II was murdered by revolutionaries. Abdullah was murdered over the question of the Jews in Palestine in 1951, but his grandson, the present King Hussein, still rules uneasily in Jordan, the state Lawrence and Churchill created. Britain kept her mandate in Palestine until 1948 when she

* FO, 608/80, Note to a telegram from Colonel A. T. Wilson.
† *Seven Pillars*, Chapter XLVIII.

had to abandon it and the state of Israel came into being. The whole area, wracked with the bitterness inherited from Britain's 'wartime Eastern adventure', still presents the same melancholy and alarming picture which Churchill saw in 1921.

But at that time, right or wrong, Lawrence felt that he had had enough: his retirement from politics was 'final and absolute'. From devoting himself to his country's welfare, he now had to turn to his own. The physical strain to which he had heedlessly subjected himself during the war, the emotional stress of the double role he had chosen to play, the elation of victory, the near-realization of a dream which had turned to bitter defeat—all these had sapped Lawrence's well-being. Yet although he believed that he had left the Middle East behind, the residue of its problems and his attempts at their solution were to plague him for the rest of his life.

11 Breakdown

Lawrence, writing Seven Pillars of Wisdom, *is in a deeply disturbed emotional state as he relives the Revolt in the desert and faces the question: was it all a fraud? His dedication to* Seven Pillars *with its mysterious S.A. is explained. He writes to Trenchard asking to be allowed to enlist in the ranks of the RAF and uses the story of an offer of a commission in the Irish Free State army to get Churchill, who dislikes the idea, to agree. Lawrence embarks on a relationship with John Bruce, a tough young Scotsman, to whom he spins an elaborate tale to prepare him for a ritual that he is planning. Lawrence is physically, emotionally, and financially exhausted when he finally receives Trenchard's permission to join the RAF, which he does under the pseudonym of John Hume Ross.*

Lawrence returned to England from Jordan and his 'settling' of the Middle East in a deeply disturbed emotional state, which eventually was to reach a condition near to madness. His travels over much familiar ground—this time by T-model Ford instead of camel—had been an unsettling experience. The twisted rails and shattered sleepers of the Hejaz railway were lasting evidence of the reality of the Revolt and of his role in it. Now he had to face what he had long postponed: the realization that the Arabian adventure was over and that there was no longer any excuse for delaying his return to civilian life. His emotional state was partly due to what could be called a post-war depression: nostalgia for the comradeship of arms; the loss of a sense of security engendered by order and discipline; the change from a life of excitement and danger in the realization of a positive ideal to one of apparent triviality with no easily recognizable goal. Life during a period of transition such as this can be difficult for anyone; for Lawrence it became almost unbearable. For he had not abandoned Arabia and the Revolt entirely: he was reliving it in writing *Seven Pillars*, and as the words ran out across the page, putting 'ink fever into me', he had to face again the fact that his role had involved him in an empty and dishonourable fraud. How much should he tell? Should he say openly that the British would have promised the Arabs almost anything in order to get them to revolt? As Newcombe had put it, '. . . he [Feisal] must have a political propaganda which will induce the people to risk their lives. It must be a clear statement, showing that they will be fighting for an Arab Govt.'.* Should Lawrence say in *Seven Pillars* that because he knew Britain had no intention of allowing the Arabs to have a government of their own, his part in the conspiracy was a shameful one? The surprising thing is that Lawrence *did* admit this, justifying his action by saying that Arab help was necessary to win the war and 'better we win and break our word than lose'. But this was written in that first chapter of *Seven Pillars* which was set up in proof and then suppressed on the advice of Bernard Shaw. 'For political reasons'† it remained unpublished until 1939, when it was included in *Oriental Assembly*. It was reinstated in English editions of *Seven Pillars* in 1940, but to date has not appeared in any American edition. So perhaps Lawrence intended to tell the whole story of the Revolt, but weakened when he realized what it would involve. At any rate, what he eventually settled for was a personal and selective narrative of one man's war, in keeping with a note he made while travelling in an RAF plane on his way to Cairo in 1919: 'Let my excuse be that I have introduced such trivia, just so that no one should mistake this narrative of mine for History. The book of battle is a large one, and each of us sees only a little page. I have written down what I thought, and saw and did, fully conscious myself that as I sometimes did ill and saw imperfectly, so also my thoughts must often be wrong. This book is the bone of history, not History herself.'‡ It is clear from this that Lawrence decided against telling the full story of the Revolt as he knew it. He was no doubt inhibited by the Official Secrets Act, but his main reason must surely have been that the real story of Britain's actions in Arabia and his own part in them he found too shameful to tell. Even the form in which he decided to write the story, his 'bone of history', involved him in analysing his motives and re-living his remorse, but still he pushed ahead, hoping that by getting it down on paper the whole affair would be somehow justified and his guilt—exacerbated by his ever-growing fame—would no longer gnaw at him. So he drove himself, ignoring his exhaustion, to finish the writing and be done with Arabia and the Arabs for ever.

* Note by Colonel S. F. Newcombe, 24 May 1917. Wingate Papers.
† A. W. Lawrence, in preface to *Oriental Assembly* by T. E. Lawrence. Williams and Norgate, London, 1939.
‡ Bodleian Library.

Alan Dawnay, a close colleague of Lawrence's during the war, said that at this period he lived like an animal. He wrote with dogged persistence, ate when he was hungry, and after eating, slept; he kept no track of time and took his meals at railway station refreshment rooms in the heart of London because they were always open. He wrote to Robert Graves, 'I nearly went off my head this spring [1922] heaving at that beastly book of mine'.

Lawrence's trouble was that recreating the forces and emotions which had driven him so powerfully for four difficult years involved him in an examination of his own character. As far as we can discover, only once had he ever done this with complete honesty and only once did he set down his conclusions in writing. It is worth examining these not only because they relate directly to *Seven Pillars* and its writing, but also to the major personal motivation for his years in Arabia.

The circumstances were these. A certain Foreign Office official who got on well with Lawrence, had asked him one night in Paris during the Peace Conference exactly what he had been up to in Arabia. The offical was amazed when next morning Lawrence handed him a three-page letter, with the request that he should burn it after he had read it. Lawrence later waived this condition, but insisted that it should remain secret until both of them were dead. Because it shows a side of Lawrence's life we have not yet examined, and because it reveals the compelling private motive behind his years in the desert, we quote it in full:

> Dear ——,
> You asked me 'Why' today, and I'm going to tell you exactly what my motives in the Arab affair were, in order of strength:
>
> (i) Personal. I liked a particular Arab very much, and I thought that freedom for the race would be an acceptable present.
>
> (ii) Patriotic. I wanted to help win the war, and Arab help reduced Allenby's losses by thousands.
>
> (iii) Intellectual curiosity. I wanted to feel what it was like to be the mainspring of a national movement, and to have some millions of people expressing themselves through me: and being a half-poet, I don't value material things much. Sensation and mind seem to me much greater, and the ideal, such a thing as the impulse that took us into Damascus, the only thing worth doing.

(iv) Ambition. You know how Lionel Curtis has made his conception of the Empire—a commonwealth of free peoples —generally accepted. I wanted to widen that idea beyond the Anglo-Saxon shape, and form a new nation of thinking people, all acclaiming our freedom, and demanding admittance into our Empire. There is, to my eyes, no other road for Egypt and India in the end, and I would have made their path easier, by creating an Arab Dominion in the Empire.

I don't think there are any other reasons. You are sufficiently Scotch to understand my analysing my own mind so formally. The process intended was to take Damascus, and run it (as anyone fully knowing the East and West could run it), as an independent ally of G[reat] B[ritain]. Then to turn on Hejaz and conquer it: then to project the semi-educated Syrians on Yemen, and build that up quickly (without Yemen there is no re-birth for the Arabs) and finally to receive Mesopotamia into the block so made: all this could be done in thirty years of directed effort, and without impairing British holdings. It is only the substitution of a 999 years' lease for a complete sale.

Now look what happened when we took Damascus: Motive (i) I found had died some weeks before: so my gift was wasted, and my future doings indifferent on that count. Motive (ii). This was achieved, for Turkey was broken, and the central powers were so unified that to break one was to break all. Motive (iii). This was romantic mainly, and one never repeats a sensation. When I rode into Damascus the whole country-side was on fire with enthusiasm, and in the town a hundred thousand people shouted my name. Success always kills the hope by surfeit. Motive (iv). This remained, but it was not strong enough to make me stay. I asked Allenby for leave, and when he gave it me, came straight home. It's the dying remains of this weakest of all my reasons which made me put up a half-fight for Feisal in Paris and elsewhere, and which occasionally drives me into your room to jest about what might be done.

If you want to make me work again you would have to recreate motives (ii) and (iii). As you are not God, Motive (i) is beyond your power. I'm not conscious of having done a crooked thing to anyone since I began to push the Arab Movement, though I prostituted myself in Arab Service.

For an Englishman to put himself at the disposal of a red race is to sell himself to a brute, like Swift's Houhynyms [*sic*]. However my body and soul were my own, and no one can reproach me for what I do to them: and to all the rest of you I'm clean.

When you have got as far as this, please burn it all. I've never told anyone before, and may not again, because it isn't nice to open oneself out. I laugh at myself because giving up has made me look so futile.

T.E.L.*

Apart from this very revealing exposure of what he now thought of his years with the Arabs—'I prostituted myself in Arab Service. For an Englishman to put himself at the disposal of a red race is to sell himself to a brute, like Swift's Houhynyms'—Motive (i) is perhaps the most interesting. We have seen Lawrence's patriotism, his intellectual curiosity and his ambition to create an Arab dominion in the Empire, but what of this 'particular Arab' Lawrence 'liked very much' and for whom he thought 'freedom for the race would be an acceptable present'? Who was this Arab?

In his letter to the official, Lawrence was very frank, much more so than in the tantalizing epilogue to *Seven Pillars*. There he is deliberately vague: 'The strongest motive throughout had been a personal one, not mentioned here, but present to me, I think, every hour of these two years. Active pains and joys might fling up, like towers, among my days: but, refluent as air, this hidden urge reformed, to be the persisting element of life, till near the end. It was dead, before we reached Damascus.'

The reader cannot help but wonder what this 'personal motive' was and why there is no other mention of it in *Seven Pillars*. What was this hidden urge, this persisting element of life? The letter in Paris takes the epilogue a stage further and answers some of the questions. We can say with reasonable certainty that the personal motive was, as Lawrence wrote in Paris, that he 'liked a particular Arab very much, and ... thought that freedom for the race would be an acceptable present'. But having solved one part of the mystery, we find that Lawrence has added another. Why did he carefully avoid using a personal pronoun and write, 'freedom for *the* race' rather than 'freedom for *his* race', or 'freedom for *her* race'? There are clues elsewhere in Lawrence's works that suggest an answer to these questions and, with the evidence of one who served with Lawrence,

* Bodleian Library.

Tom Beaumont, and who has remained silent until now, go some way to solving the mystery of the identity of this 'particular Arab'.

First, we must examine the dedicatory poem to 'S.A.' in *Seven Pillars*. The version as published is not as Lawrence wrote it, but as Robert Graves, his friend, arranged it. Graves toned down the more personal references and rewrote a complete stanza. To show what changes Graves made, here is the original with Graves's substitutions in italics:

> I loved you, so I drew these tides of men into my hands
>   and wrote my will across the sky in stars
>   [*earn*]
> To gain you Freedom, the seven-pillared worthy house,
>   that your eyes might be shining for me
>   [*we*]
>   When I came
>
>   [*seemed*]
> Death was my servant on the road, till we were near
>   and saw you waiting:
> When you smiled, and in sorrowful envy he outran me
>   and took you apart:
>   Into his quietness
>
> [*Love: the way-weary, groped to your body*]   [*our brief wage*]
> So our love's earnings was your cast off body to be held
>   [*ours for the moment*]
>   one moment
>   [*hand explored your shape,*]
> Before earth's soft hands would explore your face and the
>   [*grew fat upon*]
>   blind worms transmute
>   [*your substance.*]
>   Your failing substance.
>
>   [*that I set our*]
> Men prayed me to set my work, the inviolate house,
>   [*as a*]
>   in memory of you.
>
> But for fit monument I shattered it, unfinished: and now
> The little things creep out to patch themselves hovels
>   in the marred shadow
>   Of your gift.

Lawrence described this poem as a cipher and did his best to keep it so. He told Graves that perhaps he had been in love with S.A. and that 'S.A. was someone who had provided a disproportionate share of the Arabian adventure'.* Graves himself revealed that in 1927 one of Lawrence's oldest friends had said that S.A. was 'Sheik Achmed, an Arab with whom Lawrence had a sort of blood brother-hood before the War'—that is, Dahoum. Graves believes that S.A. is a cipher for 'Son Altesse' (His or Her Highness), and that the person concerned was Lawrence's Arabic teacher at Jebail, in Syria, before the war, Farida el Akl.

But these are only the beginning of numerous testimonies and guesses. An article in the Beirut newspaper, *L'Orient*, on 1 October 1965, claims that S.A. was Feisal. Lawrence told Liddell Hart, 'One is a person and one a place', and Liddell Hart noted beside this answer 'vague', indicating that Lawrence had evaded a clear answer. Vyvyan Richards believes that S.A. was Dahoum. Anthony Nutting believes that 'S.A. offers neither clue nor connection to the main enigma of Lawrence's life'. Professor A. W. Lawrence, his brother's literary executor, believes that S.A. represents Sheik Ahmed, otherwise Dahoum, 'but as a personification as well as a person—a combination of the person and the place, a symbol of the pre-war happiness of life at Carchemish'. Villars, the French author, says simply that the S.A. enigma is insoluble because Lawrence intended it to be—'it gave him pleasure to think that there would be an S.A. riddle, like the W.H. riddle in Shakespeare's Sonnets'. This could well be so. The Lawrence collection at the University of Texas includes Lawrence's record of the writing, printing, publication and distribution of *Seven Pillars*, and in his own handwriting at the begin-ning is a note which says, 'Dedication of book is to an imaginary person of neutral sex'. Since this does not accord with the notes Lawrence made before writing the dedication, it must be regarded as a further attempt to confuse the issue. Finally, according to Captain Somerset de Chair, Dr Ernest Altounyan, who was a close friend of Lawrence's, thought S.A. was a Jewish intelligence agent, Sarah Aaronsohn.

Let us examine these theories one by one. Sarah Aaronsohn was a Zionist who was working for British Intelligence in Palestine in 1917–18. The Turks caught her and tortured her to try to discover who her fellow agents were and her methods of contacting the British. She managed to get hold of a pistol which she had hidden and shot herself. Although Lawrence, no doubt, knew about Sarah

---

* *Letters to his Biographers*, p. 16.

Aaronsohn while he was in intelligence in Cairo, there is no evidence
that he ever met her, and even if he had met her, it is even more
unlikely—for reasons that will be explained later—that Lawrence
would have fallen in love with her. Nor does a Jewish girl accord
with Lawrence's remark to a Foreign Office official—'I liked a
particular Arab very much'.

The Son Altesse theory as explained by Robert Graves refers to
the fact that Son Altesse was the title bestowed by a troubadour
upon his mistress or his muse and the phrase is still occasionally
used by French poets, though never in connection with homosexual love. Farida el Akl was a noble and beautiful woman in
Lawrence's early life and he loved her 'as deeply as his Irish
chastity-mystique permitted him'. However, Graves claims,
Lawrence, an Irish gentleman, did not want Farida's name popularly linked with his own, so he adopted the cipher S.A. and began
his note on the provenance of *Seven Pillars* with 'Dedication of
book is to an imaginary person of neutral sex'. Graves's theory is
that although Farida, Son Altesse herself, still existed after the
war, Lawrence himself had changed, probably because of the
Deraa flogging.

This might seem a plausible explanation but for one fact: Farida
el Akl is still alive and a vigorous eighty-nine. She has been in
correspondence for some years with a friend of Robert Graves's,
Richard Benson-Gyles, who has been to see her. He is convinced
that Farida is S.A. and that information she has given him is proof
of this. However, she herself has written to at least two people
emphatically denying that she is S.A. 'I am not S.A. and this is the
truth. T.E. never fell in love with any woman. He could not ...
T.E. wished that S.A. would be a mystery that is difficult to solve.
S.A. is to me Syria-Arabia.'

This leaves the theory that Sheik Ahmed, or Dahoum, was S.A.
What is there, then, to support this claim? First, there is no doubt
that Dahoum played a very important part in Lawrence's life in the
years preceding the war. We have already seen how, during the
summer of 1911–12, when the dig at Carchemish was closed down,
Lawrence wandered about the Middle East with Dahoum as his
companion. On the spying expedition in the Sinai Desert in 1913,
when Lawrence and Woolley went along with Captain Newcombe,
Lawrence took Dahoum with him. His letters during these years
contain frequent and anxious references to him at Carchemish.
When he was only fourteen Lawrence described him as an interesting
character who could read a little and was generally more intelligent

than his colleagues. Dahoum was thinking of going to school in Aleppo and Lawrence decided that if he did he would keep an eye on him to see how he progressed. Lawrence was not too certain that he approved of the idea, except that in the country Dahoum would not be able to find much intellectual stimulation. Over the next six years it is possible to trace the steady growth of the relationship. Lawrence begins to spend an hour each morning learning Arabic 'with Dahoum and a dictionary'. He investigates Dahoum's background and discovers it to be mixed Hittite and Arab with possibly a strain of Armenian. When Dahoum falls ill with malaria Lawrence nurses him, sitting on his chest on one occasion to hold him in bed. Dahoum recovered and Lawrence was able to note that he was once again capable of wrestling better than other youths of his age.

Dahoum, who by all accounts was a remarkably handsome young man, slight, with large brown eyes and a serene expression, went to England with Lawrence and the site foreman, Hamoudi, in the summer of 1913 and Lawrence delighted in their comments on London, the Underground, the museums, and the Zoo and had Dahoum drawn at the Ashmolean Museum. Professor A. W. Lawrence, who was constantly with him, remembers him as 'an extraordinarily nice chap, of the sort that remains a countryman and would hate to become a Levantine townee'. By now Lawrence had turned Dahoum into a reasonably competent photographer, and he records the young man's growing sophistication. His interest in Dahoum was evidently reciprocated. Dahoum began to carry out assignments for Lawrence, and often used his own initiative in securing objects that he knew Lawrence would like, sometimes a small Persian carpet which he bought for a few shillings, at others a piece of pottery or an Arab saddle bag. Dahoum was not always particular about collecting his wages and once at Maan in February 1914 Lawrence, apparently short of money, paid all his servants except Dahoum who did not mind waiting.

An indication of the extent of Lawrence's interest in Dahoum is the concern he expressed early in 1916 when he could get no news of him. By that time most of the men and boys from Dahoum's district had been sent by the Turks to Constantinople and Lawrence was afraid to send and ask for news of his friend in case it was bad.

This, in outline, is the evidence for believing S.A. to be Sheik Ahmed (Dahoum) that existed up to the time of the articles that

appeared in *The Sunday Times* in mid-1968. No other person seems
to have played such an important part in Lawrence's emotional life
during the relevant period—that which preceded the war and the
Revolt. During the research for these articles we discovered among
Lawrence's papers in the Bodleian Library, a copy of a note written
by him in pencil on a blank page at the end of Sir Robert Vansittart's
The Singing Caravan:

'I wrought for him freedom to lighten his sad eyes: but he had
died waiting for me. So I threw my gift away and now not anywhere
will I find rest and peace.

Written between Paris and Lyons in Handley Page.'

This is obviously a first attempt at a dedication and here, unlike
the final effort, Lawrence makes the gender clear—'*him* . . . *his* sad
eyes . . . *he* had died'. In our assessment of this new information in
The Sunday Times we wrote: 'It is clear from the poem, the epilogue,
and the letter in Paris that the particular Arab died "before we
reached Damascus". So we are looking for an Arab man who died
before 1918, either in Lawrence's presence or just before he arrived—
"to be held one moment . . . before earth's soft hands would explore
your face".'

We came to the conclusion that during the secret trip Lawrence
claimed to have made to Damascus he had come across Dahoum,
whom he had found dead or dying of typhus. We concluded: 'This
is the only person who fits all the clues . . . Sheik Ahmed is both
S.A. and "the particular Arab" of the Kidston letter.'

After publication we received many letters attacking us for this
conclusion. Robert Graves wrote twice, the first time restating his
Son Altesse theory and the second time saying that Lawrence had
written to him in the winter of 1921–2 replying to a question about
S.A.: 'You have taken me too literally. S.A. still exists; but out of
my reach because I have changed.' Benson-Gyles wrote to say that
we had not shaken his belief that S.A. was Farida el Akl, that
Dahoum was not in Damascus at the time of Lawrence's secret
trip in June 1917, nor was Dahoum dying of typhus. Suleiman
Mousa, the Arab historian, wrote to point out that 'Sheik' was a
distinction conferred with age, wealth, position and honour and
that therefore Dahoum could not possibly have been known as
Sheik Ahmed. These are all important assertions and seriously
shook our confidence in the conclusion at which we had arrived. We
can answer Lawrence's note to Graves, however, by saying, as is

already well known, that Lawrence delighted in being enigmatic and once he realized he had created a mystery over S.A. he determined to preserve it. When Graves appeared curious about S.A.'s identity, instead of being frank, as one friend would normally have been to another, and saying who S.A. really was, Lawrence took refuge in further mystery: 'S.A. still exists but out of my reach because I have changed.' In fact, as Villars points out, 'As for Robert Graves, Lawrence seems to have taken an evil delight in misleading him'.* Lawrence's note to Graves must also be weighed against his letter to an RAF friend, Aircraftman R. A. Guy. With no need to be enigmatic or misleading, Lawrence wrote: 'People are not friends until they have said all they can say, and are able to sit together at work, or rest for long without speaking. We [ie, Lawrence and Guy] never quite got to that but we were nearing it daily—*and since S.A. died*† I haven't experienced any risk of that happening.'

The other arguments against Dahoum are all answered in a convincing manner by the evidence of Tom Beaumont, the British machine-gunner who served under Lawrence in the later stages of the Revolt. Beaumont told us that Dahoum worked for Lawrence during the Revolt as a spy behind the Turkish lines. He said that Dahoum, a grown man and past the nickname stage, was called both by Lawrence and the other Arabs by his proper name, which was not Sheik Ahmed, as so many have believed (and Suleiman Mousa has shown to be untenable), but *Salim* Ahmed. In Beaumont's own words:

'Salim was a very nice chap. He was fair-skinned, spoke some English and Turkish, and was skilled at photography and even accounts. He was not a soldier and never served as one. He was more like Lawrence's personal assistant. After he went behind the Turkish lines, Lawrence would send someone to meet him, to take him money and instructions. And the messenger would come back with news of Turkish movements. At the councils with the Arabs Lawrence would say that the Turks were doing such and such and when this turned out to be right the Arabs would say, 'How could Lawrence have known this? Allah must have told him'. It wasn't Allah, it was Salim.

'We were at Umtaiye about September, 1918. One day Lawrence

* Jean Beraud Villars, *T. E. Lawrence or the Search for the Absolute*. Sidgwick and Jackson, London, 1958, p. 305.
† Authors' italics.

told us, "Don't worry, I'll be away for a few days. I'm going to see Salim." When Lawrence came back I said to him, "Did you see Salim?" and he said, "He's finished. He's dying. He's got typhoid." I'm sure it was typhoid he mentioned because we all got emergency typhoid shots soon afterwards. Lawrence turned away and pulled his kuffieh over his face and I heard him say, "I loved that boy". When he turned back I could see that he had been weeping. I overheard the bodyguards talking and I caught the Arabic word for death and I saw them make gestures like Lawrence holding Salim in his arms.'

We have gone over Beaumont's story with him twice, and making allowances for the fact that the events he narrated occurred fifty years ago, his account was substantially the same on both occasions. The dates fit, and it seems logical that Lawrence would have used Salim Ahmed, a man whom he knew he could trust, for spying missions. It also explains the guilt as well as grief that many have detected in the dedication to S.A. and even more so in the notes: 'And now not anywhere will I find rest and peace.' For Lawrence, doubting the morality of his own role in the Revolt, may well have accused himself of having sent his friend on a mission which cost him his life.

All this makes a convincing case for saying that S.A. is Salim Ahmed, the man nicknamed Dahoum; that Salim Ahmed was an agent for Lawrence and that Lawrence was greatly disturbed by the guilt he felt at his death. We believe that not only was Salim Ahmed the strongest private motivation for Lawrence's actions in the Middle East, but that his influence lived on to affect Lawrence's post-war behaviour. In a later chapter we suggest that Lawrence never fully recovered from Salim Ahmed's death, and that later his strange employment of another youth was, in part, an attempt to recreate this relationship.

With most of *Seven Pillars* written and sent to Dawnay for checking, Lawrence now began to look round for a haven, a place of escape, not only from the fame which was pursuing him, but from himself. He chose to go into the RAF—in the ranks. In later life he admitted that he did not really know why he did this. He told Lionel Curtis that the ranks provided him with the nearest thing he could get to 'determinism complete' and that 'there lies the perfect peace I have so longed for'. He told Robert Graves that it was because of 'an inclination towards ground level . . . partly I came here to eat dirt till its taste is normal to me and partly to avoid the current of other men's thinking'.

There were, of course, no personal reasons why he should *not* join up. The house in Oxford had been sold in 1921, two years after his father's death; his eldest brother, Bob, then went out to China as a missionary-doctor and was joined by his mother a year later. Thus there were no family responsibilities to prevent Lawrence entering one of the services. There was nothing he wanted to do, except, perhaps, return to archaeology, and he would now be suspected of spying in any country where he might want to dig. After leaving the Colonial Office, in the midst of writing *Seven Pillars*, he was beset by uncertainty. At least in the RAF he would have food, shelter, a regular life and, as he put it, 'a brain sleep'.

But why did he choose the RAF rather than the army? After all, he had held army rank, even though in reality he had been a Foreign Office official. He told Hogarth, 'When I joined the RAF it was in the hope that some day I'd write a book about the very excellent subject that it was'; and he wrote to his mother, 'My plans are . . . perhaps to consider the Air Force. . . . I think that the life and the odd mind (or lack of mind) there might give me a subject to write about'. But the most important consideration of all was his veneration and respect for the Chief of Air Staff, Sir Hugh Trenchard. With Lawrence's help, Trenchard had developed his plan for air control of Mesopotamia. They had been together at the Cairo Conference and had discovered many areas of common interest. Both detested petty officialdom. Both were visionaries. Both had a family tragedy to overcome—Lawrence that his parents had never married, Trenchard his father's bankruptcy. Each had suffered from illnesses or wounds that might have justified retirement from active life (Trenchard had nearly died as the result of a lung wound in South Africa). Most important of all, both had an ambition to do something large in life.

Trenchard and Lawrence recognized in each other a similar soul. Lawrence needed Trenchard for the strength, support and understanding that hitherto he had derived from Hogarth—now too closely associated in his mind with the Arabian period—and to a lesser extent from Churchill. He needed someone with whom he felt safe and who would, he hoped, assist him in his search for oblivion.

Though Trenchard was cryptic and sometimes even taciturn in most of his relationships, he had a reputation for quickly recognizing the qualities he needed in those who were to help him build up the newest branch of the armed services, the Royal Air Force. Men who would perhaps have been misfits in other spheres of life found through Trenchard situations where they could put their talents to the best use. Often this involved Trenchard in a calculated gamble and the impatient cutting of bureaucratic corners, but he found the result worth it. In short, he recognized in Lawrence qualities which he knew the RAF needed and saw no reason why conventions should prevent him from using them. But there was never any doubt in his mind that he was dealing with a gifted, unbeloved eccentric, and although he appeared to agree to assist Lawrence in his search for oblivion, Trenchard hoped—in the beginning, anyway—that he would be able to persuade Lawrence into accepting greater responsibility; that once through his difficult period Lawrence would make a real contribution to the RAF, by writing a serious history, taking a commission in a special branch, or making use of his valuable knowledge of the Middle East. In this he was disappointed. Lawrence flatly refused to serve where he could have been of most use, rejected Trenchard's attempts to find him a job where he could be both happy and useful, and when Trenchard tried to protect him and the RAF from unwanted publicity, somehow managed to ruin the arrangements. For his own ends Lawrence capitalized on Trenchard's feelings for him and on his desire to collect for the embryonic service the finest talents the country had to offer. In Trenchard's later letters to Lawrence one senses his disappointment over the fact that Lawrence had failed him so badly, but never—even over the explosive issue of *The Mint*, Lawrence's uninhibited exposure of barrack-room life in the RAF—any sign of anger or feeling of betrayal. If Trenchard could have foreseen the difficulties that his relationship with Lawrence were to create, perhaps he would have treated his first request to join the RAF in a different way. Writing to Trenchard on 5 January 1922 Lawrence began:

'You know I am trying to leave Winston on March the first. Then I want about two months to myself, and then I'd like to join the R.A.F.—in the ranks of course. I can't do this without your help. I'm 33 and not skilled in the sense you want. Probably I couldn't pass your medical. It's odd being too old for the job I want when hitherto I've always been too young for the job I did . . .

'You'll wonder what I'm at. The matter is that since I was 16 I've been writing: never satisfying myself technically but steadily getting better. My last book on Arabia is nearly good. I see the sort of subject I need in the beginning of your Force . . . and the best place to see a thing is from the ground. It wouldn't "write" from the officer level . . .

'It's an odd request this, hardly proper perhaps, but it may be one of the exceptions you make sometimes. It is asking you to use your influence to get me past the Recruiting Officer! Apologies for making it: If you say no I'll be more amused than hurt.'*

It was a well-aimed letter, and Trenchard reacted as Lawrence expected. He replied by return post:

> My dear Lawrence,
>
> With regard to your personal point, I understand it fully—and you too, I think. I am prepared to do all you ask me, if you will tell me for how long you want to join; but I am afraid I could not do it without mentioning it to Winston and my own Secretary of State,† and then whether it could be kept secret I do not know.
>
> Why I feel I could not do it without mentioning it, is first of all I should have to override the Recruiting Office, which I could do, but then it would be no good my saying I did not know you were joining, and I feel that it would be letting my two bosses in for me to let you do this without their knowing it.
>
> What country do you want to serve in, and how? I would make things as easy as anything.
>
> Let me know if I may mention this to my two Secretaries of State.
>
> Yours, H. Trenchard.‡

Lawrence decided to keep Churchill in ignorance of his plans for the time being, but in case the RAF idea fell through he approached L. S. Amery§ to see if he could find him something. Amery suggested that he should become a coastguard or a lighthouse keeper, but it may be that to Lawrence these were clichés of withdrawal; in any event, he found neither to his taste.

Then in 1922, while still in limbo, as it were, Lawrence appears to have embarked on one of the strangest periods of his life. It was at this juncture that he began with a tough Scots youth called John Bruce

* Trenchard Papers.
† Frederick Edward Guest (1875–1937), MP. Secretary of State for Air, 1921–2.
‡ Trenchard Papers.
§ Leopold Amery (1873–1955), MP, who was at this time Parliamentary Secretary to the Admiralty.

a relationship which, Bruce says, continued until Lawrence's death thirteen years later.

Some aspects of this strange friendship are no secret. For example, Bruce is mentioned in a letter that Lawrence wrote to Charlotte Shaw on 19 July 1924 at Clouds Hill: 'Bruce (a Scotsman, inarticulate, excessively uncomfortable). He comes up here quite often on Sundays; will enter only if I'm alone, glares and glowers at me till I put some Beethoven on the gramophone, and then sits solid with a heroic aura of solidarity about him; my room after four hours of Bruce feels like a block of granite, with myself a squashed door-mat of fossilized bones between two layers. Good perhaps to feel like a prehistoric animal, extinct, and dead, and useless: but wounding also.'

But until certain details appeared in our *Sunday Times* articles in 1968, the peculiar role which Bruce played in Lawrence's life had remained a secret because, Bruce says, he made a promise to Mrs Bernard Shaw and the Hon. Edward Elliot, Lawrence's solicitor, that 'I would not write about Lawrence while Lawrence's mother was alive'. After Mrs Lawrence's death in November 1959, Bruce wrote a short memoir which he considered publishing; but at that time he did not need money, and the newspapers and magazines he approached were either not interested or not prepared to deal with his story in the way in which he insisted it must be treated. A serious illness and enforced retirement from his position as manager of an engineering company ate rapidly into his savings. By 1968 he was reduced to living on a state disability pension and began once more to consider trying to publish his memoir.

At this stage, then, Bruce admits to two main motives—he needed money, and he felt that 'a correct assessment should be made of Lawrence's sacrifice in order that others could live in respectability'. He regards Lawrence as one of the great men of his time and insists that he is proud of what occurred between them, emphasizing that his actions helped Lawrence during a difficult period of his life: 'I helped him regain his sanity, security and self-respect.' Having decided to disclose what took place, Bruce approached *The Sunday Times* and his story was investigated. Some parts of it were comparatively easy to check: for example, that for a period after leaving the RAF, Lawrence had been in the Tank Corps with Bruce; that Lawrence was god-father to Bruce's son; that from one of the Lawrence Trusts set up to handle money derived from royalties, an annual payment of £4 was made as the result of a request by Mrs Bruce for the benefit of Bruce's son, and that Lawrence made Bruce's mother, Mrs Mary Bruce, a small allocation from his RAF pay. Localities and dates of visits that Bruce claimed to have made with Lawrence were found to be correct. It is known that Professor Lawrence knew as long ago as 1937 of Bruce's existence and that there had been some sort of relationship between his brother and Bruce, but he hoped, for reasons that are understandable, that Bruce would remain silent about the relationship.* However, the difficulty of checking events of forty-seven years ago is obvious and a lot of Bruce's story—especially the pre-Tank Corps period—must be accepted or rejected on his word alone. Bruce willingly made a legal declaration that he was telling the truth and Dr Denis Leigh, secretary-general of the World Psychiatric Association, and a distinguished psychiatrist, has interviewed Bruce and accepts the basis of his story—that Bruce beat Lawrence—as being true. We are convinced that Bruce knew Lawrence and that at Lawrence's request he took part in certain beating rituals. But in the end the reader will have to decide for himself about the authenticity of Bruce's story. In this and the next two chapters his account of events has been left as far as possible in his own words.

Bruce says he first met Lawrence early in 1922 in the Mayfair flat of a Mr Murray, a friend of the Bruces' family doctor, Dr Alex Ogston. As Bruce describes it,

'I was there by arrangement with Dr Ogston, being looked over for a position which was to become vacant presently. I needed a job very quickly. My father's business in Aberdeen, a dairy milk distribution, was on the rocks after twenty years. It was only a matter of time until the Official Receivers took over. . . .

'When I left Murray's house that evening Lawrence was still there . . . I must have aroused his interest in some way or other, and to do that there must have been a reason. Lawrence did nothing without purpose, and using people was his masterpiece, and I was no exception. . . .

'I had only been back in Aberdeen a few days when Dr Ogston telephoned and asked me to go and see him. He told me I did not have enough experience for the position which Mr Murray had in mind, but the gentleman who was with Mr Murray had suggested he might have something for me, and another trip to London would be necessary. . . . There were to be conditions for my journey south,

* These facts have been established by independent investigation, not by reference to Professor Lawrence or to Lawrence's papers in the Bodleian Library.

a sort of initiative test: no rail fare, no ticket, and ten shillings in my pocket only to be used in an emergency. The appointment time was seven-thirty a.m. the following Friday in London. I was politely told: if you are not prompt, don't bother to keep the appointment. I went home and told my father, who phoned Dr Ogston, who reaffirmed the arrangements. Father had a brainwave; he went and saw one of his customers who was the Chief Steward on the London Pullman Car. It was arranged that I go as a temporary steward for the Thursday to work in the kitchen. . . . Promptly at seven-thirty I rang the door bell at the flat, knees knocking, not knowing what to expect.

'Murray came to the door and ushered me into the drawing room; Lawrence had not yet arrived. He turned up at nine o'clock, saying sleep had overtaken him. Murray left to allow us to talk in private. No sooner had the door closed, when . . . Lawrence said, "What I'm looking for is someone like you, young, strong and alert who can be trusted with highly confidential personal matters, and to do what he is told without question. He should be able to look after himself, probably others too. Everything will be legal and above board, and Mr Murray thinks you will fit. I am going to tell you something about myself, as much as need be at this stage." He said that he had been a Colonel in the Army. He now held a responsible position in the Colonial Office which would be terminated shortly. He had found himself in great financial difficulties and he might have to submit to some unpleasant things in which he might require assistance.

'When he finished talking, I looked him straight in the eyes and said, "Really I don't think I'm your man, I have no qualifications in the first place and secondly, it looks like a job for the Governor of the Bank of England." He laughed, saying, "He has already turned me down. Don't give up this easy; sleep on it; we will talk further tomorrow." The Union Jack Club* was my abode for the night. I slept little, thinking that there was a crank, if ever there was one. Morning could not come quickly enough, so that I could phone my father for advice.

'Lawrence was to have lunch with me at the club at one o'clock. I got through to my Dad and asked him to get the advice of Dr Ogston on this man. He phoned back to say the doctor wished me to go along with Lawrence; I could always back down later if I wished. This was sound enough, and put me at ease. I felt ready for Mr Lawrence—or so I thought. He arrived at one o'clock, looking very ill and worn out, so ill that I suggested he saw a doctor. His reply

* A serviceman's club in Waterloo Road in south-east London.

was, "When I left you last night I walked back to Barton Street,* wrote all night, and was at the office at eight-thirty this morning. Does that sound like a sick man?" At lunch he said he was going to have a few hours sleep in the Union Jack Club and I was to wake him at six. I let him sleep on, and he did not wake up until mid-day Sunday, twenty hours later. This made all the difference to him; he was a charming and delightful person.

'We went for a walk in Hyde Park in the afternoon. He told me that his job was coming to an end very soon, not by choice but by force and he was not yet ready to put into operation what he had in mind. He would however pay me a retainer of £3 a week to be on call; this was to last three months. I agreed to this. He came to King's Cross station and saw me on the train; homeward bound for Aberdeen, I was puzzled but pleased. I . . . still . . . had no idea what Lawrence had in mind. I was concerned only with receiving trades-man's wages. From then on I received £3 a week in cash in an envelope sent to my home.

'I heard nothing further for three weeks, then in June a telegram came saying—UNION JACK SUNDAY WITHOUT FAIL. I saw him for less than half an hour. He told me he had to give up his job, and . . . gave me a package containing twelve letters addressed to various people. Each letter had a wrapper around it with instructions for the posting; date to be posted, post offices, time of posting. It took me three or four days to get rid of them. I remember there was one in Euston, one in Westminster, two in Bishopsgate. . . . Once this was done, I was to return home . . . Lawrence said he was off to Cairo on a private mission.† I learned later Lawrence went to try and raise money to get himself out of trouble, but it was a mission without success, and from here on he was really in trouble for the rest of his life.'

While Lawrence was, according to Bruce, thus testing him by entrusting him with small assignments, he was detaching himself from the Colonial Office. (His letter of resignation was published in the *Morning Post* on 20 July 1922.) He now stepped up his efforts to get into the RAF. Churchill proved difficult: he had not wanted Lawrence to leave the Colonial Office and had in fact refused many requests by him for permission to resign. The idea of Lawrence

* Lawrence had the use of an attic in Barton Street, Westminster, above the office of Sir Herbert Baker, the well-known architect, who was a friend of his.

† There is no evidence that Lawrence left England at this stage.

wasting his talents as an aircraftman annoyed him so much that he did his best to scuttle the whole plan. He had not counted, however, on Lawrence's determination or allowed for the wiliness with which Lawrence drew the name of the Irish leader, Michael Collins, into his scheme.

On 3 December 1920 Lawrence had met Michael Collins in London, he having come there with Arthur Griffiths and other members of the Irish Free State movement to negotiate a peace treaty with the government. It was to be a treaty which would recognize an 'all-Ireland totally independent republic', but Lloyd George, as Prime Minister, had issued a warning that unless the claim for a republic was dropped and Ireland was content to accept only partial independence, Britain would pour men and arms into the country and there would be an 'immediate and terrible war' instead of the police action that had existed until then. Collins was in a difficult position. If he gave way to Lloyd George he risked condemnation from hard-line Republicans, led by de Valera. It had been a worried man who had stopped to talk to Lawrence in an ante-room in Whitehall. Lawrence described the encounter in a letter to Charlotte Shaw: 'I tried to give him confidence that night; he wanted to give in to Lloyd George, and was afraid to do so. Of course he knew and Griffiths knew, and we knew that the arrangement probably meant his death-warrant. Griffiths wouldn't have done it alone. M[ichael] C[ollins] was the keener on making peace of the two of them. Only he didn't want to be called a traitor by the De Valera people. . . . He was in a tragic position that night. I left before he saw it through: but clearly he meant to say yes. . . . Collins served Ireland very well, and best of all perhaps, by dying for her.'*

Lawrence obviously liked Collins and probably expressed sympathy for the Irish cause, because there is an unconfirmed story that in July 1922, a month before his murder, Collins approached Lawrence and offered him command of a brigade in the Free State army which was to assist in the invasion of Ulster. The thought of the 'Deliverer of Damascus' serving in the Irish Free State army would certainly have been too much for Churchill, and this could well have been what finally persuaded him to allow Lawrence to go ahead with his RAF scheme. On 17 August Trenchard signed the following agreement:

---

* In the end, Collins signed the treaty, news of which, when it reached Ireland, caused many to call him a traitor. He was ambushed and shot near Cork on 22 August 1922.

SECRET

It is hereby approved that Colonel T. E. Lawrence be permitted to join the Royal Air Force as an aircraft hand under the alias of John Hume Ross.

He is taking this step in order to learn what is the life of an airman. On receipt of any communications from him through any channel, asking for his release, orders are to be issued for his discharge forthwith without formality.

Trenchard's authority was welcome confirmation of Lawrence's hopes. He was emotionally exhausted by the writing of *Seven Pillars* and besides this was now faced with the necessity of earning a living, his Colonial Office salary of £1,200 a year having ceased. By now the third draft of his book had been set in type at the *Oxford Times* press and eight proof copies had been run off.

In the second week in July, Bruce says, Lawrence sent for him again.

'Lawrence met me at the station. He was nervous and dejected, ill at ease; he didn't look kempt, and he was very quiet. We had a cup of tea with not much being said and went straight to Barton Street. He told me something terrible had happened to him ... and that what he was about to say was in the utmost confidence and should be treated very seriously.'

The story which Bruce says Lawrence then told him upset him so much that he remembers its details vividly to this day.

First Lawrence related his family background, dwelling on the strain involved in waiting for some member of his father's family to proclaim his illegitimacy. He told Bruce of debts and of pressure from his bank. There had been, he said, only one solution: to write a book in the hope that it would sell well enough to allow him to pay his debts and have sufficient money left over for him to retire to the country. But even finding the money to live while finishing the book was proving difficult. Eventually, Lawrence continued, he had gone to a merchant bank and they had agreed to lend him money on two conditions: that he assigned the copyright of his book to them, and that he should find a guarantor. Lawrence said that his father had died in 1919, but instead of inheriting his money, as he had expected, the bulk of it had gone to a relative* (whom he

* In fact, Lawrence's father left all his money to his wife, except for £200 each to his two executors.

referred to as 'The Old Man'), whom he had gone to see in order to explain his predicament and ask him to stand as his guarantor.

Bruce continues the story:

'Lawrence said that at first The Old Man agreed to be guarantor, but that when he learnt that Lawrence had left the Colonial Office he withdrew the offer and abused him. The Old Man told him that he had dragged the family name through the gutters. He had turned his back on God, lost an excellent position at the Colonial Office, become involved financially with "the damned Jews", insulted a Bishop and insulted King George at Buckingham Palace; and ruined the life of a great Foreign Minister, referring to Lord Curzon. The Old Man called him a bastard not fit to live amongst decent people. He was told the matter was of such a serious nature that a meeting of the family would have to be called to see what was to be done with him: the alternative would be to place himself in his hands unreservedly, which meant the copyrights and everything. He was told that he had borrowed money from friends under false pretences and would probably land in court (unless the monies were paid right away), thus bringing further disgrace on his family. He was told in no uncertain terms that he would be put away where he could do no more harm. He was not even allowed to speak. He was told to get out of the house and not come back unless he was prepared to place himself in The Old Man's care for as long as he deemed it necessary . . . He was told to think it over and come back on Sunday with his answer. The conditions which were laid down must have broken his heart, because he returned to London and slept rough for a few nights on the Embankment with layabouts and the like. We have heard that his mental condition was suspect around this time. Do you wonder now? As I remember this a lump comes into my throat; I can see his face now as if he were telling me over again. He kept on saying, "He called me a bastard, and meant it. How he must loathe us for my father's sins."

'Lawrence had come to the end of his tether. He told me he had decided to agree to the conditions and there was no road back until the conditions were fulfilled to the entire satisfaction of The Old Man, which could take years. He had the option of being sent away or joining the Army as a private soldier. His business affairs would be controlled for him, including money matters. His discipline would be controlled by The Old Man personally. Any breach of these conditions would prolong the length of time. The only friends he was to have in the upper bracket were those connected with his writings. Lawrence's time was to be occupied by soldiering and writing.'

Lawrence got Bruce into the Union Jack Club for the night and left him to digest the story. He called the following morning, accompanied Bruce back to Barton Street and pressed him for his reactions.

'I told him the whole thing was ridiculous and he should tell The Old Man to go to Hell. "Too late now," he said, "I've agreed, and it must be done. I need help. There is nothing anyone can do about my outstanding debts. The money I borrowed was loaned on the understanding it would be paid back from the proceeds of the *Seven Pillars* when published. No time was specified. My bank overdraft is a private matter between my bank manager and me. There is no case for criminal proceedings. The only case I have to answer is the payment of that money at the very earliest. This I cannot do for a very long time as it would take months of continuous writing and I don't intend that my friends should wait that long in these abnormal times of uncertainty. By agreeing to The Old Man the slate would be clean. But that is not what worries me most. The Old Man has shown his hand.... I had to agree with him or he would expose the circumstances of my birth. I have my mother to consider and she comes first whatever happens to me." '

The discussion was interrupted because Lawrence had an appointment and Bruce says he was left to think over what he had been told. Bruce at this time was an unsophisticated youth of eighteen. He was nevertheless aware of Lawrence's fame and conscious of his social superiority. He believed Lawrence's story of The Old Man and believes it to this day.

There is no doubt that the story was substantially the same as that which Bruce has recounted. Professor Lawrence believes Bruce has given a true account of what Lawrence told him about the anonymous uncle and the mode of life of this non-existent relative required of him.

Lawrence's description of The Old Man in some respects fits a distant relative now dead, but he was a man of high reputation, married, and with a healthy interest in his family, and does not appear to have met Lawrence more than once or twice.

As for the rest of Lawrence's story, he certainly had not ruined Lord Curzon's life, nor become involved with 'damned Jews' (presumably a reference to money-lenders rather than Zionists). Although the story of his refusing the insignia of his two awards was common knowledge, it is extremely doubtful if he 'insulted King George'. He had not 'dragged the family name through the gutters', and if he had 'turned his back on God' he had kept the fact to himself. The accusation that he had insulted a bishop derived presumably from a letter he wrote to the Anglican Bishop of Jerusalem, Dr MacInnes, about an allegation that the Bishop disliked the idea of a Jewish national home being established. The letter's contents leaked out and Lawrence was asked either to withdraw its implications or to deny them. He refused to do either, and when pressed by the Bishop for an answer Lawrence may have written to him (there are two draft replies among Lawrence's letters) saying the Bishop should know better than to remonstrate because he was not fit to black Weizmann's (the Zionist leader's) boots.

From the careful investigation that has been made of Bruce's story and from evidence brought to light during the course of enquiries about it, it would seem that what Lawrence told him was an elaborate fantasy concocted for a specific reason. To at least one other man he spun a similar story for an apparently similar reason: to arouse compassion in order that he should assist him in a private project which had to do with the emotional crisis through which he was passing. It seems likely that Lawrence, anticipating that these confidants might doubt his story, wove into it a sufficient element of fact to persuade anyone making a superficial check that it was true, and in the case of Bruce established his persecutor in the image of this distant relative. We believe The Old Man was an invention of Lawrence's. But Bruce was not to know this, and as he waited for Lawrence to return to Barton Street he went over and over Lawrence's story, looking for a flaw.

When Lawrence got back Bruce says he confronted him:

'I asked him what he wanted me to do, thinking this would draw him and he would put his cards on the table. He said, "You understand the position I'm in, and the complications which are likely to follow . . . something I cannot face alone. Have I not made it clear to you? I'm on the edge of a precipice crying for help, and you can help, I'm sure of that." I said, "But what is expected of me?" Lawrence said, "That depends on what The Old Man has in store for me. He has mentioned that my physique requires attention, and training will be necessary. He will make me do everything I hate to do. Where you fit into things depends entirely on him. I was made to swear over a Bible that I would respect The Old Man's every wish, and that's how it's going to be. There must be no half measures regarding his instructions. Corporal punishment was mentioned, but that will be resisted." '

Bruce, who had been listening with growing concern, says that at this stage he protested. Lawrence silenced him by repeating that corporal punishment was part of The Old Man's scheme, but that it would be strongly resisted. He suggested that Bruce should go back to Aberdeen and take a job which he could leave easily when Lawrence needed him.

' "I would suggest," he said, "that if you are interested in engineering you should study that; this field is the coming thing and once I shake off The Old Man's chains, I'll only have need of your friendship. I won't be in the Army longer than necessary. The *Pillars* should be finished in about two years' time, and then I shall be in a position to discharge my debts to The Old Man and at the same time discharge myself from the Army".'

Bruce says he agreed to do what he could to help. He extended his stay at the Union Jack Club and spent most of his time at Lawrence's room in Barton Street. By this time Lawrence was looking much better. His manner was quite different and he was at peace with himself, except when he talked about The Old Man.

'August was upon us. The first week he spent out of London, I don't know where. I had learned not to ask questions. He would tell me in good enough time if he wanted me to know. The night before his enlistment was spent at Barton Street. He walked the floor most of the night and was in a heck of a state. He kept asking all sorts of questions which I could not answer, like would joining the RAF be degrading? I don't know who was most pleased when morning came. We parted company after breakfast and I did not see him again until November.'

12 Into the Ranks

The arrangements to keep secret Lawrence's enlistment in the RAF go wrong because he fails his medical examination. He is eventually passed by an independent doctor. At the training centre he suffers under the rigid and tyrannical discipline. He transfers to the School of Photography, where he incurs the disapproval of his officers, who try repeatedly to get rid of him. The newspapers discover that Lawrence is in the RAF and, following more protests from his officers, he is discharged and goes into hiding. Bruce comes to London and finds him in a bad way. Lawrence tells him he is being forced to join the Tank Corps and persuades Bruce to enlist with him.

In spite of all the precautions taken to ensure that Lawrence's enlistment in the RAF would be kept secret and that it would take place with the minimum of formality, the whole affair went wrong from the beginning. In *The Mint*, the book he wrote about his days in the RAF, Lawrence says he got by the doctors, though they were worried about the scars on his ribs and some evidence of under-nourishment. This differs from the RAF recruiting officer's version of the story, which was that Lawrence was first rejected because it was found that his references were forged—probably by Lawrence himself—but that he was admitted on orders from the Air Ministry after an outside doctor had overruled the doctors at the recruiting office.

Lawrence's version begins outside the RAF recruiting centre at Henrietta Street in Covent Garden. The date is 28 August 1922:

'God, this is awful. Hesitating for two hours up and down a filthy street, lips and hands and knees tremulously out of control, my heart pounding in fear of that little door through which I must go to join up. Try sitting a moment in the churchyard? That's caused it. The nearest lavatory, now. Oh yes, of course, under the church. What was Baker's story about the cornice?

'A penny; which leaves me fifteen. Buck up, old seat-wiper: I can't tip you and I'm urgent. Won by a short head. My right shoe is burst along the welt and my trousers are growing fringes. One reason that taught me I wasn't a man of action was this routine melting of the bowels before a crisis. However, now we end it. I'm going straight up and in. All smooth so far. They are gentle-spoken to us, almost sorry. Won't you walk into my parlour? Wait upstairs for medical exam.? "Righto!" This sodden pyramid of clothes upon the floor is sign of a dirtier man than me in front.

'My go next? Everything off? (Naked we come into the R.A.F.)

' "Ross?"

' "Yes, that's me."

'Officers, two of them . . .

' "D'you smoke?"

' "Not much, Sir."

' "Well, cut it out. See?"

'Six months back, it was, my last cigarette. However, no use giving myself away.

' "Nerves like a rabbit." The scotch-voiced doctor's hard fingers go hammer, hammer, hammer over the loud box of my ribs. I must be pretty hollow.

' "Turn over; get up; stand under here: make yourself as tall as you can: he'll just do five foot six, Mac: chest—say 34. Expansion—by Jove, 38. That'll do. Now jump: higher: lift your right leg: hold it there: cough: all right: on your toes: arms straight in front of you: open your fingers wide: hold them so: turn round: bend over. Hullo, what the hell's those marks? Punishment?"

' "No, Sir, more like persuasion, Sir, I think."

'Face, neck, chest, getting hot.

' "H . . . m . . . m . . . that would account for the nerves."

'His voice sounds softer. "Don't put them down, Mac. Say *two parallel scars on ribs*. What were they, boy?"

' 'Superficial wounds, Sir.'

' "Answer my question."

' 'A barbed-wire tear, over a fence.'

' "H . . . m . . . m . . . and how long have you been short of food?"

'(O Lord, I never thought he'd spot that. Since April I've been taking off my friends what meals I dared, all that my shame would let me take. I'd haunt the Duke of York steps at lunch-time, so as to turn back with someone to his club for the food whose necessity nearly choked me. Put a good face on it; better.) Gone a bit short the last three months, Sir. How my throat burns! "More like six" . . . came back in a growl. The worst of telling lies naked is that the red shows all the way down. A long pause, me shivering in disgrace.

He stares so gravely, and my eyes are watering. (Oh, it hurts: I wish I hadn't taken this job on.)

'At last, "All right: get back into your clothes. You aren't as good as we want but after a few weeks at the Depot you'll pull up all right." Thank you very much, Sir. "Best of luck, boy," from Mac. Grunt from the kinder-spoken one. Here's the vegetable market again, not changed. I'm still shaking everyway, but anyhow I've done it. Isn't there a Fuller's down that street? I've half a mind to blow my shilling on a coffee. Seven years now before I need think of winning a meal.'*

This account differs from that of the RAF recruiting officer, Captain W. E. Johns, the author of the famous *Biggles* books, who died in 1968. Johns said that when Lawrence presented himself and gave the name of Ross, Sergeant-Major Gee, who was assisting Johns, signalled to him that Ross seemed a suspicious character. Johns checked Lawrence's face with photographs of wanted criminals issued by Scotland Yard, then sent him away to get a reference from his last employer and a character reference. While Lawrence was away Johns had the register of births, deaths and marriages at Somerset House checked, but could find no record of a Ross which fitted the details Lawrence had given.

So when Lawrence returned Johns bawled him out and sent him away. To Johns' surprise, Lawrence was soon back, escorted by an Air Ministry messenger with an order to enlist Lawrence immediately. Johns tried to obey the order, but there was still an impediment: the RAF doctors would not pass Lawrence. So Johns went to his commanding officer for guidance, and was told to get Ross into the RAF without delay: 'And for heaven's sake watch your step. This man is Lawrence of Arabia. Get him into the Force or you'll get your bowler hat.'†

According to Johns, he tipped off the doctors, but they still refused to sign Lawrence's medical sheet. So Johns telephoned to the Air Ministry and an official there ordered the doctors to pass Lawrence. Again the doctors refused. In desperation Johns called in a third doctor. 'He signed, I signed and Lawrence was in. But I then rang up Flight-Lieutenant Nelson, my opposite number at Uxbridge [RAF training depot], to warn him who was on the way, because by this time Lawrence was making it clear that he had no

* *The Mint*. Jonathan Cape, London, 1955.
† Interview with the authors.

time for junior officers.'* Lawrence's secret was out before he had even left the recruiting office.

What had gone wrong? Trenchard had delegated the job of organizing Lawrence's enlistment in the RAF to his assistant, Air Vice-Marshal Sir Oliver Swann. It was Swann who chose the name Ross, who suggested the faked references, and who wrote to Lawrence telling him exactly where and when he should go to enlist. A copy of Swann's secret instructions was sent to Henrietta Street and acknowledged five days before Lawrence arrived. Johns always denied that he failed to carry out his instructions, and there seems no reason why he should suddenly have become obstructive. Possibly, because of some administrative failure, Swann's secret order was not passed on to him.

There is, of course, another possibility. Swann hated the whole business; the secrecy and the subterfuge went against his principles and he resented being ordered to organize the affair. Although he later insisted that not a soul in his department knew of the scheme and that no one realized who Aircraftman John Hume Ross really was, it is not improbable that some RAF officer under Swann sniffed out the secret and started a top-level passive resistance movement to sabotage Lawrence's entry.

The training depot at Uxbridge consisted of a series of corrugated iron huts, which were stifling in the summer heat. Hut 2, to which Lawrence was assigned, had whitewashed walls, a cement floor, and brown blankets on iron-hard beds. Fifty men were crowded into it —labourers, farmhands, ex-officers unable to adjust themselves to peace, clerks, factory hands, lorry drivers—all recruits to the newest arm of the Services, then barely four years old.

Having, as yet, no traditional procedures of its own, the RAF had borrowed its basic training methods from the Guards. These methods were old-established and had been tested by time, but whether they were suitable to the type of men the RAF hoped to attract is another matter. Their aim was to break a man's individual spirit and replace it with a collective loyalty, to inculcate the idea that the good of the unit must at all times precede the importance of the individual.

The process started with five weeks' physical training and fatigues calculated to break the will of the strongest recruit. The day began at 6.30 a.m. and did not end until after 5 p.m.—or later for those who had drawn punishment. The recruits scrubbed floors, emptied

* Interview with the authors.

dustbins, cleaned pigsties, and drilled and trained until their bodies ached and their minds grew numb.

At first, the senselessness of it, the deliberate degradation of the recruit (as in such things as having no doors on the lavatories), the obscenities and general behaviour of his fellow recruits worried Lawrence greatly. He wrote to Swann: 'The crudities, which aren't as bad as I expected, worry me far more than I expected: and physically [he was now thirty-four] I can only just scrape through the days.' In the same letter he could not resist a reminder—perhaps more to himself than to Swann—of his former importance: 'In case I'm wanted by the Colonial Office I'll send you a note as often as I change station . . .' He was ill after the morning physical-training session. He suffered from blisters, cuts, a fractured finger, and a sprained foot. The rough wool of the uniform chafed his skin and the harness of his pack tormented the collar bone he had broken in his air crash in 1919. Stiffy, a former sergeant-instructor in the Guards, made the airmen's life a misery* with drilling and cursing because 'he'd been cursed himself and had been thirty years an instructor and these things were the secret of smartness. We were picked men from all the nation: drill would make us look like it . . .'

In the hut there was the usual sort of horseplay that men in barracks cannot avoid. Lawrence, who had a horror of being touched, must have found this particularly offensive. The intimacy of Hut 2 at night disturbed him and he could not sleep. He wandered about the station in the dark longing desperately for privacy.

He hated his Commanding Officer, the late Bonham-Carter: 'He is only the shards of a man—left leg gone, a damaged eye and brain, (as we charitably suppose), one crippled arm, silver plates and corsets about his ribs. Once he was a distinguished soldier:—and now the R.A.F. is his pitying almoner . . . I found myself trembling with clenched fists, repeating to myself, "I must hit him, I must," and the next moment trying not to cry for shame that an officer should so play the public cad.'†

There is no reason to think Bonham-Carter deliberately picked on Lawrence. He simply held the view, not uncommon at the time, that firm handling and lots of drill made good servicemen. He was intensely proud and very self-conscious about his disabilities. Airmen had to be careful not to offend him by noticing them. 'He struggled hardly in, [to his car] unhelped; for we knew that he would

---

* The previous intake of recruits had nearly mutinied and had thrown Stiffy onto a rubbish dump.
† *The Mint*, pp. 69–71.

swipe at an offered hand with his crutch . . . I swung the engine. He waved me away while he let in the clutch and backed her round: then roared, "Now jump, you damned fool!" ' After accompanying Bonham-Carter to his house and starting the long walk back to camp, Lawrence records: 'Before I was out of earshot I could hear him loudly drilling his little children, in the garden.'

But there were better times, too, and later he remembered with nostalgia the comradeship of the recruits and their ready acceptance of someone obviously from a different social sphere into their tight and loyal little circle.

Slowly Lawrence adjusted himself, and by early autumn he felt sufficiently confident to slip up to London—out of bounds to RAF personnel—and call on Edward Garnett, who was preparing an abridgement of *Seven Pillars*, and Eric Kennington, the artist, who was doing the portrait drawings for the book. Kennington, whom Lawrence had approached with this commission in 1920, thought the RAF had improved Lawrence, certainly as far as care for his appearance was concerned. 'Every line always perfect, from set of hat to spacing of the puttees,' Kennington wrote. 'Never a dull button, or speck on the boot, and how the well-cut uniform showed the strength of his neck and drive of his jaw.'*

Early in November Lawrence was transferred to the RAF School of Photography at Farnborough. The basic training continued, and to add to his burden he was going through Garnett's abridgement of *Seven Pillars*. He wrote to Hogarth saying, 'My mind wobbles between the need of money and the desire to be withdrawn . . . I wish the beastly book had never been written.'

Bruce describes what happened next:

'Several letters had passed between us. I had been kept informed about his likes and dislikes. There can be no doubt: he hated the place and everything that went with it. He hinted on several occasions that The Old Man was not satisfied with the easy life he was leading in the Royal Air Force and had told him he had no right to be there at all, as it had been arranged that he join the Army, and he had disobeyed his instructions.

'Then in November Lawrence asked if I would go down to Farnborough as there were things that needed to be discussed and which could not be written. I got there two days later and found him most distressed. He told me a birch had arrived. There had

* *T. E. Lawrence by his friends*, p. 275.

13

been a small note from The Old Man with it, saying further instructions would follow. We agreed I'd get digs in town and wait developments. I told him then he had to put his foot down right away. He said, "That's impossible. I've already told you I agreed to his conditions without reserve and if I kick now this hellish life could go on indefinitely. I'm fit enough now to take a few over the buttocks and if that's what he wants, that's what he will get. Anyway, this is the penalty for cheating. But it won't happen again. I'm supposed to be in the Army, but I knew the RAF would be cushier. I hoped he wouldn't realize it. I'll never cross him again in my life."

'I went back to Barton Street and sorted out some stuff for him, then on to Aberdeen. I was perturbed about this new development. If he allowed this to take place, God knows where it might lead, and the consequences could be serious. I wrote to him that same evening pointing these things out, and begged him not to allow anything like that to happen or at least make some endeavour to have that cut out of his arrangement. This he refused to do, saying that if he was a willing party that was all there was to it.'

Not that Lawrence seemed perturbed. At Farnborough he continued to go over his officers' heads if he could not get what he wanted. He wrote to Swann on 9 November 1922 complaining that the CO had put him down for a photography course starting in January because he had missed the start of the November course by a day. He said he was already as good as the men passing out and asked Swann to put him straight into the school for his technical training. When Swann, who was doing his best to discourage Lawrence from communicating with him, failed to reply, Lawrence wrote again ten days later, this time to Swann's house, repeating his request. This time Swann acted, sending an order to the CO at Farnborough, saying, 'Ross is rather urgently needed for employment in a unit and I wish him passed on his course'.*

It is easy to understand that this led to resentment in Lawrence's superior officers, who by now knew his identity. They could not understand why Lawrence should want to serve in the ranks and, casting about for a reason and suspecting him of communicating with the Air Ministry, decided that the only possible explanation was that he was a Ministry spy sent to report on them. There is no truth in this, but it inflamed the dislike that some officers had for Lawrence. His Commanding Officer at Farnborough, Wing-Commander W. J. Y. Guilfoyle, wanted a quiet, uncomplicated command

* Bodleian Library.

and he became worried in case Lawrence's presence should upset this. Guilfoyle, a staunch traditionalist, felt that a man of Lawrence's class should not have enlisted in the ranks. Lawrence's friendship with several airmen, particularly with one, whom Lawrence called either 'Poppet' or 'Rabbit', could hardly have reassured him and when the time came for him to have his say, he pointed out how Lawrence's presence made matters difficult for the officers.

The result was that by December—that is to say, within a month—everyone at Farnborough knew who Aircraftman Ross really was. As Lawrence wrote to Bernard Shaw, 'They [the recruits] treat my past as a joke and forgive it me lightly. The officers fight shy of me: but I behave demurely, and give no trouble.' By mid-December the knowledge had spread more widely. The CO reported that two reporters, one from the *Daily Mail* and the other from the *Daily Express*, had been snooping round the camp and had talked to officers and airmen. Lawrence's comrades among the recruits had rallied to protect his privacy and although they were offered large sums of money for a photograph of Lawrence, no one betrayed him. Jock Chambers went as far as smashing a pressman's camera. After Guilfoyle had written to the Ministry saying that this was 'not in the best interest of discipline' and that he hoped 'some definite procedure will be taken', there was a meeting at the Air Ministry. It was decided that it would be best to ignore the newspaper enquiries and allow Lawrence's training to proceed normally.

It was no use. On 27 December 1922, the *Daily Express* broke the story:

Uncrowned King as Private Soldier

Lawrence of Arabia

Famous War Hero Becomes a Private.

Surprisingly, there was little immediate official reaction. No questions were asked in Parliament and it took the Air Ministry until January to do something about the matter. Lawrence blamed 'one of the beastly officers' for having given him away. Robert Graves agrees that it was an officer who did so and says that he sold the information to the newspaper for £30. Bruce says Lawrence told him that The Old Man paid the £30. Swann said it was 'solely due to carelessness at the Colonial Office in letting it be known that Lawrence had been requested to call there, and to Lawrence's unfortunate love of drawing a veil of mystery about himself'.

When the Ministry again examined Lawrence's case the reports were stacked against him. It is apparent that resentment among the officers—one, Squadron-leader G. C. Breese, said later that he had tried three times to get Lawrence discharged*—and the embarrassment that they claimed to have felt in having a former colonel serving under them, were major factors in the Ministry's decision that Lawrence would have to go. Trenchard tried to avoid this. He offered Lawrence a commission, but Lawrence refused it and thereupon Trenchard told him to regard his discharge as final. Pressed for a reason by Lawrence, Trenchard said, 'As you know I always think it foolish to give reasons!! But this case is perhaps different. I think the reason to give is that you had become known in the Air Force as Col. Lawrence instead of Air Mechanic Ross, and that both you and the officers were put in a very difficult position, and that therefore it was considered inexpedient for you to remain in the service.'†

Yet Lawrence did not give up without a fight. In order to avoid further publicity he had cancelled a contract with his publishers, Jonathan Cape, for an abridged version of *Seven Pillars* (tentatively called *Revolt in the Desert*), which was a considerable sacrifice because he had estimated that the book would have brought him £6,000 in one year. Then he wrote a letter to T. B. Marson, Trenchard's secretary, asking Trenchard to give him another chance by posting him to some remote station where he would not be an embarrassment to the CO. 'I've had a lurid past which has now twice pulled me down and of which I'm beginning to despair, but if my CO was a decent size he'd treat me as average and I'd be average.'

But this appeal failed, and by the end of January he was out of the service and on the run from the newspapers. Bruce says Lawrence had written to him in December saying that his real identity was known at Farnborough and expressing anxiety about his future in the Force. When Bruce read in the newspapers about his dismissal, he came immediately to London to try to help him.

'I searched everywhere but I couldn't find him. I knew that he would have to go to Barton Street sometime, or make arrangements about his mail to be forwarded to where he was, so I went back to Aberdeen and sent him a telegram asking him to contact me right away. This he did three days later, by letter. He said he was broke and had been sleeping rough, and I wired a five pounds' money

* *Daily Express*, 28 January 1955.
† Bodleian Library.

order. Broke and sleeping rough! Where were all his friends now?
Those who in later years said, "If only we had known?" Why
didn't they? He told plenty he was broke, but he only told those
who could afford to help in the hope they would without being
asked. No blame can be tagged to his own family, because he made
sure they were unaware of the circumstances. The sacrifice was for
them, and his alone. He had even pawned his watch in order to
buy food. I saw the ticket.'

Broke and sleeping rough was an exaggeration but not untrue.
Lawrence wrote that he spent several nights during this period
sleeping in the sidecar of his motorbike.

'It was now about the end of January 1923. By this time I had
already sent him several money orders without a reply. I was considering getting in touch with his solicitor or his banker, whose
address I had, but was afraid in case I started something which
could do more harm than good. I had only a little money myself,
and running between Aberdeen and London was getting expensive.
I decided to go to London and stay there until I found him. I got a
night's work on the Pullman express, washing dishes to save the fare.
The following day in London I got a job as bouncer at a kind of
night club in Paddington.
'I left a message at 14 Barton Street telling Lawrence where I
was and to contact me at the club as soon as possible. Days passed
and still nothing happened. Then early one morning, when the club
was closing up, I went outside to get a cab for a client and there he
was. When I saw him my eyes filled with tears; not at seeing him,
but the mess that he was in. He looked ragged, worn out and dirty.
It was to hell with the cab and the clients. I got him downstairs to a
back room and the first thing he said was "Jock, I'm ashamed at the
state I'm in." He put both hands over his face and cried like a child.
I got him something to eat while he cleaned up, and we went back
to my digs in Praed Street, where he had a hot bath. I sent him
straight to bed and I slept in a chair for the rest of the morning. He
woke about mid-day. He told me that for the past two weeks he had
been staying in a Salvation Army hostel at a shilling a night and
that he had no more shillings left. I was glad he had no more
shillings, because he was found, and that's what mattered most. I
was pleased that he came to me, not for vanity's sake but because it
proved the trust he placed in me.
'As far as I was concerned, it was now obvious that someone had to

look after him until he found his feet. I wanted him to confide in his family, but this he flatly refused to do. His solicitor and friends? Again no. Who then? "The Old Man is the only one who can help now," he said, "and I must see him." He did, but I was never told what took place at that meeting. All Lawrence said when he came back was, "It has *got* to be the Tank Corps, nothing else".

Again there is a discrepancy between what Lawrence is said to have told Bruce he was doing and what he was actually doing. While giving Bruce the impression that he was a broken man who was being forced into the Tanks Corps by The Old Man, he was busy trying to get back into the RAF or, failing that, shopping around to find something else. L. S. Amery wrote to him on 2 February: 'Sam Hoare* assures me it was nothing but the embarrassment of junior officers and others of knowing . . . your real identity . . . Trenchard [is] still thinking of trying to find something for you to do . . . Meanwhile I spoke to Beatty [about] finding you something under the Intelligence somewhere.'† While friends of Lawrence's were looking round on his behalf, Bruce was preparing to join the Tank Corps, too. He says by then he had regretted making the decision to join up with Lawrence, but was worried that Lawrence was getting out of his depth.

'Lawrence told me his fears: "I'll be found out sooner or later, then it'll be the same thing all over again." I asked him, "Would you feel safer if I joined with you?" He said, "Oh, Jock, would you do that for me? I'm not worth it but honestly, I wanted to ask if you would, and I daren't in case you refused." I said to myself inwardly, "My God, what have I done?" Then I told him that I would join only on the condition I could get my discharge at any time for the asking. He said that would present no problem.

'I worked at the club until the end of February, but we saw each other every day. He told me on one of these occasions that he had told The Old Man about me and that my offer to join up with Lawrence seemed to please him. He said that The Old Man would be writing to me once I was in the army. We made arrangements that I should return to Aberdeen to straighten my personal affairs and that I should join up there.'

* Sir Samuel Hoare, Bt (1880–1959), later Viscount Templewood. Conservative politician and at this time Secretary of State for Air.
† Bodleian Library.

13 Private Shaw, Tank Corps

Lawrence uses his influence at the War Office to arrange his enlistment in the Tank Corps. He considers the army 'muck, stink, and a desolate abomination' from which he finds refuge at Clouds Hill, a small cottage near the camp, which he rents from a relative. The fantasy he has been weaving for Bruce reaches a climax and the first of several ritual birchings takes place. Lawrence's friends try to get him out of the army; among them is Bernard Shaw, who writes to the Prime Minister, but without result. Lawrence is in a low emotional state and in December 1924 Bruce prevents what appears to be an attempt at suicide. Lawrence continues to try to get back into the RAF. His efforts to do so meeting with no success, he threatens to kill himself. The threat works, the Prime Minister intervenes, and Lawrence is given a transfer.

It was thanks to his contacts at the War Office that Lawrence was able to smuggle himself into the Tank Corps. Sir Philip Chetwode* had been commander of the Desert Column of the Egyptian Expeditionary Force during the desert war and later of the XX Corps, which took part in the advance on Jerusalem. In 1923 he was Adjutant-General to the Forces and when Lawrence formally applied to be allowed to join the army as a private the decision whether or not he should be accepted was Chetwode's. On 17 February he wrote to Lawrence: 'I have received this morning a letter from Elles who is prepared to consider your proposal and sees no very great difficulty about it. He ... asks you to write to him at HQ Tank Training Centre, Bovington Camp, Wool, Dorset, marked personal. ... If you come to a satisfactory arrangement, would you call here at the War Office to see General Vesey† ... as there are certain matters which he would have to arrange with you before the affair is carried through.'‡

On 12 March 1923, under the name of T. E. Shaw—a name he

---

* Later Field-Marshal Lord Chetwode (1869–1950), chief of the Imperial General Staff.
† Director of Organization at the War Office.
‡ Bodleian Library.

said he had chosen at random—Lawrence enlisted at Bovington. Bruce had enlisted at Aberdeen. The army had organized things rather better than the RAF and everything went smoothly. Lawrence was in, as he wrote to Hogarth, for 'seven years guaranteed. I haven't any longer the mind to fight for sustenance.' Bruce says his entry was smoothed for him. 'The sergeant said to me, "Is your name Bruce?" When I said yes I was taken to an inner office and there was a bit of a pow-wow. I signed the forms, had my medical and next day they sent a car to my house to collect me.'

Bruce says he was sent south and met Lawrence by arrangement in Bournemouth, and together they entered the guard-room of the Tank Corps depot at Bovington Camp, where they were assigned to B. Company, Hut 12. In his letters Lawrence, thinking nostalgically of the RAF, has described the atmosphere at Bovington—'the Army is muck, stink, and a desolate abomination'; but at least he had Bruce as a bodyguard to take care of him. With a kind of smouldering rage Bruce recalls the camp in these early days:

'The hut itself was one of many in a row. It was the usual type of Army hut. Inside there was a partition in the middle, dividing it into two, but without a door. There were beds on either side and two large stoves, one in each section. Lawrence took the bed against the partition on the top section. I took the bed which was second to the partition on the first section, and on the opposite side.

'On the Friday evening some of the inmates had more drink than they could hold. The filth that followed before and after lights out has been adequately described by Lawrence himself, and he was not exaggerating. They didn't know who Lawrence was, but it was obvious some of the chaps in the hut wanted to pal up with him, and this could have led to trouble. There was only about a handful of them fit to be in his company, and we arrived at a short list of two: Privates Russell and Palmer. Russell was a nice fellow, thick-set and strong, and looked as though he could use himself if need be. He was my choice for that reason. Palmer was Lawrence's choice. He was a gentler kind of chap, without brawn, and seemed to have read a little. . . .

'The squad was now formed. Company sergeant-major was Thorpe, squad sergeant was Sylvester; squad corporal, Dixon; recruits, twenty-two, and as raw as carrots. Training, sixteen weeks' duration. By this time we had everyone in the hut sized up. It was the bad ones I had to keep my eyes on, especially the drinkers, who were continually touching Lawrence for money. . . . I came into the hut and heard a fellow giving Lawrence a mouthful of filth because he refused to give him a pound. I jumped him there and then and one hell of a fight took place. We both spent the night in the guard room; seven days' each next day . . .

'Some two weeks later we were doing physical training and the squad had to run across country for three miles. I knew Lawrence was not up to that and I kept with him. Eventually we got back last and were laughed at by one of the instructors. Lawrence said something to him which I did not hear, but it certainly annoyed him. He went to move forward to Lawrence, so I said, "Could we do the run on our own this evening to see if we could make better time?" He said "Yes, and I'll come with you!"

'We set out as arranged. I tailed myself off quite a bit. We had not very far to go when Lawrence had to give up altogether. This annoyed the instructor, who gave him a mouthful. We were both in bad now.'

Luckily Lawrence had a refuge from the constricted and vaguely menacing life of the camp. He had taken the small derelict cottage called Clouds Hill, at Moreton, a mile and a half from the camp, which he rented from a relative at half-a-crown a week. He set about renovating the place and when life at the camp became unbearable he would slip away for a few hours to the cottage. But to Bruce the cottage was another piece in a sinister pattern.

'Lawrence had told me that The Old Man was to pay his debts in return for the copyright in his writings, control of his finances, choice of friends, and complete domination of his life. From The Old Man's point of view, as Lawrence put it to me, all this made him easier to control by keeping him away from his friends.'

Lawrence now had a job in A Company's stores, a not very demanding occupation which left him enough time to push ahead with plans for the subscribers' edition of *Seven Pillars*.

There were to be about one hundred subscription copies at thirty guineas each, which would bring in enough money to cover the cost of printing; no more was necessary—Lawrence insisted that he would not profit from the venture in any way, as a matter of principle. By this time he had become uneasy in his conscience over his part in the Arab Revolt. About *Seven Pillars* he wrote to Mrs Thomas Hardy: 'It is meant to be the true history of a political movement whose essence was a fraud—in the sense that its leaders did not believe the arguments with which they moved the rank and file . . . .' And he told another friend, 'Do you know I so hate the Arabian business that I would give all the world (if it were mine) to wipe the record off the slate.'*

His unease was accentuated by the fact that Lowell Thomas was planning to publish *With Lawrence in Arabia*, a book which was to give permanent form to the glamorous image of this part of his life. (The odd thing about both the Lowell Thomas lectures and the book is that it was first thought that Lawrence had nothing to do with them. In Thomas's book there was a note saying: 'The publishers desire to state that Colonel Lawrence is not the source from which the facts in this volume were obtained, nor is he in any way responsible for its contents.' But, as Thomas later admitted, Lawrence had helped 'in a lot of ways' with the lecture and 'he also worked with me on my book', but 'at that time he was exceedingly anxious that no one should know this.')

Yet at this moment, worried though he was about Thomas's book, coolly calculating the advantages and disadvantages of publishing his own great work, considering its libel risks, and writing long letters about it to, among others, Bernard Shaw, E. M. Forster, David Garnett, Jonathan Cape, C. M. Doughty, and Eric Kennington, Lawrence was preparing to embark on an extraordinary adventure with Bruce. What happened between them now was the first of several such incidents, and to Bruce the experience was such a shock that he appears to have no difficulty in remembering it in detail forty-five years later:

'Lawrence asked me to go to see him in A Company stores. He was nervous and upset. He said he had heard from The Old Man and that he was in disgrace. He had failed to attend church parades and had been a disappointment in many ways.

'Lawrence said The Old Man had decided he must be punished, and the sentence was to be twelve strokes of the birch. He handed me an unsigned, typed letter which he said was from The Old Man. It was on blue paper. It said that a birch had been despatched to a nearby railway station and I was to administer the punishment with it. I would be paid for it. Afterwards I was to report in writing if I had done so, and I was to describe Lawrence's demeanour and behaviour under punishment. I said I wanted nothing to do with it, but Lawrence said it would have to be done, "otherwise The Old Man will publish my ancestry to the world". In the end I said I

* Bodleian Library.

would be a willing party only because Lawrence was a willing
party'.

It is easy at this remove to be critical of Bruce. Yet it must be
remembered that he was only nineteen at the time and although
well able to look after himself among his equals, was out of his
depth in the sophisticated world represented by Lawrence. 'To
be associated with the élite like he was made me feel a bit silly.
He was a person of more than usual dignity and I was merely a
sparrow. It was my idea that what I was to do to him would get
him out of bondage.' So Bruce collected the birch and thrashed
Lawrence the same afternoon.

'He kept his trousers on and lay on the bed. He never murmured.
It was a disgrace. This first one was not a beating at all. Anyway,
he went to see The Old Man the same afternoon. The Old Man
said it was not good enough and it was to be done with his trousers
down. So I put rugs over his back and left only his small buttocks
exposed. After I had given him the twelve he said: "Give me another
one for luck." It is nasty. The prongs go into the skin and break
little blood vessels and it bleeds. He just lay there and gritted his teeth.
He never moved. He was as tough as a rail. When I did this beating
I saw no other scars. He went straight off to see The Old Man again
and came back with his thumbs up. He said: "That's done the trick."
Lawrence gave me a blue envelope and said "Thanks! Good job."
I cannot remember how much it was. Not much. A few quid. I
shared it with Lawrence. I always shared my money with Lawrence,
or else he would say he needed it to pay a debt.'

According to Bruce, he was not the only man to beat Lawrence
in this manner. At any rate, not long after this first birching Lawrence
handed Bruce an unopened letter which he said was from The Old
Man—it was a confidential communication to Bruce himself:

'He wanted to know if Lawrence's conduct had improved since
he had joined the Tank Corps; if any famous people had been
to see him? Was he attending church parades? Was he working
excessively hard and impairing his health? Was there anything
that he should know that I knew about and had not been reported?
Was the money he was receiving from the Army adequate to get him
necessities? The Old Man said my answers were to be direct and
honest and I was not to show the correspondence to Lawrence. This

put me in a spot and after I read the letter I told Lawrence I was
going out for ten minutes.

'We were in the store hut and I purposely dropped the letter on
the floor and made for the door. He said, "Jock, you've dropped
something", I called back, "Yes, I know", and left. When I came
back he played hell with me. He said my dropping the letter was
dishonest and I was never to do such a thing again, although I
think he was pleased. I asked him, "What about my reply?"
Lawrence said I should do exactly as The Old Man had requested.
On the Saturday morning I gave Lawrence my letter to The Old
Man. I left the envelope unsealed. Lawrence took the letter and
sealed it.'

From this moment all correspondence between Bruce and
The Old Man was carried on in this manner—that is to say, with
Lawrence as the intermediary. Bruce believes this was because of
the nature of the trust which existed between him and Lawrence,
but if The Old Man was a fantasy figure created by Lawrence this
would, of course, have been the only way for the correspondence to
be conducted.

Although Bruce did not know it, his time in the army was drawing
to a close. After quarrelling with an NCO who had been borrowing
money from Lawrence, he reported the sergeant for an offence,
expecting him to be reduced to the ranks. This did not happen and
instead the sergeant had Bruce transferred to Lydd, in Kent. Bruce
says Lawrence tried but failed to get Bruce returned to Bovington.
Early in 1925, after Bruce had been in the Tank Corps about two
years, he was excused all duties without warning and sent on leave.
From the Tank Corps station at Lydd he went to Clouds Hill
cottage to meet Lawrence. Bruce says Lawrence told him what had
happened: the newspapers were chasing the Lawrence story again
and Bruce had been identified as Lawrence's bodyguard. When
Bruce tried to end his state of uncertainty by reporting back to the
Tank Corps he says he was discharged without being given a reason.
He pressed the authorities for one, but all an officer would say was,
'Why don't you ask the Arab?'

Bruce took a job at a garage in Bournemouth, about an hour's
drive from Clouds Hill, because 'Lawrence asked me to stay until
Seven Pillars was finished'. Bruce says that while he was in Bournemouth, Lawrence would come to do physical training, under his
instruction, at a local gymnasium. Bruce told us: 'On one of these
occasions I noticed there were marks on Lawrence's legs, high

above the knees. When I asked what they were he flushed, saying "Nothing really." I was not happy about this and told him so and insisted he tell me how they got there. "A birch," he said. "Good God, no," I said, "I understood you had agreed there was to be no more of that." I managed to get out of him that it had been an employee of The Old Man who had done it. Then he said, "Forget it", and refused to talk about it any more.'

Nothing in the overt activities of Lawrence at this time could have suggested to anyone that he was leading this bizarre double life. As well as occupying himself with the subscribers' edition of *Seven Pillars*, he had been continuing his campaign to get back into the RAF, to which end he had enlisted the support of several eminent friends. One of these, Bernard Shaw, had written to the Prime Minister, Stanley Baldwin, saying it was a scandal that Lawrence should have to serve in the ranks and that all who knew about it felt that 'the private soldier business is a shocking tomfoolery and are amazed to find that Lawrence is not in a position of a pensioned commanding officer in dignified private circumstances'.*

Before sending the letter to the Prime Minister, Shaw asked Hogarth to read it and check certain details of Lawrence's career. This Hogarth did, returning the letter to Shaw with a perceptive appreciation of Lawrence's character. 'The fact is,' Hogarth wrote, 'that money weighs much less with him than mode of life. I cannot now conceive any Government post, such as the P.M. could offer, which Lawrence would accept, or if he accepted, retain. He begins at once to talk of moral prostitution and quits. . . . Lawrence is not normal in many ways and it is extraordinarily difficult to do anything for him. . . . He will not work in any sort of harness unless this is padlocked onto him. He enlisted in order to have the padlocks rivetted onto him.'†

Shaw's appeal having brought no result, he applied to the new Prime Minister, Ramsay MacDonald. The fact is that there were few politicians who could tolerate Lawrence. He recognized this and remarked on it later with agreeable irony: 'The Labourites think I am an Imperial spy, and the diehards thought I was a bolshie and Lord T says I am a self-advertising mountebank.'‡ But his determination to get his own way never failed him; he had set his mind on getting back into the RAF, and he continued to

* *Letters*, p. 446.
† Bodleian Library.
‡ Ibid.

try every possible approach, particularly since life in the Tank Corps had grown worse because Bruce was no longer there to protect him: 'My face [was] damaged and my lately broken rib rebroken, (I think) by four drunks in the hut . . . Night terrors after proof-correcting had revived war memories . . . [I] kept the barrack room awake five nights running. They gave me a sort of barrack court-martial to keep me quiet. This was humiliating and rather painful.'*

At one stage there appeared an opportunity for a change. In May 1924 Trenchard offered him a post in the RAF: he was to write the official history of the Royal Flying Corps and the Royal Air Force in the war. He thought the proposal over for a night and then declined it, on the ground that the responsibility would be too great and 'it's no use having gone through the grind of climbing down to crowd-level once to give it up for three years' decent living'.

One can well imagine how discouraged Lawrence's friends became in their efforts to help him. When he had been in the Tank Corps for twenty-one months, nearly everyone had given up and thought that Lawrence had done so too. In fact, by about mid-1925, he had reached an emotional crisis to which, according to Bruce, he could see only one solution: suicide. Bruce was present at Clouds Hill on the weekend when the crack-up seemed to threaten.

'He poured out his heart to me, and told me what had been going on, saying it could not go on much longer. . . . He said he had been to see The Old Man and there had been a row and he had been beaten at The Old Man's place. The neatness of his own cottage was more noticeable than usual. His desk was cleared and tidy. . . . While he had been talking he was sitting on the chair beside the table, and I could not help but notice that he was a bundle of nerves. . . . Intuition told me to keep alert. I knew there was a revolver in a chest in the box-room opposite to where we were. That was where we also kept the sleeping gear. As the evening wore on I said I would get the gear ready. I went to the chest and at the same time I looked to see if the gun was still there. It was, but it was loaded—this never used to be. I took the bullets out of the gun and took away the box which contained the rest of them. I put the gun back and put the cartridges into my sleeping bag. There was no lavatory in the cottage and before retiring one had to go outside. I went outside first and when I came back Lawrence went.

'As soon as he was safely out of the door I looked in the chest.

* Ibid. Letter to Dawnay, 27 July 1924.

The gun had gone. I took six cartridges and went down to the door.
Lawrence had obviously gone further than was the custom and was
away longer than usual. In the still of the night I heard a "click".
When he came back to the door, holding the gun, I asked if he had
been looking for something. He said "No". I asked, "Not even these?"
holding out the cartridges in my hand. He said, "Give them to me",
and tried to snatch them from me. A little scuffle took place. He was
trying to get the cartridges and I was trying to get the gun. I bashed
his hand against the wall until he dropped it. Then he cried like a
child. I got him up the stairs but I'm afraid there was no sleep for
either of us that night. There is no doubt he planned to end it,
because the next day we destroyed eighteen letters which he had
written to various people before I had arrived, including one to his
mother in a very large envelope.

'We talked most of Sunday morning, but he was very embarrassed,
and kept his head low most of the time. I suggested we go and have
lunch in Dorchester and he could go and see Thomas Hardy at
Max Gate and pick me up later. He liked that idea. He was very
fond of Hardy, and off we went. We met again at six and we went
straight back to the cottage. I had put the gun in the sleeping bag.
It was a service Webley and too heavy to carry around. I now gave
him the gun and the cartridges, saying "It's all yours". He said,
"Take it with you. I don't want to see it again. You have a solid
gold promise that I will never do that again—ever." When he said
that I was very relieved, but I wondered why he had changed his
mind, and still do. He was suddenly more cheerful. "By this time,"
he said, "the big wheels are grinding for me, and I'll be back in the
Royal Air Force soon." '

Lawrence had started the wheels some months earlier. He wrote
to Trenchard: 'February is supplication month . . . so for the third
time of asking—Have I no chance of re-enlistment in the RAF,
or transfer?'* He added that he was now 'clean and whole in mind
and body' and could pass the monthly medical inspections of the
Tank Corps. As Trenchard was slow in replying, Lawrence began
to lobby on the political level, getting Winston Churchill's secretary,
Eddy (later Sir Edward) Marsh, to talk to his master on his behalf,
because if Churchill moved in 'upon S. Hoare, S. Hoare will run
obediently. . . .' Lawrence devised an 'accidental' meeting with
John Buchan, author of the Richard Hannay books and a prominent

* Trenchard Papers.

member of the Round Table: when they met, apparently by chance in the street one Sunday, Lawrence sought Buchan's help. Then, on 13 June 1925, in a letter to his literary adviser Edward Garnett, he threatened suicide: 'Trenchard withdrew his objection to my joining the Air Force. I got seventh-heaven for two weeks: but then Sam Hoare came back from Mesopot and refused to entertain the idea. That, and the closer acquaintance with *The Seven Pillars* . . . have together convinced me that I'm no bloody good on earth. So I'm going to quit. . . . I shall bequeath you my notes on life in the recruits' camp of the RAF. . . .'*

It is hard to judge the seriousness of this threat. Trenchard had heard Lawrence say things like it and knew how to deal with him. When once before Lawrence had threatened suicide, Trenchard calmly replied, 'All right, but please go into the garden. I don't want my carpets ruined.'† Lawrence smiled and the remark became a private joke between them. In this instance, however, Garnett felt the threat might be serious, and he wrote at once to Bernard Shaw. Shaw was alarmed, too, and replied: 'I have sent your letter to Downing Street with a card to say some decision should be made [about the RAF] as there is a possibility of an appalling scandal, especially after Lowell Thomas's book.'‡

Buchan had appealed to Baldwin, who had become Prime Minister again, and Baldwin now decided to intervene. The result was that on 16 July, soon after the cheerful prophecy to Bruce, Trenchard signed his approval of Lawrence's transfer. On 19 August Lawrence left the army and the nightmare of the Tank Corps—relieved only by the haven of Clouds Hill—was finally over.

It would not have been surprising if Bruce's role in Lawrence's life had ended at this point. Lawrence had got, as he said, 'the only thing I care about . . . surely nothing but time and physical decay will uproot me now'. In some respects he had no more need of Bruce and the relationship might easily have been allowed to run down. But it continued. Bruce went back to Aberdeen to study engineering—at which he later enjoyed a successful career—after having agreed to come back any time Lawrence needed him.

Bruce says they next met late in 1925 when they spent four days together at the gymnasium in Bournemouth, and thereafter saw each other intermittently until Lawrence was posted to India in December 1926. According to Bruce:

* *Letters*, No. 266.
† Andrew Boyle, *Trenchard*. Collins, London, 1962.
‡ *Letters*, p. 477.

'Just before Lawrence left for India there had to be another beating. It was at Barton Street and on The Old Man's orders was a ferocious one. It was The Old Man's last fling because he knew that when Lawrence was in Karachi *Revolt in the Desert*, the abridged version of *Seven Pillars*, would be published and it would pay all of Lawrence's debts plus a lot of money left over. The Old Man wanted his pound of flesh. Twelve strokes. When Lawrence returned from India in 1929 it was another twelve. Again at Barton Street. In September the same year he had a flogging at my house in Aberdeen. For this issue he came all the way from Cattewater, Plymouth, had breakfast and a flogging and caught the next train back. The worst beating of all was in 1930. In August that year I had received a letter which had apparently come from The Old Man. It said Lawrence would be spending a period of his leave with me in the north around September. The Old Man understood there were some quiet seaside coves just north of Aberdeen in the Cruden Bay area where safe swimming was to be had and that nearby there were vast areas of waste land where horses could be galloped. Could I arrange to rent a cottage in one of these places? Also hire three horses and a groom for the period of Lawrence's stay. I made the necessary inquiries and when I was satisfied I wrote and told The Old Man so—via Lawrence, envelope unsealed—but reminded him that the water was so cold at that time of the year that even the locals would not bathe in the sea. I had a reply within the next few days telling me to go ahead with the arrangements.

'The place I had chosen was Collieston, sixteen miles north of Aberdeen. The cottage belonged to a Mr Ross, of Aberdeen. Three horses were hired . . . and the groom was a James Nicolson. He was not a groom really, but knew about horses and he was safe to have around. For Lawrence to agree to all these suggestions of The Old Man was madness—he detested horses and disliked riding them. As for swimming in the North Sea at that time of the year, it just wasn't done. The water was freezing cold and very rough. His programme was to be: rise at six-thirty; swim in the sea for fifteen minutes—he had not far to go as the cottage was practically on the jetty. Then breakfast at the Post Office, which was a café and general store as well; then riding on the links from ten until twelve; lunch; riding from two until four; swimming for half an hour; then a meal and retire.

'Lawrence arrived in Aberdeen on 13 September and we went straight to Collieston. Nicolson was already there with the horses. Next day was wild. The waves and wind were lashing the side of the cottage, but Lawrence insisted on going on to the moors with Nicolson. After riding for an hour they were back because they had had to give up. I could see Lawrence was running a temperature and I was perturbed in case he became ill. I dosed him up with toddy . . . he kicked at having to take it because he did not like the taste of the whisky. However, he drank it and was tucked safely in bed. The result was effective, for in the morning he was all right again, and he asked for the formula in case anything like that should happen again.

'This went on for six or seven days. On the last day birches arrived and I had to give him a severe beating. Jimmy Nicolson was supposed to watch as a witness and I was supposed to write an account of the beating, which made Jimmy sick and he had to leave the room.

'To try and understand Lawrence is near impossible. The letter he wrote to Doubleday, the American publisher,* from Collieston can be seen by all. Here is a man subjecting himself almost beyond human endeavour, willingly, and in the midst of it all he writes a four-page letter in the gayest possible manner. This was not an isolated incident. It happened all the time I knew him. There was one letter he showed me which he wrote to Mrs Bernard Shaw from Collieston. Although he did not tell her everything that was happening, he missed out little and what he did miss he left to her imagination.

'There was another beating in 1931 at Aberdeen and another in 1934 at Maitland Buildings, Elm Row, Edinburgh. On this last occasion The Old Man made him travel up from Bridlington on his motor bike. He had a meal, his usual dose and rode back. He told me later that he rode back standing up in the saddle.

'I saw him six or seven times after that—in Perth, Edinburgh, London and Aberdeen—before his death in 1935. When I heard about the accident I went straight to Bovington, but the security surrounding him was too much for me. I went to the funeral, and looking around at all the great people who were there I wondered if any of them had any idea of the mental agony he had suffered through The Old Man. There were not many there I knew and fewer who knew me. As far as I was concerned the Lawrence association had ended. Then it came up again because of Mrs Shaw. I was asked to go to meet her in July 1935 in a solicitor's office. I think she knew about the beatings. Anyway, we had a private talk. She said that we were the only ones who were privileged to have

* *Letters*, No. 421.

Lawrence's confidence, which was an honour which must be respected.

'The only people it would benefit, she said, if some things became known would be the owners of the juicy Sunday papers, and Lawrence did not belong there. His relations and personal friends were very concerned and they were endeavouring to get people to give an undertaking not to publish confidential matters concerning Lawrence. Mrs Shaw then said, "I understand that you are not willing to co-operate." I asked her how his life story could be written in full if the past ten years were not accounted for in detail. She said that *The Mint* would take care of that, but I told her that it would be incomplete. She asked if it was my intention to publish my story and if this were the case, would I not consider Lawrence's mother? I said that publishing my story had never entered my mind and if it was his mother they were all concerned about, then I would give my word of honour that I would publish nothing while she was alive.'

Bruce has had some astonishing things to say. His memory, after forty-seven years, may be shaky on some points and he may have coloured some incidents. But even if one were to discount everything else, there can be no doubt about the truth of the basic point of his story—that he beat Lawrence at Lawrence's own request.

Weight is given to the basis of Bruce's story by another account of Lawrence's peculiar behaviour: '. . . in 1933 as Mr "E. Shaw" he wrote to Mr G. D. McGee, who ran a riding and hunting establishment in Southampton, for riding instruction for his recalcitrant nephew "Ted", warning, "he will not be an easy pupil." Then as Ted he would show up for the lessons and later receive a report on himself from the riding instructor addressed to Mr E. Shaw.'*

It is clear that for periods at this stage of his life Lawrence was emotionally sick. What had happened to him?

* Paper by John E. Mack, MD, American Journal of Psychiatry, 8 February 1969.

14 The Unknown Element

Lawrence's personality is examined for hidden drives which might explain his actions. His early life seems happy and uncomplicated, yet it was there that the seeds of his later emotional disturbances must have been planted. Did something occur to him during the war to change his personality? According to what Lawrence said on some occasions (but which he contradicted on others), he was buggered by a Turkish Bey at Deraa. New information throws doubt on the authenticity of this story. Lawrence's medical history provides clues which could explain his post-war actions and his masochistic practices.

It is now time to pause and look more closely, more critically, at Lawrence, the little man with a big head, so familiar in a number of favourite poses—in his gold-adorned kafiyeh, fingering the Meccan dagger at his belt; in crumpled khaki uniform at GHQ in Cairo; in RAF uniform on his Brough Superior; in polo-necked jumper and civvies; or on his bicycle before the long ride to Clouds Hill. So far we have seen Lawrence as the stoic, the man preparing himself for a task that lies somewhere ahead, as an intelligence agent with a direct line to Whitehall, as a romantic follower of the Round Table, the reader of Arthurian legend, the creator (in fantasy) of a Brown Dominion. We have read of him as a man obsessed with pain, disliking most women, children and animals, yet remarkably kind to his youngest brother; fond as well as proud of his female racing camel Ghazala, and jealous of old Motlog el Awar, who owned el Jedha, 'the finest she-camel in North Arabia'. To cap it all, here was a man who suddenly decided to renounce both fame and fortune (and even though he gave a lot of it away, he had always had a keen sense of money) for life as a ranker in the RAF and then in the army. Can any consistent pattern in Lawrence's life and personality be traced, any hidden drives which might explain the mainspring of his actions?

Men of genius, like heroes, are rarely subject to the motives and desires of the herd. There is an element of the unknown in all such men, which in Lawrence presents particular problems, for it is clear that at times he was a deliberate and imaginative liar. Any attempt at a psychological interpretation of Lawrence's character must therefore be made with considerable circumspection and with a recognition of our relative ignorance of the inner workings of a man so talented, so brave and so tragic.

We shall begin with the charge most often made against Lawrence: that he was a homosexual. This was hinted at by Brémond: 'He was always strictly shaven in a country where the lack of a beard gave rise to suspicions which he was not spared.' Even the sympathetic biographer Villars considered that Lawrence was 'in his intimate nature . . . certainly homosexual'. Dahoum is seen as a 'pretty ephebe' and Lawrence's descriptions of homosexual behaviour among the Arabs as 'pointless and . . . nothing to do with . . . the war in Arabia'. Villars believes that these references were an attempt by Lawrence to explain his own feelings.

It is certainly true that Lawrence showed a marked lack of any sexual interest in women and that at least one man was physically attracted to Lawrence: Vyvyan Richards, an intelligent and sensitive person. Richards has admitted the strength of his feelings for Lawrence and has said that he could not have been treated more delicately, more kindly and yet more firmly in the rejection of his overtures. This, indeed, was one of the appealing facets of Lawrence's character—his kindness and understanding of other people's feelings, whether they were simple Bedouin, British troopers or airmen, an explorer like Doughty, or the sexually inhibited Charlotte Shaw. In human relations Lawrence was, for the most, a delicate person in the best sense of the word, sensitive to others, self-questioning, thoughtful and tolerant. Yet in some ways he was curiously immature. He had a high-pitched voice, a beardless chin, and an embarrassed giggle; not that these things by themselves indicate that he was either an overt or a latent homosexual.

True, he wrote about homosexual acts, but anyone who has served with non-European troops east of Suez is familiar with the often intense relationships which develop between man and man and, like the artist he was, Lawrence vividly depicted them. Also, in order to play his appointed role, it was necessary for Lawrence to penetrate every aspect of the Arab mind and of Arab behaviour. *Seven Pillars of Wisdom* is an attempt to transport the reader into the midst of his experience, to feel the rough winds of the high desert, the lust for killing, the relief of tension in a sexual activity which

in many cases had to be between man and man because there was
no other outlet. So there would seem to be no special significance in
the references to homosexual activity in *Seven Pillars* (or in a passage
of the original manuscript, deleted on Bernard Shaw's advice),
and it would be a mistake to place too much emphasis on them.

What else remains to suggest that Lawrence was homosexual?
The Deraa episode? The fact that he preferred the companionship
of social and intellectual inferiors? That in none of his writings does
he express any heterosexual feeling? Such evidence is extremely
flimsy and must be rejected by anyone who relies on evidence rather
than intuition or some far-fetched psychological theory.

We now turn to the question of masochism, and this involves
going back to Lawrence's childhood. Here the accepted view of
him as the sensitive yet rebellious son of parents of diverse social
backgrounds, who were unable to marry and as a result lived a
closed and unsociable life in Oxford, is not entirely borne out
by the facts. Nor do the facts show Mrs Lawrence to have been as
great a tyrant as has been suggested, attempting to break her son's
will when necessary by beating him. It is not unknown for parents
to beat their children's bottoms without turning them into heroes or
neurotics. One is struck by the apparently happy nature of Lawrence's
early life and manhood, by the close ties between one member of the
family and another. This at least is the picture revealed in the
Home Letters, perhaps of all Lawrence's writings the most interesting
and revealing for being the freest from that self-examination,
ambiguity, pretentiousness and artificiality that characterize his
post-war letters. The little bungalow at the bottom of the garden in
Oxford—so strange to some—is described by Lawrence for what
it was to him, if not to all his later biographers, a haven of quiet.
He felt that if his brother Frank lived at home then he should use
the bungalow—not for the reason that Lawrence himself used it,
but so that Frank could be noisy. Anyone with a growing family
of five boys in a house none too large can realize that two extra rooms
for study were a sensible addition to the house in Polstead Road,
particularly at a time when Lawrence had shown promise from an
early age of unusual mental development. On his travels he bought
stamps for Arnie, his youngest brother, carpets and antiquities for
his parents and friends, gave advice to his brothers on their careers,
commiserated with his father in that Lawrence did not see how the
boys would ever be able to support their parents in their old age.

One had become a missionary, one was thinking of becoming a teacher, one was in the army, one—Lawrence—was footloose, and one was still an infant. As Lawrence himself realized, these were hardly the professions which would enable them to make a lot of money, but he saw this as relatively unimportant compared with the satisfaction they hoped to achieve from their endeavours.

Digging was 'tremendous fun', he enjoyed life, he had adventures, he had seen the Mediterranean at Aigues Mortes for the first time at the age of nineteen and the experience had impressed him so deeply that he felt like buying a ticket and sailing for Greece immediately. He had written *Crusader Castles*, come under the patronage of the remarkable Hogarth, travelled with him in the Hauran, seen 'the pilgrim route, the great Haj road', and enjoyed a déjeuner in the buffet of the railway station at the junction town of Deraa where he was fascinated listening to Hogarth, as at home there as in Oxford, playing the cosmopolitan traveller, switching without effort from English to Turkish, to German, to Greek, to French, to Italian, and back to English again. Lawrence felt that now he was really out of Europe, away from a culture that he knew and understood, far from the influence of the Renaissance in the exotic and stimulating atmosphere of the Middle East. For any young man it was a memorable experience; for a young man of Lawrence's personality it was a great adventure. There is an ebullience, a real delight in living, in the letters of these years before the war, a manly and healthy satisfaction in overcoming the physical hardships and illnesses such as dysentery and malaria inherent in the type of work in which Lawrence was engaged. It has been alleged that his illegitimacy created in him a shyness, a compensatory and overwhelming conceit, a capacity for deception and other characteristics which depend more on interpretation than on fact. If he is to be believed, he knew that he was illegitimate for certain when he was ten, yet the knowledge did not seem to interfere with his friendships or affect his behaviour at school, at Oxford, or on his archaeological trips. The response to illegitimacy is very varied; there is nothing unusual in Lawrence's reticence in later life about his parent's situation, and nothing in the *Home Letters* to suggest that he felt himself crucified by his knowledge of it. Even if this were the reason for his running away to join the Royal Artillery, which his mother denied, this would have been a most unusual response. The *Home Letters* do not reveal Lawrence as a tortured, pathological personality, nor Mr and Mrs Lawrence as tyrannical parents. They suggest, on the contrary, that they received some unusually fascinating, fond and moving letters from the three brothers, Ned, Will and Frank.

So far there is no sign of the post-war Lawrence, the neurotic, the masochist, the exhibitionist, the imposter, the poseur, to mention but a few of the depreciatory expressions used about him. On the contrary, we get the picture of a high-spirited, intellectually and physically lively person carrying out congenial work and thoroughly enjoying himself. The occasional oddity is there; his friendship with a young Arab donkey boy who poses for him in the nude, and with a Syrian ruffian; a tendency to embellish a situation, or maybe even to invent one; the attraction which he had for young men such as Vyvyan Richards without any reciprocal feeling being apparent on his part; and his lack of interest in women. This is hardly the picture of a tortured soul—nor indeed was his response to the outbreak of war in any way 'neurotic' or unusual. He had been trained for war. He was an intelligence agent. He knew the dispositions of the Turkish army, its units, the names of their officers; he had participated in the impudent survey of the wilderness of Zin under the very noses of the Turks. Of course he must be 'in', to root the Turks out of Syria. It would be 'good fun'. He was twenty-six, a remarkable shot with rifle and revolver, could speak Arabic fluently, if badly, had been hardened by seven years in the Middle East, was with good companions, and had Hogarth behind him.

For the first two years he carried out intelligence duties at GHQ in Cairo, his province being the area from European Turkey to Arabia and Mesopotamia. Then in June 1916, the Arab Revolt broke out. Henceforth the old Lawrence slowly begins to disappear from view. A more mature, more complex and more mysterious person emerges. During the years of the Revolt he experienced the joys of independent command of men, of submitting his body to the rigours of campaigning in a hard and pitiless country; he felt the thrill of action, and he killed men in cold blood and in the heat of battle. Above all, he imposed his will on violently emotional, wayward and savage peoples and on their fickle and divided masters— petty rulers of desert kingdoms too small in stature for his and the British Empire's grand design. How could a man fail to be influenced by this kind of life, which, if Lawrence is to be believed, proved to be the activator of those seeds of later emotional disturbances that were lying dormant in his mind? What happened to him at Deraa has been accounted decisive in the shaping of this new personality. Captured while on a mission and subjected to torture, he is said to have yielded to the homosexual demands of a brutal Turkish Bey.

How accurate is this generally accepted account of the nightmare of Deraa?

According to Lawrence, Deraa appealed to him as the best place to cut the Medina railway. It was a junction of major strategic importance and a local capital. A successful raid would not only have considerable military advantages but would demoralize the Turkish garrison. Late in November 1917, Lawrence decided to test the feasibility of such a raid. In *Seven Pillars* he describes what happened when he went to spy out the land. (The extracts given here are from the Oxford edition—the version set by the *Oxford Times*, which remained in galley form. This differs from the subscribers' edition published in 1927, in which Lawrence made certain changes and omitted certain passages included in the Oxford edition.)

'My plan was to walk round the railway station and the town with Mijbil, and to reach Nisib after sunset. Mijbil was my best companion for the trip, because he was an insignificant peasant, old enough to be my father, and respectable. The respectability seemed only comparative as we tramped off in the watery sunlight, which was taking the place of the rain last night. The ground was muddy, and we were barefoot, and our cheap clothes showed the stains of the filthy weather to which we had been exposed all the week. I was in ragged cotton things, with a torn Haurani jacket, and was yet limping from the broken toe gained when we blew up Jemal on the railway [on a previous raid]. The slippery track made walking difficult, unless we spread out our toes widely and took hold of the ground with them: and doing this for mile after mile was exquisitely painful for me. . . .

'We stepped up onto the head of the curving bank of the Palestine railway, and from its vantage looked at Deraa station, but the ground on this side was too open to admit of our ever making a surprise attack across it. We decided to walk down the east face and examine the defences closely: so we plodded on outside the fence, noting the German stores, the barbed wire here and there, the rudiments of trenches. Turkish troops were passing between their tents and the latrines which were dug out on our side, and everything was unbuttoned and unsuspecting. However, all the east face was also too exposed for an advance in force. We reached the corner of the aerodrome at the south end of the station, and struck over it towards the town, as there was no wire there. We meant to cross the railway, and go up into the village to complete our survey. There were two or three old Albatross machines in the sheds and a few men lounging about. One of these, a Syrian soldier, came up to us and began to question us about our villages, and where they lay, and if there was much "government" in our districts. He was probably an intending deserter, fishing for the offer of a refuge. We shook him off at last and turned away, when someone called out in Turkish. We walked on deafly, but an N.C.O. came after us, and took me roughly by the arm, saying, "The Bey wants you". There were too many witnesses for either fight or flight, so I went with him readily. He took no notice of Mijbil, who wisely slipped away at once.

'I was marched through a tall fence into the compound which was set about with many low temporary huts and a few buildings. We passed some of these to a mud room, outside which was an earth platform, where, on a green tent canvas, sat a fleshy Turkish officer. One leg was tucked under him, and he hardly looked at me when the sergeant brought me up and made a long report in Turkish. He asked my name: I told him Ahmed Ibn Bagr. "An Arab?" I explained I was a Circassian from Kuneitra. "A deserter?" "But we Circassians have no military service."* He then turned round and stared at me curiously, and said very slowly, "You are a liar. Keep him, Hassan Chowish, till the Bey sends for him".

'They led me into a guardroom, mostly taken up by large wooden cribs, on which lay or sat a dozen men in untidy uniforms. They took away my belt, and my knife, but let me sit on a spare place, made me wash myself carefully, and fed me with their own food: I passed the long day there unmolested. They would not let me go on any terms, but tried to re-assure me. Tomorrow, perhaps it would be permitted, if I fulfilled all the Bey's pleasure this evening. The Bey seemed to be Hajim,† the Governor, though what he was to do with me I could not gather. . . .

'Soon after dark they called me. I was waiting for the summons, but three men came with me, and one held me all the time. I cursed my littleness. They took me over the railway, where were six tracks, besides the sidings of the engine shop. We went through a side gate north of the platform, and there turned to the left down a street, past a square, and finally to a detached house . . . there was a sentry at the door, and a glimpse of one or two others lolling in the dark entry. They took me upstairs into the Bey's room, which I was astonished to see was his bedroom.

* Lawrence was wrong. Circassians did have military service.
† Changed to Nahi in the published version.

'He was another bulky man, a Circassian perhaps, sitting on his bed in a night gown, trembling and sweating as though with fever. When I was pushed in he kept his head down, and waved the guard out. Then in a breathless voice he told me to sit on the floor in front of him, and after that was dumb for several seconds, while I gazed at the top of his great shaven head, on which bristling hair stood up stiffly, no longer than the dark stubble on his cheeks and chin. At last he looked me over and told me to stand up: then to turn round. I obeyed, and he flung himself back on the bed, and dragged me down with him in his arms. When I saw what he wanted I twisted round and up again, glad to find myself equal to him in wrestling.

'He then began to fawn on me, saying how white and clean I was, and how fine my hands and feet, and how he was all longing for me and would get me off drills and duties, make me his orderly, and pay me, if I would love him. Incidents like these made the thought of military service in the Turkish army a living death for wholesome Arab peasants, and the consequences pursued the miserable victims all their after life, in revolting forms of sexual disease.

'I was obdurate, so he changed his tone, and sharply ordered me to take off my drawers. When I hesitated he snatched at me, and I pushed him back. He clapped his hands for the sentry, who hurried in and seized me. The Bey then cursed me horribly, and threatened me, and made the man holding me tear my clothes away bit by bit, till I stood there stark naked. His eyes rounded as he saw the half-healed places where the bullets of Jamal Pasha's guards had flicked through my skin a little while ago. Finally he lumbered to his feet, with a glitter in his eye, and began to paw me over. I bore it for a little, till he got too beastly, and then jerked up my knee and caught him hard. He staggered back to his bed, and sat there, squeezing himself together and groaning with pain, while the soldier shouted for the corporal and the other three men of the guard to come and hold me hand and foot. As soon as I was helpless the Governor recovered courage, and spat at me, saying he would make me ask pardon. He took off his soft slipper, and hit me with it repeatedly in the face. He leaned forward and fixed his teeth in the skin of my neck, and bit till the blood came. Then he kissed me. Afterwards he drew one of the men's bayonets. I thought he was going to kill me, and was sorry—but he only pulled up a fold of the flesh over my ribs, worked the bayonet point through, after considerable trouble, and gave it a half turn. This hurt, and I winced a little, while the blood wavered down my side in a thin stream, and dripped on to the front of my thigh. He looked pleased and dabbled it over my stomach with his fingertips.

'I got angry and said something to him. His faced changed, and he stood still, then controlled his voice with an effort and said significantly, "You must understand that I know all about you, and it will be much easier if you do as I wish". I was dumbfounded by this, and we waited silently for another moment, staring at one another, while the men who had not seen an inner meaning shifted about uncomfortably: but it was evidently a chance shot, by which he himself did not, or would not, mean what I feared. I could not again trust my twitching mouth, which faltered always in emergencies, but at last I threw up my chin, which is the sign for "No" in the East, and then he sat down, and half whispered to the corporal to take me out and teach me till I prayed to be brought back.

'They kicked me to the landing at the head of the stairs, and there threw me on the guard-bench and stretched me along it on my face, pommelling me. Two of them knelt on my ankles, bearing down with their arms on the back of my knees, while two more twisted my wrists over my head till they cracked, and then crushed them and my ribs against the wood. The corporal had run downstairs, and now came back with a Circassian riding whip, of . . . single thongs of supple black hide, rounded, and tapering from the thickness of a thumb at the grip (which was wrapped in silver, with a knob inlaid in black designs), down to a hard point much finer than a pencil.

'He saw me shivering, partly I think with cold, and made it whistle through the air over my head, taunting me that before the tenth cut I would howl for mercy, and at the twentieth beg for the caresses of the Bey, and then he began to lash me across and across with all his might, while I locked my teeth to endure this thing which wrapped itself like a flaming wire about my body. At the instant of each stroke a hard white mark like a railway, darkening slowly into crimson, leaped over my skin, and a bead of blood swelled up wherever two ridges crossed. As the punishment proceeded the whip fell more and more upon existing weals, biting blacker or more wet, till my flesh quivered with accumulated pain, and with terror of the next blow coming. From the first they hurt more horribly than I had dreamed of, and, as always before the agony of one had fully reached me, another used to fall, the torture of a series worked up to an intolerable height.

'To keep my mind in control I numbered the blows, but after twenty lost count, and could feel only the shapeless weight of pain, not tearing claws, for which I was prepared, but a gradual cracking apart of all my being by some too great force whose waves rolled up my spine till they were pent within my brain, and there clashed terribly together. Somewhere in the place was a cheap clock, ticking loudly, and it troubled me that their beating was not in its time.

'I writhed and twisted involuntarily, but was held so tightly that my struggles were quite useless. The men were very deliberate, giving me so many, and then taking an interval, during which they would squabble for the next turn, ease themselves, play a little with me, and pull my head round to see their work. This was repeated time and again, for what may have been no more than ten minutes. They had soon conquered my determination not to cry, but so long as my will would rule my lips I used only Arabic, and before the end a merciful bodily sickness came over me, and choked my utterance.

'At last when I was completely broken they seemed satisfied. Somehow I found myself off the bench lying on my back on the dirty floor, where I snuggled down, dazed, panting for breath but vaguely comfortable. I had strung myself to learn all pain until I died, and no longer an actor, but a spectator, cared not how much my body jerked and squealed in its sufferings. Yet I knew, or imagined, what passed about me.

'I remembered the corporal kicking me with his nailed boot to get me up: and this was true, for next day my left side was yellow and lacerated, and a damaged rib made each breath stab me sharply. I remembered smiling idly at him, for a delicious warmth, probably sexual, was swelling through me: and then that he flung up his arm and hacked with the full length of his whip into my groin. This jerked me half over, screaming, or, rather, trying impotently to scream, only shuddering through my open mouth. Someone giggled with amusement, but another cried, "Shame, you've killed him." A second flash followed. A roaring was in my head, and my eyes went black, while within me the core of my life seemed to be heaving slowly up through the rending nerves, expelled from its body by this last and indescribable pang. . . .

'I next knew that I was being dragged about by two men, each disputing over a leg as though to split me apart: while a third astride my back rode me like a horse. Then Hajim called. They splashed water in my face, lifted me to my feet, and bore me, retching and sobbing for mercy, between them to his bedside: but he now threw me off fastidiously, cursing them for their stupidity in thinking he needed a bedfellow streaming with blood and water, striped and fouled from face to heel. They had laid into me, no doubt much as usual: but my indoor skin had torn more than an Arab's.

'So the crestfallen corporal, as the youngest and best looking on the guard, had to stay behind, while the others carried me down the narrow stairs and out into the street. The coolness of the night on my burning flesh, and the unmoved shining of the stars after the horror of the past hour made me cry again. The soldiers now free to speak tried to console me in their fashion, saying that men must suffer their officers' wishes or pay for it, as I had just done, with still greater suffering.

'They took me over an open space, deserted and dark, and behind the Government house to an empty lean-to mud and wooden room, in which were many dusty quilts. They put me down on these, and brought an Armenian dresser, who washed and bandaged me in sleepy haste. Then they all went away, the last of the soldiers whispering to me in a Druse accent that the door into the next room was not locked.

'I lay there in a sick stupor, with my head aching very much, and growing slowly numb with cold, till the dawn light came shining through the cracks of the shed, and a locomotive began to whistle in the station. These and a draining thirst brought me to life, and I found I was in no pain. Yet the first movement brought anguish, but I struggled to my feet, and rocked unsteadily for a moment, wondering that it was not all a dream, and myself back five years ago in hospital at Khalfati* where something of the sort had happened to me.

'The next room was a dispensary, and on its door hung a suit of shoddy clothes. I put them on slowly and clumsily, because of my swollen wrists: and from the drugs chose some tablets of corrosive sublimate, as a safeguard against recapture. The window looked north onto a blank long wall. I opened it, and climbed out stiffly. No one saw me, which perhaps was the reason why I had been shut up in so weak a place. I went timidly down the road towards the village, trying to walk naturally past the few people already astir. They took no notice, and indeed there was nothing peculiar in my dark broadcloth, red fez and slippers: but it was only by restraining myself with the full urge of my tongue silently to myself that I refrained from being foolish out of sheer terror.

---

* Between Aintab and Urfa in Syria. It is impossible to say what Lawrence meant by this. In the later version he altered it to read: 'Five years ago, a timid recruit at Khalfati, where something less staining of the sort had happened.' This could refer to the occasion when he says he was mistaken for a Turkish deserter and imprisoned.

The atmosphere of Deraa seemed inhuman with vice and cruelty, and it shocked me like cold water when I heard a soldier laugh behind me in the street.

'By the bridge were the wells, with men and women already about them. A side trough was free, and from its end I scooped up a little water in my hands, and rubbed it over my face: then drank, which was precious to me: and afterwards wandered aimlessly along the bottom of the valley for some minutes, towards the south, till out of sight of both town and station. So at last was found the hidden approach to Deraa for our future raiding party, the purpose for which Mijbil and myself had come here it seemed so long ago. . . . I was feeling very ill, as though some part of me had gone dead that night in Deraa, leaving me maimed, imperfect, only half myself. It could not have been the defilement, for no one ever held the body in less honour than I did myself. Probably it had been the breaking of the spirit by that frenzied nerve-shattering pain which had degraded me to beast level when it made me grovel to it, and which had journeyed with me since, a fascination and terror and morbid desire, lascivious and vicious, perhaps, but like the striving of a moth towards its flame.'

This account contains only what Lawrence and his literary advisers considered fit to be published. Most of those who have sought to find an answer to the question: did these things really happen or did Lawrence make the story up? seem to have decided that Lawrence told the truth. Of his major biographers, Graves, Liddell Hart, Villars and Aldington (with reservations) consider the story to be reasonably accurate. Another, Nutting, is unable to decide; but Suleiman Mousa, the Arab historian, says frankly that he finds the whole story 'highly implausible'. Anyone trying to probe the truth of the Deraa incident at this distance in time will find his investigations strewn with traps. In the researches necessary for the articles which appeared in *The Sunday Times* in June and July 1968, we came upon evidence which we believed offered an answer to the question beyond reasonable doubt and quoted two documents in support of this. The first, the secret report of June 1919 from Lawrence to the Chief Political Officer at GHQ Egyptian Expeditionary Force in Cairo (see Chapter 7) recounts the story much as it appears in *Seven Pillars*, except that there is no mention of Lawrence's being flogged and he is unequivocal in stating that the Bey 'never reported my capture and escape'.

The second document is a letter to Charlotte Shaw in which

Lawrence is much more specific as to what occurred. It is dated 26 March 1924:

'About that night. I shouldn't tell you, because decent men don't talk about such things. I wanted to put it plain in the book, & wrestled for days with my self-respect ... which wouldn't, hasn't let me. For fear of being hurt, or rather, to earn five minutes' respite from a pain which drove me mad, I gave away the only possession we are born into the world with—our bodily integrity. It's an unforgivable matter, an irrecoverable position: and it's that which has made me forswear decent living, & the exercise of my not-contemptible wits & talents.

'You may call this morbid: but think of the offence, and the intensity of my brooding over it for three years. It will hang about me while I live, & afterwards if our personality survives. Consider wandering among the decent ghosts hereafter, crying "Unclean, unclean!".'

Lawrence says that he gave way to the Bey's homosexual demands. Yet in the passage quoted from *Seven Pillars* (see page 209, par. 3) he specifically asserts that he resisted the Bey. What, then, is the truth of the matter? The Cairo report and the letter to Charlotte Shaw seemed to point to the fact that (a) Lawrence was captured because the Turks knew he was in the area; (b) he had been betrayed by Mohamed Said and Abd el Kadir, who not only warned the Turks that he was coming, but also described him in detail; (c) the Bey, when he said, 'You must understand that I know', meant that he knew his prisoner was Lawrence; (d) the Bey, an active homosexual, forced Lawrence to submit to him, then, fearing his superiors' wrath if they knew he had allowed Lawrence to escape, suppressed the news of his capture; and (e) Lawrence, broken by the way the Bey had used him, was never—despite the unusual methods he was to adopt—able to heal the wound which the experience had inflicted on his psyche.

On the evidence before us at the time these seemed valid conclusions. The only Arab who might have been able to say whether Lawrence went to Deraa or not was killed during the war, so admittedly all the evidence was either circumstantial or depended on Lawrence's own account; and, to bedevil the matter still further, for every person to whom Lawrence had sworn that his account was true there appeared to be one to whom he had confessed it to be a fantasy. For example, Bernard Shaw wrote in a note which is attached*

* Arents Collection, New York Public Library. This note was written by hand.

to an early copy of *Seven Pillars:* 'Even my wife, always friendly and a
help to him, said to me, when, after his unusually long absence
from our house, I asked whether there was any quarrel—any
unpleasantness: "No, no quarrel, no unpleasantness. But he is
such an INFERNAL liar!" He was not a liar. He was an actor.
But I must add that neither was he a monster of veracity. One of
his chapters (LXXXI) tells of a revolting sequel to his capture by
the Turks and his attraction for a Turkish officer. He told me that
his account of the affair is not true. I forbore to ask him what
actually happened.'

In Paris during the Peace Conference, Lawrence told the Deraa
story to Colonel R. Meinertzhagen, a member of the British delegation whom he had met in Palestine in 1917. According to
Meinertzhagen, Lawrence said he had been seized, stripped and
bound, then buggered by the Governor of Deraa, and afterwards by
the Governor's servants. He added that he did not intend to publish
the true account of this incident because it was too degrading and
had 'penetrated his innermost nature'. Meinertzhagen at first
accepted Lawrence's story as true, but after Lawrence's death he
wrote, 'the Deraa incident is false'.*

There is conflicting testimony, too, about Lawrence's escape.
Jock Chambers, Lawrence's friend from the RAF, remembers
having once asked him, 'How did you get away from Deraa?'
Lawrence replied, 'I had to kill the sentry with a stone . . . horrible
business. It took a long time.'

After the articles had appeared in *The Sunday Times*, we continued our investigations into the Deraa incident. With more time
available it seemed worthwhile to try to discover what had become
of the one other person who could, if he were willing, tell us the
truth about Deraa—the Bey himself. The more we considered this,
the more difficult it seemed to understand why none of the writers
on Lawrence had apparently been able to find and interview the Bey.

We decided to do so, but were too late—by three years: the
Bey died at Izmir in Turkey in 1965. We have, however, spoken
to his son, examined the Bey's diaries, and interviewed some of his
associates and several of his enemies, with results that cast considerable
doubt on Lawrence's story.

Hacim Muhittin Bey was known in Turkey as an aggressive
heterosexual who had little difficulty in getting girls at Deraa and
was in almost every respect unlike Lawrence's description of him.
As a clever and patriotic official he would have been most unlikely

* *Middle East Diary, 1917–56*. The Cresset Press, London, 1959.

to let Lawrence escape once he had caught him. Finally, there is no mention of Lawrence in the Bey's diaries, although the Bey knew of him and referred to him in conversation as 'my opponent'.

Hacim Bey, Ottoman War Medal, the Iron Cross, and Independence Medal, came from a prominent noble family of Anatolia. He was chief of police in Izmir from 1914 to 1917, and became Governor of Hauran, based at Deraa, in March 1917. His son, Targan, remembers his father's referring to Lawrence as 'my opponent who wants to capture Deraa'. Targan also told us that his father never at any time mentioned having met Lawrence and gave no indication he had even so much as known what he looked like.

In the Bey's diaries, which he began to keep only two months after the apparent date of the Deraa incident, there is no reference to Lawrence, but there are frequent references to women: 'We spent the night in Damascus and enjoyed ourselves with . . .' (a list of girls' names follows). Another entry refers to the Bey having contracted gonorrhoea. A nephew of the Bey said to us 'There is no one in the family who did not know of his weakness for women', a view also expressed by Yakup Karaosmanoglu, journalist, novelist, and a prominent figure in the early days of the Turkish Republic, who knew Hacim as a young man: 'I knew him well. If he had ever had any homosexual tendency I would certainly have known about it. He was in the first nationalist parliament in Ankara, and that parliament was a puritanical affair. If Hacim had exhibited any homosexual leanings he would not have lasted as a member.'

Several of Hacim Bey's friends pointed out that he had been under strong attack in Turkey when, as Governor of Bursa in 1920, he retreated before the invading Greeks. A committee of inquiry decided that he had been acting under orders, but before its findings were published he was bitterly assailed in parliament and in the press. Yet although all kinds of allegations were made against him, there was never any hint of homosexuality.

Karaosmanoglu's brother, Fevzi Lutfi, had no cause to respect the Bey's memory. A writer and poet, he was arrested on his instructions in the early 1920s when Hacim was head of a tribunal set up to root out counter-revolutionary activity. Fevzi Lutfi's offence was that he had written a poem that was critical of Ataturk. Although still bitter about his arrest and prepared to believe the worst of Hacim Bey, Fevzi Lutfi would not accept that the Bey could have been a homosexual.

While it would be understandable if Hacim Bey's family should defend him against a charge of pederasty—even if it were true—it is significant that people who had no reason to like or defend him—who, on the contrary, might have supported such an allegation in order to pay off old scores—were adamant that, whatever else he might have been, he was not a homosexual.

So what really happened? All the evidence points strongly to Hacim Bey being innocent of the charge of having assaulted Lawrence. It is possible, of course, that Lawrence was captured at Deraa and buggered by someone else. The garrison commander at Deraa was Bimbashi Ismail Bey and the militia commander Ali Riza Bey. Lawrence may have confused one or other with Hacim Bey. In the original version of the story Lawrence says, 'The Bey *seemed* to be Hajim'. But in the Cairo report he is emphatic: '[I] was identified by Hajim Bey, the Governor. . . .' Or he could have been buggered by the guards: 'I next knew that I was being dragged about by two men, each disputing over a leg as though to split me apart: while a third astride my back rode me like a horse.' It is also possible that Lawrence was captured and beaten but not buggered. And, finally, it is possible that the description of the incident was imaginary.

Nevertheless, it would be unwise to reject the story out of hand. The brutality of the Turks was well known in all the Arab countries under their hand, and whether Lawrence was assaulted by the Bey or by someone else is immaterial: his ordeal, real or imaginary, was none the less horrifying.

Yet we believe that the major reason for the change in Lawrence's personality will be found not in an incident as traumatic as Deraa but simply in his medical history. Here, as with so many aspects of his story, there is a good deal of conflicting evidence—some of it provided by Lawrence himself. To Robert Graves he wrote: 'I got malaria in France when I was sixteen: and have had it so often since that it's hardly worth mentioning. Malta Fever at eighteen. Dysentery, typhoid, black-water, smallpox etc. since (and once nearly murdered).' In fact, so far as is known, he never suffered from Malta fever, typhoid, blackwater, or smallpox, and doubt has been cast on the attempt to murder him. As a boy he was healthy and vigorous (except for a broken leg at about the age of thirteen and an attack of mumps at the same age). It was when he was at Aigues Mortes in the Camargue in the summer of 1906, when he was nearly eighteen, that Lawrence was ill with what was most probably malaria. The area was highly malarial, the parasites being of a type that produces benign tertian malaria, a recurrent form of the disease which may persist for years. Thenceforth for the rest of his life Lawrence was to suffer from repeated attacks of fever, which he treated with quinine and later with some sort of arsenical preparation. While he was at Safed when he was twenty he had a bout of malaria; at Halifat, when he was twenty-one, he was 'tormented' by it, and a year later had a 'double extra-special bout'. In addition to these recurrent bouts Lawrence suffered repeated attacks of dysentery which began in Syria when he was twenty-two. A particularly exhausting attack occurred on the ride from Abu Markha in March 1917. 'Dysentery of this Arabian coast sort used to fall like a hammer blow, and crush its victims for a few hours, after which the extreme effects passed off; but it left men curiously tired, and subject for some weeks to sudden breaks of nerve.' To cap all this, quarrelling broke out amongst his followers and one was killed. For the sake of unity and to prevent a blood feud, Lawrence had to shoot the murderer, which must have been all the more disturbing to a man suffering 'a bodily weakness which made my animal self crawl away and hide till the shame was passed'. Attacks of fever and dysentery on top of the anxieties of a campaign in which fire had to be breathed continually into Feisal's soul and the tribes kept together by a mixture of gold, promises, and the prospects of booty, drained the energy from Lawrence's mind and body, leaving him the prey to self-doubt, introspection and self-reproach. 'Hardly one day in Arabia passed without a physical ache to increase the corroding sense of my accessory deceitfulness towards the Arabs, and the legitimate fatigue of responsible command*.... Instead of facts and figures, my note-books were full of states of mind, the reveries of self-questioning induced or educed by our situations, expressed in abstract words to the dotted rhythm of the camels' marching.'†

What was called shell-shock in World War I and battle fatigue in World War II, are states which result from overstraining of the human organism. It is not the mind alone that breaks down under stress; the body, too, shows its failing resistance by physical break-down—in tropical countries by repeated attacks of malaria or dysentery, in other climates by unco-ordination of the mind and body that lead to increased risk-taking, soreness of the muscles, and bodily fatigue. Lawrence went into the war 'a pocket Hercules—as muscularly strong as people more than twice my size and more enduring than most.' He came out of it at the end of his tether.

* *Seven Pillars*, Chapter LXXX.
† Ibid., Chapter CIII.

He was down to under six stone. He had a bad hand and his broken toe still bothered him. Apart from his exertions during the Revolt, Lawrence had sustained personal losses through the deaths in action of his brothers Frank and Will, and of the particular Arab whom he loved, and six months after his leaving Damascus his father died from influenza.

There are frustrating gaps in the documentation of these years which make it impossible to assess the affects these losses had on Lawrence, but the combination of mental and physical depletion would have meant for most men the end of the road. For many of the shell-shock cases of World War I there was no recovery. Lawrence's inherent toughness now showed itself, for he was able to go on for another five years before succumbing. And it was during these years that he was writing *Seven Pillars of Wisdom* and reliving his experiences in a state of great emotion. By the time he joined the RAF on 28 August 1922, the manuscript was finished. He was nearly done with it, but not quite; the subscribers' edition had now to be prepared, and that took another three years; he was not quit of the book until 1926, when it appeared in all its bibliophilic glory. During the four years between his leaving Damascus in 1918 and his joining the RAF in 1922, Lawrence had managed to contain his inner problems, probably by means of furious activity and the remains of that enthusiasm for life which he had known as a boy and a young man.

First, he had the excitement and exertions of the Peace Conference, the struggle for mastery—this time not of primitive peoples, but of politicians of the Great Powers, with himself in Arab robes standing at Feisal's right hand, his Grand Vizier. Second, he had his book to write, enabling him to relive his exploits and to try to explain his motives. Nearly always creative activity of this sort to a Romantic and a 'Half-Poet' such as Lawrence provides an emotional experience of greater depth and significance than that of achievement. He had the insight to see that his political efforts were failing, that the Revolt had been a house built upon sand, almost as empty as the desert, and was to be followed by catastrophe for the main pro-tagonists—Feisal thrown out of Syria by the French, old King Hussein eventually defeated by Ibn Saud and exiled to Cyprus; murder everywhere over the years to come. Lawrence had seen enough to be thoroughly disillusioned. As he wrote in the letter to a colleague in Paris, his motives had been mainly personal—fondness for a particular Arab, patriotism, intellectual curiosity, and ambition. Now he had given up—'I laugh at myself because giving up has made me look so futile'. Slowly but surely his life force was draining away.

With the completion of *Seven Pillars* he was ready for the next step—the most difficult to understand and the most unusual—his enlistment in the ranks of the RAF. Various explanations of his decision have been given both by Lawrence and his biographers. For Lawrence it was in order to obtain material for a book on the RAF; to get away from his family, particularly from his mother, who had given him 'a terror of families and inquisitions'; to eat dirt and experience degradation; to be alone in the only place where it was possible to be alone—a crowded place; to find a fresh plane of activity, 'for it is very difficult for me to do nothing, and I've tried soldiering, and science, and politics, and writing: and manual labour seemed the obvious next', to escape from the world and its obligations. To Graves he wrote: 'Honestly, I couldn't tell you exactly why I joined up: though the night before I did (a very wonderful night, by the way: I felt like a criminal waiting for daylight) I sat up and wrote out all the reasons I could see or feel in myself for it. But they came to little more than that it was a necessary step, forced on me by an inclination towards ground-level: by a despairing hope that I'd find myself on common ground with men: by a little wish to make myself more human than I had become in Barton Street: by an itch to make myself ordinary in a mob of likes. . . . All these are reasons: but unless they are cumulative they are miserably inadequate. I wanted to join up, that's all: and I am still glad, sometimes, that I did. It's going to be a brain-sleep, and I'll come out of it less odd than I went in: or at least less odd in other men's eyes.' In a letter to Lionel Curtis, he wrote that the army seemed safe against enthusiasm, a place for mind-suicide and for self-degradation, and 'yet despite the pervading animality of spirit' which saw it as quite natural 'that you should job a woman's body, or hire out yourself, or abuse yourself in any way. . . . My masochism remains and will remain, only moral.' Yet there is a passage in *The Mint* which shows how aware Lawrence was of the relation between the infliction of pain and sexuality. 'I have been before at depots, and have seen or overseen the training of many men: but this our treatment is rank cruelty. While my mouth is yet hot with it I want to record that some of those who day by day exercise their authority upon us, do it in the lust of cruelty. There is a glitter in their faces when we sob for breath; and evident through their clothes is that tautening of the muscles (and once the actual rise of sexual excitement) which betrays that we are being hurt not for our good, but to gratify a passion.'*

The significance of the Deraa incident, whether true or false, is that it provides a classical example of a situation in which sexual pleasure flooding the whole body occurs in a response to the infliction of both pain and humiliation. Lawrence's description of the Circassian riding whip, with its 'single thongs of supple black hide, rounded, and tapering from the thickness of a thumb at the grip (which was wrapped in silver, with a knob inlaid in black designs) down to a hard point much finer than a pencil' is typical of the masochist's preoccupation with details of the instruments of his punishment, and is well recognized in the literature on the subject. The conclusion seems inescapable that Lawrence did indeed experience abnormal reactions to pain and its infliction, and was well aware of the sexual connotations of this, and that accompanying these reactions was an inner drive towards degradation and abasement. What was the reason for this inner drive? The answer can perhaps be traced through Lawrence's association with Bruce.

Their relationship began, according to Bruce, when Lawrence was nearly thirty-four and Bruce nineteen. It continued for thirteen years, slowly fading in intensity. In some respects it is reminiscent of the relationship with Dahoum: a younger person of lower social status is chosen as a companion and is allowed to enter certain aspects of Lawrence's life. He is tested with activities of a private and confidential nature, then ultimately accepted as an accessory in the performance of secret and shared activities. The whole operation is conducted in a manner not unlike the recruitment of an intelligence agent. In Lawrence's disturbed state of mind it seems possible that with Bruce he was attempting to recreate and relive his earlier, happier adventures with the Syrian donkey-boy of whom he became so fond, whom he recruited for British intelligence and for whose death he blamed himself. Lawrence had taught Dahoum English and photography and had led him out of Syrian village life into a wider world. Similarly he introduced Bruce to music, literature and high politics, and on his discharge from the army encouraged him to take up engineering. The strain of Lawrence's double life during his Middle Eastern period and especially during the Revolt, was probably alleviated by the fact that it was in some small respects shared by Dahoum, whom he loved. Alone after Dahoum's death, Lawrence in a disturbed state of mind

* *The Mint*, p. 102.

attempted to recreate the same sort of relationship with Bruce, a person on whom he felt he could depend, a youth physically strong and reliable who would not ask too many questions.

The beatings administered by Bruce may have provided some sort of expiation for the feelings of guilt and self-reproach that Lawrence felt about Dahoum's death. It would seem certain that they were not simply a sexual phenomenon, but rather a complex ritualistic pattern of self-punishment, self-degradation and mourning, combining an element of self-gratification, or at least of relief from suffering. The seeds of Lawrence's masochism must clearly have been planted in childhood, although the dearth of solid information regarding his emotional development as a child precludes anything but broad speculation. In some ways he had identified himself with his father, taking up, as he had, cycling and photography, but Sir Robert remains a figure too shadowy to provide any valid comparison. Of his mother, too, we are offered only glimpses now and then. In the vast correspondence between her and her sons little emerges about her as a living personality. The post-war Lawrence found her 'very exciting. She is so set, so assured in mind. I think she set many years ago: perhaps before I was born.' She made impossible demands for love, transformed her husband from a hard-drinking, larger-than-life person into a teetotal, domesticated character, a careful spender, as indeed he had to be, with five sons and an income of only £300 or £400 a year. After his death the demands for love made by his mother annoyed Lawrence, who wrote to Charlotte Shaw: 'She has so lived in her children, and in my father, that she cannot relieve herself, upon herself, at all. And it isn't right to cry out to your children for love. They are prevented, by the walls of time and function, from loving their parents.'

There is nothing unusual in this, the rejection of an over-possessive, dominant mother by her son. But Lawrence's letters to her in the post-war years have a coldness, a distance, and indeed a cruelty which appear to be out of proportion to what we know of his mother's demands. And here is the nub of the Lawrence problem, the stumbling block to any really objective study, for the traffic is all one way; we do not know what his mother and father wrote to him, nor for that matter his brothers, or Charlotte Shaw. Whatever happened to Lawrence, it seems to have alienated him from what remained of his family, as is shown by the pre-war relationships mirrored in the *Home Letters*. We cannot explain his early development for lack of information. Nor, until the Deraa episode, is there anything in his letters which might suggest he was wrestling with a serious psychological problem. His British and French companions in the Revolt, apart from Colonel Brémond, never suspected any deep-seated trouble; but then Brémond hated him. He was certainly an unusual person, but few could have foreseen the course his life was suddenly to take. And yet, after the furious activity of the Revolt, of Paris, and of the writing of *Seven Pillars*, there suddenly appears the worn, shrunken, shabbily dressed little figure at the doors of the RAF recruiting office. What explanation can there be?

The clinical picture of Lawrence at this time is that of a man suffering from depressive illness, an illness in which guilt and self-reproach are prominent features and madness sometimes not far away. To a man like Lawrence, who had made a god of self-control, the conflicting cross-currents of his emotions released by depression must have produced an emotional turmoil for which one can only feel pity and sympathy. Luckily, he was slowly to find his sanity again, aided by a multitude of friends who could accept him for what he chose to be and in the company of men who made no demands on him. This is not, of course, the whole psychological story of this complicated, brilliant and likeable man. But it is clear that his emotional state improved—despite flare-ups of depression in times of stress—in the RAF and that he even found happiness there. This perhaps he knew obscurely on that night of anguish and yet of hope when he first enlisted. Despite his unfavourable first experience at Uxbridge, he came to love the Air Force and he certainly realized how important a sanctuary it was to him when, after a period of desperate unhappiness in the Tank Corps, he was finally allowed to return to being an aircraftman.

15 Back in the RAF

At Cranwell, the RAF Cadets' College, Lawrence settles down in the RAF, but cannot resist doing a little counter-intelligence work. To avoid publicity when Seven Pillars of Wisdom *and its abridgement,* Revolt in the Desert, *are published he applies for, and is granted, a posting to India. In Karachi, as the months slip uneventfully by, he takes out the notes he made on his life in the RAF, revises them and calls the resulting book* The Mint. *He sends a copy to Trenchard, who is horrified and gets Lawrence to promise not to publish the book before 1950, if ever. A revolt breaks out in Afghanistan and Lawrence, by a bizarre chain of events, is accused of being behind it. The Afghanistan government issues an order for his arrest and the Government of India requests his recall. The RAF agrees to this, but there is a dispute over the manner in which his recall is to be carried out. Questions are asked about him in the House of Commons and he goes there to try to stop them. He is posted to a new flying-boat station at Cattewater on Plymouth Sound.*

On 21 August 1925, Lawrence reported for his medical examination at the RAF station at West Drayton in Middlesex, before being sent to Uxbridge and then on to the Cadets' College at Cranwell in Lincolnshire. He was very content: 'I wrote to a man yesterday and said how breathtaking, how arresting was the having received all at once you had ever asked for, or ever wanted from life.' Cranwell was all Lawrence hoped the RAF would be. He revelled in the work—preparing the training machines for the cadets, refuelling the little Bristol fighters, and keeping the records for his group. At thirty-eight he could write, 'I'm foolishly happy, and propose to stay "put" till ninety years old'.

This second spell in the RAF was to last nearly ten years and is one of the least-known periods of Lawrence's life. It was his chance to escape from the Arabian legend he had grown to detest and (if it was sincerely his wish), to bury himself in the ranks and find the peace and contentment he said he now valued above all else. Yet his old love of intrigue contrived to make this impossible: like Bernard Shaw's Private Meek in *Too True to be Good*, he could not resist an opportunity to lead from the ranks if such an opportunity presented itself. Even in India, when he served on the North-West Frontier on a remote and isolated station, he was unable to escape accusations of intrigue, and in Britain, in the final stages of his term of service his manipulation of authority enabled him to effect, indirectly, changes in RAF regulations without most of the Force realizing that he had had any responsibility in the matter. In fairness to Lawrence he only intervened when, in the words of his former commanding officer, 'he felt that there was some abuse which would not otherwise have come to light'. This desire of Lawrence's to have both the right to an anonymous refuge in the ranks and at the same time the right to exercise authority when he considered it necessary, was the main cause of his difficulties in these years. He could not stand by when he saw wasteful or inefficient methods in use or when he believed morale and efficiency could be improved by changing the regulations. Consequently what he attempted— and sometimes achieved—in the RAF bore no relation to his rank.

In this respect it was like the early days of the war in the Middle East, when Lawrence, nominally a second lieutenant, tried to ransom General Townshend and his troops. In the RAF, though only an aircraftman, he was responsible at various times for making suggestions about the recruitment of officers, developing a new branch of the service, lobbying MPs, helping to prepare a parliamentary bill, writing a paper on the role of the RAF in the event of war, expressing his views on how many new airfields and aircraft were needed, and towards the end of his life, helping to design an early version of a hovercraft.

The intrigues began at Cranwell. Lawrence was fortunate in that his commanding officer was 'Biffy' Borton, who had flown with the Royal Flying Corps in the desert and knew Lawrence there. ('I came in a Handley Page bomber and Lawrence told me with a great amount of laughter that the Arabs said the war was as good as over because the biggest aeroplane in the world was on our side.') Lawrence arrived at Cranwell without Borton's knowledge—'I walked in one day and saw Lawrence in an airman's uniform. I was furious with Trenchard for not letting me know. Fortunately I kept my head and didn't say anything, but being taken by surprise like that I could have easily let the cat out of the bag. I went to my quarters and sent for him.' No doubt they discussed the affairs of the station from time to time, as the following incident suggests: Lawrence had become friendly with Arthur Lippet, who worked in the station's X-ray department and had treated Lawrence for a fractured wrist. According to Lippet, 'One afternoon after tea-time Lawrence was waiting for me outside our mess. He told me he needed my help. About six o'clock a parcel would be dropped from a motor cycle on to the road passing through the camp or on to the road passing outside. Lawrence said, "You go to the outside road and keep watch. If anything is dropped bring it back to me. Don't stay after dusk." I did as he asked, but the drop was made on the road Lawrence was watching. It was a parcel containing hundreds of subversive pamphlets. Lawrence took them away.'* Lippet said that it was common knowledge that there were a number of Irish Republican Army sympathizers in the camp and minor explosions had occurred. It seems clear that Lawrence, either on his own initiative, but more probably with the knowledge of the authorities, had made it his business to keep an eye on the IRA elements and, when possible, upset their schemes.

While busy with his duties, Lawrence was still preparing the subscribers' edition of *Seven Pillars* for publication. The printer, Manning Pike, had premises in London at 44 Westbourne Terrace North, W2, which he leased from George H. Noble at £1 a week. Lawrence would ride his motorcycle from Cranwell to check on progress and sometimes would stay overnight, sleeping on a make-shift bed on the hot water pipes in the basement.†

As publishing time grew closer it became clear that the interest the subscribers' edition would create, plus the plan to publish the abridgement, *Revolt in the Desert*, in March 1927, and the substantial sale of Lowell Thomas's book would all add up to a considerable stir. This realization forced Lawrence to take a decision he had been dreading. He made up his mind in June to leave the country before the publicity began and applied for a posting to India, where 'nobody will know or care'. Trenchard told him this was not necessary, but Lawrence insisted, and sailed for Karachi in the troopship *Derbyshire* on 7 December 1926. He hated the voyage and wrote a sickening description of it which he kept for what would probably have been the final section of *The Mint*. In it he describes a flooded lavatory and how a tough orderly officer clears a drain blocked by sanitary towels. (It is published as Letter 292 in *The Letters of T. E. Lawrence*.) On his arrival he was stationed at Drigh Road, six miles outside Karachi, where he was posted to the engine-repair section and soon took over the station's clerical

* Interview with the authors.
† Letter from Noble to George Wren Howard of Jonathan Cape, 20 February 1955.

work as well. The job was light and easy, leisure hours were long, and in the drowsy heat of India Lawrence soon slipped into the limbo of 'airmanland': 'I haven't been out of camp since arrival,' he wrote to Lionel Curtis in March 1927. 'The India business is too big for me to tackle . . . so it's better to stay in and not meet anyone . . . You have driven yourself very hard for twenty-five or thirty years: and the equivalent of the RAF is perhaps your due. There comes a great peace upon the spirit when the will finally gives it over.'*

Meanwhile in Britain the subscribers' edition of *Seven Pillars* came out with a flurry of publicity. Hogarth wrote a three-column review of it for *The Times*, describing how the book had been written. Within weeks *The Times* personal column was carrying advertisements offering £20 for a loan of the book and subscribers who were willing to sell their copies could get between £300 and £400 each for them. In March 1927 *Revolt in the Desert* was published simultaneously in Britain and the United States and quickly became a best-seller. The reviews were, in general, good. Bernard Shaw, who reviewed the book for the *Spectator*, described it as 'one of the great histories of the world'. Churchill said it ranked with 'the greatest books ever written in the English language'. Not everyone was so fulsome. Sir Arnold Wilson, the former Civil Commissioner in Iraq and an old enemy of Lawrence's, hit hard. In a review in the *Central Asian Journal* he blamed Lawrence for 'the estrangement of Anglo-French relations in the Middle East . . . and for the present deplorable situation in Syria'. Wilson said the Arab Bureau 'helped induce [Britain] to adopt a policy which brought disaster to the people of Syria, disillusionment to the Arabs of Palestine and ruin to the Hejaz'.

Controversy added to the sales of the book and money began to roll in, revealing in Lawrence's handling of it that he was not without business acumen. He admitted that he had spent an extra £1,000 on bindings at the last moment, 'when I saw that otherwise I was going to have too much money in hand. The residue is going to the RAF Memorial Fund and there is no sense in giving them a gold mine.' He suggested to Curtis that he should sell a dagger which he had given him: 'Some Yank would pay pots for it, now it's got a pedigree.' He advised his financial adviser not to accept any film offers for the book and instead to write to the famous producer, Rex Ingram, at Ciné Studios in Nice, because 'his touch would be more favourable to the subject' and he could film it in Tunis, 'which, while not Arabia, would be better than California or Arizona'.

* All Souls College Library, Oxford.

Lawrence's overdraft was now paid off and the RAF Memorial Fund was about to receive a handsome donation. (The existence of this Fund was not widely known at the time and the general belief was that Lawrence was now a rich man.) He could afford to feel some satisfaction—even though he himself was not benefiting by as much as a penny. He wrote to Trenchard, 'The book profits, being derived indirectly from my part in the Arab Revolt, had to go to the way of the rest . . . I would not feel so seagreenly incorruptible otherwise. Tons and tons of dirt on my hands and head, but not a morsel swallowed.'* In the elation of knowing his book was a success he could not resist a stab at the French. When his bank manager wrote to tell him that the French rights had been sold, he replied that he would never have agreed to a French edition unless the publishers had promised to print a notice on the book-jacket that the profits were to be devoted to the victims of French cruelty in Syria.

The months in India slipped by in a routine relieved only by the arrival of mail. Lawrence appeared to be content, but in a frank letter to Trenchard he confessed, 'I hold my safety-valve down with both hands, every night after lights out, trying not to want it [a posting home]: because I'll only make myself ill if I start vainly thinking'.†

On 6 November 1927, Hogarth died. Only a few months earlier Lawrence had confided 'I value him very specially. It was he who first encouraged me to visit Syria: who put me on to the Carchemish Staff: who got me the Sinai Survey job: who recommended me for the Geographical section of the War Office: who assisted me into Arabia, and in Arabia. He shines out across Oxford as a man.' Lawrence's distress at the loss of Hogarth can easily be imagined. 'I . . . feel benumbed. Somehow I never thought that special thing would happen.'

They had not been as close since the war as during the Revolt and the preparations for it, but during his early period Hogarth had been the main influence on Lawrence and his death must have left him the poorer. Hogarth may have viewed Lawrence's later development with some disappointment and Lawrence may have turned from Hogarth to other father figures, but the bond of Arabia was never completely severed while Hogarth lived. With his death the desert adventure came to a clearly defined end and Lawrence began to look to a new future—a literary one. Early in 1928 he dragged from his tin trunk his notes for *The Mint*, which he had

* Trenchard Papers.
† Ibid.

started to copy out in Karachi, and sent the MS off to the critic, Edward Garnett. The next day he wrote to Trenchard about it. The letter, which has not been published before, is interesting because it reveals how Lawrence himself felt about this controversial book:

'In 1922, when you let me enlist, I promised that the C[hief] of A[ir] S[taff] should see, first, any book I wrote on the R.A.F.... I posted something rather like one yesterday to Edward Garnett: and you'd better hear about it. In those days I hoped to turn as much of me as had survived the war into a writer; and I thought the R.A.F. was a subject. So I made full and careful notes of Uxbridge... In Karachi I took them up ... and I sweated on them for months, till they were all out straightly in a little note-book of 176 pages (70,000 words) called *The Mint*. *The Mint* because we were all being stamped after your image and superscription. This note-book it was which I posted yesterday ... if you care to see it you may ... Garnett will not hawk the thing about; only his son [David Garnett] will read it . . . after I'm dead someone may censor out of it an edition for publication . . . It's a worm's eye view of the R.A.F.—a scrappy, uncomfortable thing . . . Any word used in barrack rooms has been judged good enough to go in; wherefore Scotland Yard would like to lock up the author. The general public might be puzzled, and think I didn't like the R.A.F., whereas I find it the only life worth living for its own sake. Though not the Depot. Uxbridge was bad, and I'd have written and told you so, only that it seemed implicit in your letting me join, that I should take my stuff quietly.'*

Trenchard did not read *The Mint* immediately, but hastened to write to Lawrence expressing his dismay. He said that Lawrence had probably written 'What is quite comprehensible to you and me as we both understand the position'. If, however, the newspapers got hold of the book they would say what a hopeless Air Force it was, how badly it was run, what hopeless officers it had, and, as Trenchard pointed out, 'it cannot go on continually being abused by everybody'. Trenchard said he had enough to worry about. A quarrel between Ibn Saud and Feisal Al Dawiss had flared up and there were rumours of 30,000 tribesmen gathering for battle, but with patience and the Air Force he hoped he might yet make peace between the two Arab leaders. 'Perhaps you will say this is impossible. Could you do it?' It was a personal and rather sad letter—'I do not feel a bit annoyed with you.

* Trenchard Papers.

I feel I always thought you would do it, though I hoped you would not. Anyhow, I am going to see Garnett when I can, and I hope he will not publish it or let it be published . . . You know you did promise me years ago, and it is not for myself I care twopence, but for the Air Force that I have tried so hard to get going in the right way.' There was a p.s.: 'When do you want to come home?'*

Lawrence replied with a four-page letter, 'the longest, I think, I have ever written'. It is an amazing letter and ranges over an assurance that *The Mint* would not be published before 1950, or even 1970, a page of praise for Trenchard's work in building the RAF, and of Trenchard as a man ('If my father had been as big as you, the world would not have had spare ears for my freakish doings'), to a long exposition of how Lawrence would handle the Feisal Al Dawiss–Ibn Saud feud, and a revealing paragraph—published here for the first time—giving the reasons for Lawrence's transfer from Karachi to another station in India. (This had nothing to do, as might have been supposed, with an article in the *Daily Express* which had revealed his whereabouts.) It was at Lawrence's own request because he wanted to get away from an officer who had threatened him. According to Lawrence, 'This one is reported to have sworn he "had me taped" and was "laying to jump on me" when he got the chance . . . I'm pretty tired of fighting, and of risks and my past makes my service character brittle.'

Lawrence's views on the Feisal Al Dawiss–Ibn Saud clash are interesting in that they disclose that he had not changed his mind on the practicability of a united independent Arab nation—'I don't believe you can yet unite, or federate, or crush into one tyranny, even, any two Arabic-speaking districts; *yet*'—and as his suggestion for settling the feud shows, he felt some nostalgia for the days of the Revolt: 'The fellow you need to influence is Feisal Al Dawiss . . . If I were at Ur, my instinct would be to walk without notice into his head-quarters. He'd not likely kill an unarmed, solitary man . . . He would make a wonderful border-warden, if he once got out of the ruck . . . I beg you not to order your Political Officers to execute this suggestion straight away or Feisal may execute your P.O.'s. Such performances require a manner to carry them off. I've done it four times, or is it five? A windy business.' Here we have a glimpse of the old Lawrence still lurking behind the uniform of Aircraftman T. E. Shaw, the Lawrence who could walk into the tent of a troublesome Arab leader, win him over for Britain, and indefinitely keep him sweet.

While he was on the topic of Middle Eastern politics Lawrence

* Ibid.

could not resist a mention of St John Philby. 'Let me warn you against Philby. His "red" complexion, in English affairs, is an index of his judgment. His politics are Corsican: that is, they include blood-feuds and personalities . . . I am afraid of Philby, sometimes, lest he go wrong, wilfully.' (There is a peculiar irony in the fact that Philby's son, Kim, a senior British Secret Intelligence Service officer, fled to Russia in 1963 after having secretly served the Russians for over thirty years.)

By July Trenchard had seen *The Mint*. 'I read every word of it', he wrote. 'And I seemed to know what was coming each line, and I feel no soreness, no sadness, about your writing, and yet again I feel all of a tremble in case it gets out and into the hands of people who do not know life as it is.'* Again Lawrence assured Trenchard the book would not be published before 1950, even though, if it were, 'I would get £10,000 and a reputation as a writer . . . I must hasten to say that even if you dismiss me the force tomorrow in circumstances of the utmost barbarity, even then I shall not publish it. It will only come out before 1950 if I am made to hate the Air Force, somehow . . . and as I have survived spells of Bonham Carter and Guilfoyle, and still like the Service, that will be very hard to make come about.' Trenchard apparently accepted Lawrence's word because although there is an Air Force file, No. S44G8, marked 'Precautions for Preventing Publication of *The Mint*', it seems that none was taken. Trenchard continued to correspond with Lawrence and their relationship appeared to remain on the same cordial level.

By May, Lawrence's request for transfer had been approved and he moved to a frontier station at Miranshah, about ten miles from the border with Afghanistan. It was the smallest RAF station in India, on the edge of a no-man's-land where Pathans made frequent raids. 'We are behind barbed wire, and walls with towers,' Lawrence wrote, 'and sentried and searchlit every night. It is like having fallen over the edge of the world.' In the same letter he asked for Trenchard's approval to extend his period of service by another five years. 'You said, as I left England, that my application . . . would or might be favourably considered, if I could pass the doctor when the time came. The time comes tomorrow: and I could pass all the M.O.'s in the RAF.'

Trenchard agreed to allow Lawrence to sign on for another five years. He had decided this, he said, despite considerable pressure from 'various people' who had implored him to bring Lawrence back to England. Among them was Lawrence's friend, the architect,

* Trenchard Papers.

16

Sir Herbert Baker, who had approached Montagu (later Lord) Norman, Governor of the Bank of England, to see if Lawrence could be found a job in the bank. For a while the Bank considered Lawrence for the post of night porter. Lawrence had been reminding his friends that when he did leave the RAF in 1935 he wanted a job as 'bachelor–night-caretaker of a block of City offices or buildings', so that he could get on with his writing. Norman thought something could be done, but when at a meeting with Trenchard he heard that Lawrence had signed on for another five years in the RAF, it was obvious that nothing definite could be decided. 'If on his return to civilian life Lawrence should still desire to come to the Bank his case will then receive sympathetic consideration.'* Lawrence was pleased that Trenchard had resisted attempts by his own friends to decide his future for him: 'They seem to disbelieve in my capacity to lay out a course for myself.' (This refusal to accept help from his friends sometimes caused ill-feeling. Lionel Curtis, writing to Eddy Marsh said, 'Herbert Baker and I raised £1,000 to send him to China to buy pottery . . . but he just treated us like dirt and defeated us, . . . poor tragic being.')†

In December 1928 Trenchard resigned, saying that he had been Chief of Air Staff long enough. Lawrence heard the news first on the radio and then in a letter from Trenchard a week later. It is clear that he regretted it greatly: 'There'll never be another King like you in the RAF . . . Allenby, Winston, and you: that's my gallery of chiefs, to date. Now there'll be a come down.'

But before Trenchard's term was up, Lawrence's stay in India came to an abrupt end. As was to be expected with Lawrence, it was no minor affair and before it was over, the Foreign Office, the India Office, the Viceroy of India, the British Minister in Kabul, the Chief of Air Staff, three overseas stations of the RAF, the Royal Navy, and two Members of Parliament had become involved. Even Trenchard, who was obliged to order Lawrence's recall, never learnt the whole story and it has been possible to piece it together now for the first time only because the records of the British and Indian governments relating to the affair are no longer secret.

The trouble started in November 1927 with a rebellion of the Shinwari tribe in Afghanistan which touched off a civil war. Lawrence had nothing whatever to do with this, but on 16 December 1928, the *Empire News*, a now defunct British weekly newspaper, published an article by a Dr Francis Havelock, whom it described

---

* Trenchard Papers.
† Curtis Papers.

as a well-known medical missionary just returned to London from Afghanistan. According to the article:

'Col. Lawrence arrived in Afghanistan during the 3rd week in November. He had an interview with the King, the Chief of the Police and the War Minister, then departed as suddenly as he had come . . . Somewhere in the wild hills of Afghanistan up the rocky slopes by the cave-dwellers, perched high by the banks of mountain streams, a gaunt holy man wearing the symbols of the pilgrim and man of prayer proceeds along his lonely pilgrimage. He is Col. Lawrence, the most mysterious man in the Empire. He is really the ultimate pro-Consul of Britain in the East. The battle is now joined between the Apostle of Hatred and the Apostle of Peace. Lincoln (Trebitsch Lincoln, ex-spy, ex-British MP, ex-forger, the tool of the Soviet Government in China) has gold and rifles. Hillsmen love both. Lawrence has unknown resources and a silver tongue . . .'

The story was a complete fabrication, probably concocted in a Fleet Street bar. The Indian Government could find no trace of any-one called Dr Francis Havelock ever having been in India and the *Empire News*, challenged to produce him, was forced to publish the following retraction: 'Although the source from which these articles came appear to be reliable, the *Empire News* is now in possession of further facts which make it clear that they were not written by anyone possessing the authority claimed. Moreover, the statements regarding the alleged presence in Afghanistan of Col. Lawrence and Trebitsch Lincoln were in every material respect, contrary to fact . . .'

But it was too late to stop the damage. An agency, the Free Press Mail Service had relayed the *Empire News* story to India where it was widely published. In Lahore a genuine holy man was beaten by a crowd who thought he was Lawrence. More serious was the inter-vention of the British Minister in Kabul, who sent a telegram to the Government of India on 3 January 1929 saying that the rumours about Lawrence, added to the fact that he was serving as a clerk under the name of Shaw at a station near the Afghan border, 'creates ineradicable suspicion in the mind of the Afghan Govern-ment that he is scheming against them in some mysterious way'.* He pointed out that these ideas were being encouraged by the Turkish and Russian ambassadors and, of course, by the French mission. Contradicting the stories, he said, would now have no effect

* National Archives of India, New Delhi.

and he suggested that the RAF be requested to move Lawrence a long way from the Frontier. The Indian Government spoke to Sir Geoffrey Salmond, in command of the RAF in India, and the next day he put the whole matter before Trenchard:

SECRET

Y6 4/1 personal and private

Lawrence's name has been associated for some time past with the disturbances in India. It was stated recently by the vernacular press that he had been behind the bombing outrages ... at Lahore. ... Inspired in some cases by Russian propaganda the vernacular press stated as soon as the Afghanistan trouble started that Lawrence was behind the rebellion of the Shinwaris and that he had, for this reason, been stationed at Miranshah. In a communiqué this was denied. After consultation with the Foreign Office the Secretary had a discussion with me as to the desirability of sending home Lawrence. This was clearly stupid, so I objected, as Lawrence had every right to expect an asylum in the Royal Air Force. I am now however informed by the Foreign Secretary that it is reported ... that great propaganda is being made in Kabul to the effect that we are at the back of the rebellion and Lawrence is organising it. It is considered by the Foreign Secretary, that Lawrence's presence anywhere in India under present conditions is very inconvenient ... May your views be communicated to me? It is my opinion that canard ... will persist, whatever we do. The Government will be assisted however by the transfer from India.*

The reputation Lawrence had gained for himself in Arabia had again caught up with him. Sitting quietly in Miranshah he had been drawn into events with which he had had no connection and through no fault of his own he was now about to be kicked unceremoniously out of India.

Trenchard received the telegram on a Saturday, recognized the seriousness of the situation and acted immediately. He looked into the possibility of sending Lawrence to Somaliland for a year, but hesitated when he learnt that the detachment there comprised one officer, one rigger, and one fitter. He replied to Salmond:

* Trenchard Papers.

SECRET

Cipher telegram immediate

AM 25A 5/1. Private and Personal. Your Y6 4/1. It is agreed that, whether we move Lawrence or not and whatever we do, the propaganda about him will continue and people would not believe us. I concur in his transfer from India, however, in view of the definite request that has been made. Would you enquire from Lawrence whether he would like to go to Aden, or to a small detachment in Somaliland consisting of two or three men, or to Singapore for a year or whether he would like to return to England. I want to help him as much as I can. . . .

Trenchard telephoned and then wrote to Sir Arthur Hirtzel, Under-Secretary of State for India, telling him what had been arranged and adding, 'Both ourselves and Lawrence are anxious that there should be as little publicity as possible and I hope that it will not be necessary for the India Office to issue a statement to the Press that Lawrence is being sent away from India'. Hirtzel agreed to this and sent a private telegram to the Viceroy asking that there should be the least possible publicity. He did not, however, tell Trenchard that he also sent the Foreign Department of the Government of India the following telegram:

66 SECRET

From Hirtzel for Bray*

No. 53 Lawrence. It might be well that Government of India should have him closely watched lest when confronted with departure from India he should bolt. If both he and Omar† 'disappeared' it would be very awkward.‡

A copy of this telegram reached Trenchard, who reacted vigorously, with some justification. He was co-operating with the India Office in removing Lawrence from India because of completely unfounded rumours, and here was the India Office behaving as if

* Sir Denis Bray, Foreign Secretary to the Government of India.
† Sadar Mohammed Omar Khan, a political refugee from Afghanistan, who had been living in Allahabad under British surveillance. He disappeared on 31 December 1928, probably to cross the border to join the rebellion against the Afghanistan government.
‡ Trenchard Papers.

the rumours might be true. He complained to Hirtzel, 'I am amazed to see this morning that while the question of Lawrence was being discussed on the telephone with me on Saturday morning, you sent a wire to Bray lending colour to the rumours that are circulating without even consulting us on it. . . .'

Meanwhile Lawrence had been whisked away from Miranshah on 8 January and was flown to Lahore and then to Karachi. A letter awaited him at Lahore from Salmond explaining what had occurred. Lawrence said he preferred to return to England, so Salmond arranged a second-class passage for him in the *Rajputana*, which left Bombay on 12 January. His instructions were to proceed to Tilbury, where the ship was due on 1 February, and to report to the Air Ministry. But when the *Rajputana* reached Port Said on 20 January Lawrence was handed a noted from Trenchard, ordering him to disembark at Plymouth, where he was to be met by an officer in plain clothes. Lawrence was to do as much as he could to avoid being interviewed.

The *Rajputana* arrived at Plymouth on the morning of 2 February. Wing-Commander Sydney Smith, of Cattewater RAF station, met Lawrence on board and gave him a letter from Trenchard containing two pounds, '. . . in case you may want it'. He was, he said, 'out to help you all I can' and offered to let Lawrence stay at his house in Hertfordshire. 'I don't want to see a lot of placards to the effect that the Air Ministry have spirited you away in fast motor-boats and cars.'* But this is exactly what Trenchard did see. The Air Ministry's handling of the affair had only served to arouse the Press's curiosity, on the assumption that 'if Lawrence was not up to anything in India, then why all the secrecy about his return?' A naval tender went alongside the ship, Lawrence received a special customs clearance, and then boarded the tender by descending a rope ladder. Ashore, he had a meal with the Plymouth naval commander, then took the boat train to London. At Paddington station, where he was met by a crowd of reporters, he said, 'I am Mr Smith'. It was wonderful material for the more sensational newspapers. The *Daily News* carried the full story with a photograph of Lawrence's arrival at Plymouth. The story was headed, 'Great Mystery of Colonel Lawrence. Simple Aircraftman—or what?' Two days later a Labour member of Parliament, Ernest Thurtle, questioned the Air Ministry about Lawrence's 'false' name of Shaw, a point Thurtle had first raised in the House of Commons on 30 January. Lawrence went to the House that same afternoon and eventually persuaded

* Ibid.

Thurtle to drop the matter. What worried Lawrence was not the suggestion that he was using a different name because he was a spy, but that his illegitimacy might be revealed if Thurtle pressed the matter. Lawrence wrote to Trenchard, 'I have explained to Mr Thurtle, privately, the marriage tangles of my father (you probably know of them: he didn't, and is asking questions which might have dragged the whole story into the light) . . .'.* Then, since he had embarked on a plan to quieten public interest, Lawrence decided he should tackle the Press as well, so he went to the *Daily Express* office and consulted the editor, R. D. Blumenfeld, who was a friend of his, on the best way to end the newspaper stories. Unfortunately the version of these visits which reached Trenchard became distorted in the telling—Lawrence, it was said, had been lobbying and had been to the *Daily Express* to make a statement. Trenchard, fed up with the whole affair, told Lawrence that he was to keep away from politicians and newspapers. He was to go on a month's leave and then report to Wing-Commander Smith at Cattewater in March. Lawrence defended himself in a short note in which he said, 'As for the House of Commons raid, I think I was right. . . . Will you please shut up the *Daily News*. It goes on chattering, and a word from you to Sir Herbert Samuel saying that it was my wish, would end the business. . . .' Lawrence could not resist a small gesture to show how uncalled for he considered Trenchard's strictures: 'Perhaps I should report that Sir P. Sassoon has asked me to lunch on Thursday next: and that I'll go, unless you say no, meanwhile.'

It is clear that Lawrence's irritation at being whisked out of India through no fault of his own still lingered. He was now forty-one, a few white hairs had appeared in the gold. He was plumper, could not see as well as in earlier days, was occasionally hard of hearing, and felt the cold. In short, he was slipping into middle age. A desire to feel settled and secure had started to grow in him and it was with the anticipation that he was on the brink of finding what he wanted that he rode his new motor-cycle down to Cattewater to join Wing-Commander Smith's Squadron of flying-boats. His hopes were to be fulfilled; the next years were to provide Lawrence with his happiest and most productive period.

* Ibid.

16 Leading from the Ranks

While he is a clerk at the RAF flying-boat station on Plymouth Sound, Lawrence initiates a series of service reforms ranging from unbuttoning greatcoats to the abolition of the death penalty for cowardice. His activities annoy the Minister for Air and he is ordered to confine himself to the duties of an aircraftman and to keep away from prominent people. A flying-boat crashes, killing most of its crew, and Lawrence realizes that an important operational principle is involved. He intrigues with Lady Astor to have RAF regulations changed to prevent a recurrence of the accident. Also, as a result of the crash, he becomes interested in the development of high-speed launches for rescue work and devotes himself to this branch of the service. Arabia is forgotten as Lawrence works on sea-plane tenders, target-boats, and a forerunner of the hovercraft. For a friend on The Round Table *he writes a paper on defence which discusses the future of the Royal Air Force and the Royal Navy and is remarkably prescient in its ideas.*

Lawrence's commanding officer at the new flying-boat station at Cattewater—later re-named Mount Batten—was Wing-Commander Sydney Smith, a sympathetic officer who understood Lawrence's difficulties, and managed by a blend of firmness and friendliness to create a relationship that embarrassed neither. Lawrence, acting as a clerk, quickly settled into the daily routine of the new station, but it was not long before he was again tempted to lead from the ranks and we find him writing to Trenchard and Ernest Thurtle, the MP whom he had confronted at the House of Commons, making suggestions for improving not only the RAF but all three of the armed Services. In writing to Trenchard it was the irksome details of spit and polish that Lawrence wanted to change—the wearing of bayonets at church parades, the compulsory buttoning of the top button of great-coats, the carrying of canes, and the embarrassment of kit inspection. As he told Liddell Hart, 'It shouldn't be a parade or beauty show. . . . There is no need for us standing by. That makes us hot and ashamed. . . .' To Thurtle, with whom he had become friendly, it was about policy matters that he wrote—the abolition of the death penalty for cowardice in war, and a modification of enlistment arrangements, so that in peacetime servicemen could leave the Forces by giving notice and paying an indemnity. It is a measure of Lawrence's influence that Trenchard initiated the first of his suggested reforms—the unbuttoning of greatcoats—within weeks of getting Lawrence's letter; and that Thurtle, after a long campaign during which he was frequently advised on tactics by Lawrence, succeeded during the following year in introducing a bill to abolish the death penalty for cowardice.

Lawrence had less success with the new Labour Minister for Air, Lord Thomson, who did not like his flow of ideas and the network of influential friends he used to push them. When Lawrence was involved in an incident at the Schneider Cup* meeting in September, Thomson used this as a reason to crack down on him. Lawrence was on duty to assist with the organization of the meeting, so the Air Ministry went to some lengths to ensure that he did not receive any publicity. But the race attracted a lot of celebrities and nearly every day Lawrence was summoned by one or other of them. One day, after he had cleaned the slipway where the Italian planes were housed, he was seen in conversation with Lord Thomson. (There is reason to believe that Thomson had asked Lawrence why a British aircraftman was cleaning the Italian slipway.) Their encounter made an irresistible photograph—the Air Minister and the aircraftman—and it appeared all over the world. Thomson was angry and grew even angrier when Trenchard told him that Lawrence had applied for permission to crew in a Moth civil aircraft belonging to a friend on a trip to France, Switzerland, Italy, Germany and Holland. What Thomson said can only be judged by the tone of Trenchard's letter to Lawrence on 16 September 1929:

> My dear Shaw,
> Since writing a letter to you today about your trip with Major Nathan round France, Italy and Germany, and after having seen the Secretary of State I am writing to say you cannot go on this trip.
> You must come and see me as soon as you get your leave as I want to speak to you. Will you cancel my previous letter.†

* An international seaplane race over a twenty-seven-mile triangular course above the Solent. The last race was in 1931.
† Trenchard Papers.

They met a fortnight later. Trenchard, on instructions from
Lord Thomson, told Lawrence he had come very close to being
kicked out of the RAF again. Henceforth he was to stop leading
from the ranks and was to confine himself to the duties of an aircraftman. He was not to leave the country, he was not to visit or
even speak to any 'great men'—and this included most of the leading
political figures of the day—and he was not to fly in government
aircraft. Lawrence was not unduly upset and since Thurtle had not
been mentioned by name, Lawrence continued to intrigue with him.
He advised Thurtle on a way of getting round the ban on servicemen, commenting on military matters, so that Thurtle could quote
him to the House of Commons when introducing his Bill on the
death penalty: 'I cannot prevent your quoting what I said then
[*ie*, before he joined up], so your best tactics are to say, "As Colonel
Lawrence said some years ago . . .".'

Lawrence also continued to see Lady Astor, MP for Plymouth,
and the first woman to sit in the House of Commons. She was one
of five sisters from Virginia known as the Gibson girls. As leader of
the 'Cliveden Set' and a witty political hostess, she enlivened British
public life for over half a century. She became friendly with Lawrence
after writing to him in 1924. 'I am one of the people who are very
wealthy and would like a copy of your book, but I don't promise to
read it. However, as that is your wish you won't mind.' Lady Astor
was one of the 'great people' specifically forbidden to Lawrence, but
his friendship with her, with its banter, its flippancy, and its gossip,
seemed harmless enough to him, so he ignored the ban. And it was to
Lady Astor that he turned when in February 1931 an event occurred
which made him decide that despite the risk he would again have to
assume command.

At Mount Batten there were three Blackburn Iris flying-boats,
used for instruction and exercises. At least one of them went up on
most days and the people of Plymouth had become accustomed to
seeing them over the city and the Sound. On 4 February, Iris S238
was returning to base after its first flight since an overhaul. The Iris
had a crew of twelve. At the controls, undergoing instruction, was
Wing-Commander C. G. Tucker, an experienced pilot of ordinary aircraft, but a novice with flying boats. The co-pilot was
Flight-Lieutenant M. Ely, an experienced flying-boat pilot, but
junior in rank to Tucker. The day was fine and sunny. There was
little wind and the sea was calm. At about 11.30 a.m. the Iris prepared
to land. Lawrence was standing at the shore end of Mount Batten
watching the plane. It came out of the haze and circled over his

head, flying normally. Wing-Commander Tucker throttled back its engines and glided down steeply as though to alight on the water. 'Then she struck the water just under the pilot's seat, forward near the bow. The tail of the machine came left, her main planes crashed into the water and folded back altogether. The hull dived straight down to the bottom.'* Lawrence rushed to join a rescue boat and when he reached the crash he found the duty-launch and a pilot boat collecting survivors.

Nine men died in the crash, including Wing-Commander Tucker. At the inquest, Flight-Lieutenant Ely described the flying-boat's last minutes. He and other members of the crew had been reluctant to go up with Tucker. (Lawrence said in evidence that he would have flown with Tucker only if he had been ordered to do so.) When the Iris was coming in to land, Ely said, he had twice tried to take the controls, but each time Tucker had resisted, on the second occasion knocking his hands away. The jury decided that the crash had been due to the inexperience of Wing-Commander Tucker and made a recommendation that in the future a commanding officer appointed to a squadron should receive full flying instruction at another station before assuming his appointment.

This verdict caused an uproar. Newspapers said the Air Ministry was in the dock because it had known for six months that to have as commanding officer at Mount Batten a man not competent to handle a flying-boat was an unsatisfactory state of affairs, but had done nothing about it. Lawrence, with his ability to probe things to the core, saw that a more important principle was involved. In the air sole command should belong to the pilot—irrespective of rank. Then the risk of a senior though perhaps inexperienced officer, using his rank to assume command and so send the plane and its crew to their doom could never happen again. Also, when a crash occurred on the water it was no use attempting to carry out a rescue in slow duty-launches. If some speedier means of transport had been available perhaps more of the crew of the Iris could have been saved. This was the sort of situation in which Lawrence was at his best. It was obviously no good for an aircraftman to speak out at the inquest or to write out a report to his commanding officer. A knowledge of how the Air Ministry worked, influence in the right quarters, and the right public pressure were the sorts of things that counted, and in matters of this kind Lawrence was a master. He contacted Lady Astor and together they began to 'move levers' so successfully that Lawrence

* Lawrence's evidence at the inquest, as reported in the *Western Weekly News*, 21 February 1931.

was able to write to her in March: 'I *think* the battle is won. The Coroner was a perfect pet. He asked all the nibbly, difficult, hurtful questions, so innocently and so smoothly that everything came out ... and the Press followed up ... scaring the Air Ministry almost to death ... They have set the reforms afoot ... I am watching very closely and will move another little lever or two when or if it is necessary ... I need hardly say how grateful I am to you for your help. It is such a pleasure to get a thing done cleanly and naturally, without fuss. Nobody knows that anything has been done, and yet, I fancy, there will not be another case of this sort in our memories.'*

Just how many things Lawrence got done 'cleanly and naturally' in the RAF without anyone's knowing is hard to say. There is some indication, however, of what he *planned* to get done. A list among his papers in the Bodleian Library specifies a range of reforms he obviously intended to take up either with Trenchard or Thurtle, or with Lady Astor or some of his other influential friends. Part of this list reads:

> flying-boat hulls and policy: coastal area: imitation [?] of C.O. and reduction of staff: simplification of drill book and drill: damp halls and huts: machinery for men, dishwashing: cancellation of kit bags for suitcases; tool kit allowance: clothing allowance for civvies: six months' notice on either side: vacuum cleaners: reduction of N.C.O.'s: short arm inspection abolish; improvement of bad station: aero salvage: crash boats.

This seems a formidable programme of reform for an aircraftman to undertake, even an aircraftman as remarkable as Lawrence. But after the Iris crash he immersed himself in a sphere of amphibious operations which interested him above all others and which was eventually called air/sea rescue. Until the end of his RAF service four years later he devoted his abilities and energy to the development of high-speed launches. He personally worked on, tested, modified and helped to design boats which created a minor revolution in the shipbuilding world. In 1929, when he first became interested in design, RAF launches were of a standard Admiralty pattern. They were heavy, slow and costly. When Lawrence left the RAF in 1935, not one type of RAF boat in production was of naval design. 'We have found, chosen, selected or derived our own sorts,' he wrote. 'They have (power for power) three times the speed of

* *Letters*, No. 434.

their predecessors, less weight, less cost, more room, more safety, more seaworthiness ... the German, Chinese, Spanish, and Portuguese ... governments have adopted them.... In inventing them we have had to make new engines, new auxiliaries, use new timbers, new metals, new materials.'*

Lawrence had at last found his niche in the RAF and to everyone's amazement (and relief) he settled down to this new work with enthusiasm and dedication. Arabia was forgotten ('What a long time ago it was,' he wrote to Tom Beaumont) and his love of intrigue was now limited to pushing his boat project. He went to the British Power Boat Company at Hythe, near Southamptom, where he put in more engine-hours in the company's craft than did anyone else in the RAF. Up and down Southampton water he went, the newly-designed launches flinging the cold spray into his face while he and another aircraftman took turns to steer and to check the instruments. His letters to his friends decreased in frequency and his main literary effort in the summer of 1931 was the writing of a manual *Notes on Handling the 200 Class Seaplane Tender*, which dealt with the hull, engines, steering, fuel system, controls, electrical equipment, instruments, maintenance and handling of these craft. David Garnett wrote that it was 'a masterpiece of technology, running to some 80 foolscap pages'.

Lawrence presently extended his work to the testing of the launches' stability when towing targets for RAF bombing practice. Until September 1932 all went well; then it appeared that Lawrence's bane, newspaper publicity, had returned to ruin everything. Articles began to appear about the new launches, dramatizing Lawrence's part in developing them. Memoranda began to circulate in the Air Ministry and it was decided to return Lawrence to ordinary duties at Mount Batten. At first he did not seem to mind. The work at Hythe had tired him and Mount Batten allowed him to recover. But after a while the routine grew irksome and after much consideration he decided in March 1933 to invoke the release clause of his contract and return to civilian life. The RAF seemed prepared to let him go, until his friends began to ask questions. Trenchard, who had become Commissioner of the Metropolitan Police at Scotland Yard, wrote: 'Are you leaving the Air Force, or have you been kicked out? Let me know sometime. I would like to have a talk with you.'† Lawrence replied, 'I'm not being turned out. Coastal Area are very obstructionist, and won't let us do anything from Batten, in the way

* *Evening Standard*, London, 20 May 1935.
† Trenchard Papers.

of boat testing or experiment. The savour of living here in barracks is not what it was. So I put in to go, as from April 6—unless my services are for any purpose specially required.'

Trenchard understood what Lawrence meant by this. So did the Under-Secretary of State for Air, Sir Philip Sassoon, an old friend of Lawrence's, and the wheels began to turn. Lawrence had an interview with Sir Geoffrey Salmond, who was about to become Chief of Air Staff. Salmond had a long talk with Lawrence's Commanding Officer and wrote two letters to Sassoon. The démarche worked, as Lawrence no doubt knew it would. On 21 April an Air Ministry memorandum was issued saying, 'Lawrence of Arabia [not A/C Shaw!] has decided to stay on in the Air Force. As he knows a good deal about motor boats he has been given a fairly free hand to go round various motor boat firms in the country. . . .'* The memorandum said Lawrence had ideas on high-speed craft that were worth considering and proposed that he should be employed to watch the Ministry's interests at contractors' yards. He was to wear civilian clothes—except when on RAF property—to avoid publicity.

For the next eighteen months Lawrence moved about the countryside from his base in Southampton, concentrating mainly on the development of armoured target launches. It was hard, exacting work and the hours were long, but he appeared to enjoy it. The contractors, at first wary of this small, quietly-spoken man in baggy flannel trousers and a fisherman's sweater, came to respect his ability and application; a respect that increased when, for some of the early trials of the target-launch, Lawrence took the controls himself and drove the boat while the aircraft made their bombing runs. (He discounted the danger, saying that the planes used only smoke bombs.) It was his interest in high-speed craft that led him, in the last stage of his career in the RAF, to be associated with a project of an unusual nature: helping to design, develop and test models of a new type of 'aerodynamic boat' which was to run over the water on a cushion of air, a forerunner, in fact, of the hovercraft.†

Lawrence's part in this project began, when in December 1934 or January 1935, he met Edward Spurr, a young engineer from Bradford. Spurr and Lawrence had an immediate rapport and in discussing motor boat design discovered that they had each, separately, developed ideas on the same lines involving the application of aerodynamic principles. Put as simply as possible, this means that a boat built in the shape of an aeroplane wing would, when travelling

* Trenchard Papers.
† H. F. King, former editor, *Flight International.*

at speed over the water, be lifted clear of it by the creation of a cushion of air under the nose of the hull and because air pressure would be reduced over the top of the hull. The same principle by which an aeroplane is designed to fly would in theory lift such a boat clear of the water. As Spurr put it: 'The boat when travelling at speed on occasions when the hull is clear of the water...is aerodynamically balanced. In any condition, either in or out of the water, the boat is perfectly stable.'* Lawrence and Spurr constructed some seventy models of their boat, which was eventually built in conditions of great secrecy by the engineering firm of R. Malcolm Limited, of Slough, a company experienced in aircraft rather than boat construction. The boat was called 'Empire Day' and she was launched three years after Lawrence's death, on 24 May 1938. The nose of the boat carried an inscription, 'To L. of A.: *à compte*'.

Lawrence's years in small boat development made him reflect on the possible role of such boats in a future war, and then on the whole question of how best to defend Britain in an age of increasingly rapid technological progress. Once he had reached his conclusions he went into action to try to have them adopted. His contacts at high level had, if anything, improved as the years passed. Many of the young men with whom he had been friendly in the early postwar years had now risen to positions of power and importance. Lawrence felt no hesitation in expressing his views to them, and those who were members of the Round Table were usually anxious to hear what he had to say. Writing from the Union Jack Club (1s 9d a night) to Lionel Curtis, Lawrence expressed views on defence that would have seemed more appropriate if they had come from, say, a Shadow Minister rather than from an aircraftman. 'The defence question is full of snags and is being ineptly handled by Lords Rothermere and Beaverbrook. I agree that the balance of expenditure on Navy, Army and R.A.F. is wrong: but, I do not want the R.A.F. expenditure increased. Our present squadrons could deal very summarily with France. [Still Lawrence's *bête noire* in spite of the increasing threat from Germany.] When Germany wings herself—ah; that will be another matter, and our signal to reinforce: for the German kites will be new and formidable, not like the sorry French junk.' Lawrence went on to suggest that Britain, if she were to have the capacity to expand the RAF when necessary, needed fifteen new aerodromes, each costing £20,000; aircraft firms well-equipped with up-to-date designers, designs and plant; and 'brains

* *Flight International*, London, February 1966.

enough inside our brass hats' to employ them. He was outspoken: 'Our Air Marshals are rather wooden-headed, and some of the civilian A.I.D. inspectors and technicians who handle design are hopeless. Consequently our military aircraft are like Christmas trees all hung with protruding gadgets, our flying-boats are a bad joke, our civil aircraft are (almost) the world's slowest; and air tactics and strategy are infantile. Research [should be] made into flying-boat development (after sacking the present authorities) and wireless-controlled aircraft. Also to develop the art of sound-ranging, and anti-aircraft gunnery. If I had my way, I would constitute a new Flying-Boat department of Air Ministry, and have a dozen good naval men to give it a start.'

He gave Curtis the benefit of his small-craft experience.

'Our air bombs are not going to sink capital ships; but will render them useless as fighting platforms and probably uninhabitable. This in only three or four years time. The defence of surface craft against aircraft will be found in manoeuvre: in being able to turn quicker on the water than the plane can in the air—not difficult, with small ships, as water gives you a firmer rudder. So I expect to see the surface ships of navies in future limited to small high-speed manoeuverable mosquito craft, none larger than the destroyers of today.

'There are controversial points in the above, and to argue them one must consider smokescreens, the one pounder pom-pom, trajectories, dive-arcs, b. bombs; all sorts of technical things. But I am prepared to maintain my thesis in most company. Do not, however, take this exposition of it as exhaustive or even fair. To deal with imponderables, layer upon layer of imponderables, more resembles faith than argument.

'I wish I could have run through your *Round Table* argument and talked it over with you.'*

This was a very prescient letter, made even more so by its being written by a man who, to the world in general, was nothing more than an aircraftman. It is certain that few of the mechanics or fitters he mixed with during most of his working hours could have guessed that A/C Shaw was capable of writing a paper on Britain's defence policy in the modern world. But then they could not know that he was corresponding with Lady Astor, John Buchan, or Winston Churchill, and few would have dreamed that he had for many years

* *Letters*, No. 513.

enjoyed a relationship with the wife of a famous man which had started before he went into the RAF and had flowered beyond the expectation of both. It was not with Nancy Astor, nor with any of the great hostesses who had their own performances to consider, and who showed that restless energy which often characterizes women who dominate society. It was with someone retiring and sympathetic: Charlotte Shaw, the wife of Bernard Shaw. Charlotte understood Lawrence as no woman—not even his mother—ever had. Their relationship lasted thirteen years, and in it both found the encouragement, sympathy and companionship they had been seeking all their lives.

17 The Two Shaws

The relationship between Lawrence and Charlotte Shaw, which had started in 1922, provides him with inspiration and encouragement. Bernard Shaw helps Lawrence in writing Seven Pillars of Wisdom. *Lawrence makes suggestions about Shaw's plays and there is a reciprocal unburdening of emotions between himself and Charlotte. He tells her about a major literary project he plans for his retirement, but as the time approaches for him to leave the RAF he becomes preoccupied with growing old.*

Lawrence had met Bernard and Charlotte Shaw at their house in Adelphi Terrace in London on 25 March 1922. They were introduced by Sir Sydney Cockerell, director of the Fitzwilliam Museum at Cambridge, and a prominent member of Curtis's Round Table. Sir Sydney later recalled: 'Great warmth was shown on both sides and a friendship was there and then started that was fraught with happy consequences for all three of them.'

In August—a fortnight before he went into the RAF—Lawrence reminded Shaw of a promise to help with *Seven Pillars* and three weeks later sent him a bound copy of the book. This made a formidable bundle and GBS put off reading it. Charlotte, sensing Lawrence's anxiety, wrote to him on 31 December 1922:

> Dear Mr Lawrence,
> If you've been 'mad keen' to hear about your book, I've been mad keen to write to you about it ever since I read it, or rather ever since I began to read it, and I simply haven't dared. I got from it an impression of you as an Immense Personality soaring in the blue (of the Arabian skies) far above my lowly sphere, and that anything I could say in the way of admiration, or comment, or question, could only be an impertinence. But the latest developments of your

career* have been so startingly unexpected, and your later letters so human, that I take my courage in both hands and send you a word.

How is it conceivable, imaginable that a man who could write the *Seven Pillars* can have any doubts about it? If you don't know it is 'a great book' what is the use of anyone telling you so? I believe (though he has never said anything of the sort) that G.B.S. thinks you are 'pulling his leg' when you ask him. I devoured the book from cover to cover as soon as I got hold of it. I could not stop. I drove G.B.S. almost mad by insisting upon reading him special bits when he was deep in something else. I am an old woman, old enough at any rate to be your mother; I have met all sorts of men and women of the kind that are called distinguished; I have read their books and discussed them with them; but I have never read anything like this: I don't believe anything really like it has been written before. When I find in your letter such suggestions as 'should it be without the first person singular?' 'Is there any style in my writing?' 'Anything recognisably individual?' I think—are you laughing at us! Why, foolish man, it could only have been written in the first person singular: it is one of the most amazingly individual documents that has ever been written: there is no 'style' because it is above and beyond anything so silly.

You have been the means of bringing into the world a poignant human document, and now—have faith in the Power that worked through you. . . .

Your book must be published as a whole. Don't you see that? Perhaps little bits about the French, and such things as your scarifying account of Meinertzhagen (splendid, that is!) might be toned down . . . but don't leave out the things an ordinary man would leave out: the things people will tell you are 'too shocking'. Publish the book practically as it is, in good print, in a lot of volumes. I am sure Constables will do it for you that way.

Both G.B.S. and I have lots of experience about books and we would both like to put it at your service. By the way, don't call him "Mr" Shaw!

Yours sincerely,

C.F.S.   (Mrs G.B.S.!)

* It was now known publicly that Lawrence was serving in the ranks of the RAF.

This was the budding of a relationship which lasted until Lawrence's death thirteen years later. It was an unlikely and unusual relationship, but in each other Charlotte Shaw and Lawrence found a spiritual companionship such as they had both been searching for all their lives.

It was an unlikely relationship because no one could have foreseen that the hero of the imperialist Right and the wife of the darling of the literary Left would have the slightest thing in common. Yet their friendship became so intimate that after his wife died in 1943 and Bernard Shaw had been through her correspondence with Lawrence, he said to a friend, 'I lived with Charlotte for forty years and I see now that there was a great deal about her that I didn't know. It has been a shock.'

Theirs was an unusual, perhaps peculiar relationship because the Shaws' marriage was not a real one. Charlotte had met Shaw in 1896, and a lively courtship had followed. They married in 1898 but Charlotte regarded the begetting of children as the most repulsive of all physical functions and insisted that the marriage must never be consummated.

When she met Lawrence she was sixty-five—old enough to be his mother. She was a plump, dignified figure, fond of flowered hats, fur collars, and veils. Her eyes sparkled behind rimless glasses and she had a sympathetic smile. She would have made an excellent mother, and her self-frustrated maternal instinct had already expressed itself in the showering of affection on several of her husband's young disciples. Before Lawrence it had been the playwright–actor–producer, Harley Granville-Barker, but he had drifted away after a divorce of which the Shaws disapproved. Lawrence filled his place, and as this unusual relationship progressed and deepened, Charlotte directed onto Lawrence all the possessive maternal affection she had suppressed for years. In his turn Lawrence found with Charlotte a tender understanding that had evaded him all his life. She became the successor to his various mentors, to Hogarth, his Intelligence chief, to Allenby, his commanding officer, to Churchill, his Colonial minister, and to Trenchard, his chief in the RAF. She was the last and most important person in a line of substitutes for the parents from whom he had emotionally isolated himself.

There were few secrets between them. Lawrence told Charlotte of his hopes and his fears. He confessed the difficulties he had experienced with his mother and the emotional turmoil she had caused him. He told her that he had been buggered by the Turks at Deraa.

He sent her one of his typescripts of *The Mint*, complete with its four-letter words. It may be possible that he even told her about the beatings given him by John Bruce. Charlotte, in turn, told Lawrence about her difficult family life, her guilt about her mother's death—of which she had been glad—and of her love for her brow-beaten father. Lawrence became a regular visitor to the Shaws' country house at Ayot St Lawrence in Hertfordshire, where the servants in time called one of the guest-rooms 'Lawrence's room'. Lawrence and Charlotte corresponded regularly, and when the Shaws went off on one of their long sea-cruises, Charlotte drew up a mail itinerary for Lawrence to follow. She corrected the proofs of *Seven Pillars*, badgered Bernard Shaw to suggest improvements and became worried when Lawrence seemed to lose heart. She delighted in giving him presents, and every Christmas, no matter where he happened to be, she sent him a parcel of festive food. And always, above all, there were the letters; more than six hundred passed between them in the thirteen years they knew each other. Lawrence kept only a few of hers; she kept about three hundred of his and bequeathed them to the British Museum. Both parties (chilling as it may sound) sensed that they were writing for posterity. 'Perhaps', Lawrence said in one letter, 'I am not writing to you, but for my some day "life and letters".'

After the letter from Charlotte praising *Seven Pillars* and offering to put herself and GBS at Lawrence's service to help with its pub-lication, there was a long delay. After a quick skimming of the book Shaw could not get down to making a serious study of it. When Lawrence sent Shaw the first pages of the subscribers' edition, instead of the literary criticism he expected, Lawrence received a long letter lecturing him on punctuation and the law of libel and strongly recommending certain cuts. There is a vein of semi-serious leg-pulling in the letter which suggests that Shaw was substituting some typical mock analysis for the judgement he had reached at his first reading. His enthusiasm for 'one of the great histories of the world' seemed to have lessened.

> Confound you and your book, you are no more fit to be trusted with a pen than a child with a torpedo. . . . I in-vented my own system of punctuation, and then compared it with the punctuation of the Bible, and found that the authors of the Revised Version had been driven to the same usage, though their practice is not quite consistent all through. The Bible bars the dash, which is the great refuge

of those who are too lazy to punctuate: Richard Brinsley Sheridan the author of *The School for Scandal* uses dashes and nothing else. I never use it when I can possibly substitute a colon; and I save up the colon jealously for certain effects that no other stop produces. As you have no rules, and sometimes throw colons about with an unhinged mind, here are some rough rules for you.

When a sentence contains more than one statement, with different nominatives; or even with the same nominative repeated for the sake of emphasizing some discontinuity between the statements, the statements should be separated by a semicolon when the relation between them is expressed by a conjunction. When there is no conjunction, or other modifying word, and the two statements are placed baldly in dramatic apposition, use a colon. Thus:

Laurens said nothing; but he thought the more. Laurens could not speak: he was drunk. Laurens, like Napoleon, was out of place and a failure as a subaltern; yet when he could exasperate his officers by being a faultless private he could behave himself as such. Laurens, like Napoleon, could see a hostile city not only as a military objective but as a stage for a coup de theatre: he was a born actor ...

Colons are needed for abrupt pull-ups: thus, Laurens was congenitally literary: that is, a liar. Laurens was a man of many aliases: namely, Private Shaw, Colonel Lawrence, Prince of Damascus, etc., etc., etc. .... You practically do not use semicolons at all. This is a symptom of mental defectiveness, probably induced by camp life.

But by far the most urgent of my corrections—so important that you had better swallow them literally with what wry faces you cannot control—are those which concern libels. ...

I spent fifteen years of my life writing criticism of sensitive, living people, and thereby acquired a very cultivated sense of what I might say and what I might not say. All criticisms are technically libels; but there is the blow below the belt, the impertinence, the indulgence of dislike, the expression of personal contempt, and of course the imputation of dishonesty or unchastity which are not and should not be privileged as well as genuine criticism, the amusing good-humoured banter, and (curiously) the obvious 'vulgar abuse' which are privileged. I have weeded out your reckless sallies as carefully as I can.

Then there is the more general criticism about that first chapter [which dealt with the politics of the Revolt]. That it should come out and leave the book to begin with chapter two which is the real thing and very fine at that, I have no doubt whatever. You will see my note on the subject.

I must close up now as Charlotte wants to make up her packet to you.

Ever,
G. Bernard Shaw.

From this moment Shaw and Charlotte were involved in helping to edit *Seven Pillars*, Shaw with advice on deletions and punctuation, Charlotte with proof reading, suggestions for cuts (the original text was reduced by 100,000 words) and strengthening Lawrence's will to see the whole thing through. She arranged for Shaw to vet Lawrence's contract and, according to Stanley Weintraub, author of *Private Shaw and Public Shaw*, drafts of Lawrence's contracts show massive interlinear emendations by Shaw, who 'loved the ritual bargaining with publishers'. The Charlotte–Lawrence relationship was strengthened by this literary link, and Lawrence recognized its value by presenting Charlotte with an early copy of *Seven Pillars*. It also became the precedent for her performing a similar function with Lawrence's other works. She criticized *The Mint* and suggested projects for Lawrence to undertake when he left the RAF. In fact, in the literary sphere Charlotte did for Lawrence exactly what she did for Bernard Shaw.

As she gained Lawrence's trust, his letters began to grow franker. She accepted and respected his confidences, but quietly reprimanded him when he became conceited or intolerant. The first occasion for this was after Lawrence had dissuaded Bernard Shaw from writing a preface to *Seven Pillars* and when she suggested Sir James Barrie in his stead. Lawrence was outraged and tore into Barrie, who was a friend and neighbour of the Shaws in Adelphi Terrace. 'Surely my self-respect would be nothing if I let a man who writes so vilely help to publish me? He's everything that Mr Shaw is not: a cozener and deceiver, a soft-sayer, a sentimentalist, a fraud: one who plays deep tricks ... with the real stuff of literature, in order to flatter people whose tastes are already beast-low. Has he a single redeeming work or feature? I don't want to be harsh, but he seems to me as vile as Belloc.'

It was too much for Charlotte and she hit back. It might have caused a crisis in their friendship, but Lawrence accepted her rebuke.

He was constantly trying to analyse their relationship, and over the years he devoted occasional paragraphs to it.

In 1928:

'Let me acquit you of all suspicion of "mothering me". With you I have no feeling or suspicion of that at all. You are (probably) older than me: you are one of the fixed ones, socially and by right of conquest: yet I talk to you exactly as I feel inclined, without any sense that I'm talking up, or you down. Which is very subtle and successful of you. I think it represents reality too, in your attitude, as well as mine.'

In 1929:

'As for feeling "at home" with you: that is not the word. I do not wish to feel at home. You are more completely restful than anyone I know, and that is surely better? Homes are ties, and with you I am quite free, somehow.'

And in 1930:

'You remain the solitary woman who lets me feel at ease with her, in spite of all the benefits you heap on me. Usually I am a very grudging taker, too.'

One can only guess at the mainspring of this friendship. Both Lawrence and Charlotte were of Anglo-Irish stock—Lawrence being more conscious of his nationality than is generally realized. Both were Irish nationalists, expatriates who dreamed of home: Charlotte of the farm where she grew up, Lawrence of the Irish estate denied him because of his illegitimacy. In Lawrence Charlotte found the empathy she lacked with Bernard Shaw. She and Lawrence were searchers, but Shaw arrogantly implied that he knew all the answers. His realization on reading Charlotte's correspondence with Lawrence that, after forty years, he had not known his wife as well as he had imagined, came as a considerable shock to him. Although Shaw no doubt admired certain of Lawrence's attributes, other facets of Lawrence's character irritated him. He never really understood why Lawrence chose to bury himself in the RAF, and on at least one occasion said exactly what he thought about it:

Lawrence and Feisal on a visit to HMS Orion *before the Paris Peace Conference.*

Churchill, Gertrude Bell, and Lawrence in Cairo, 1921.

Charlotte Shaw.

John Bruce, 1923.

Lawrence on one of his motorcycles.

Lawrence leaves the RAF, 1935.

'Nelson slightly cracked after his whack on the head after the battle of the Nile, coming home and insisting on being placed at the tiller of a canal barge and on being treated as nobody in particular, would have embarrassed the Navy far less. A callow and terrified Marbot, placed in command of a sardonic Napoleon at Austerlitz and Jena, would have felt much as your superior officers must in command of Lawrence the great, the mysterious, save in whom there is no majesty and no might.... You talk about leave as if it were a difficulty. Ask for three months' leave and they will exclaim, with a sob of relief, "For God's sake, take six, take twelve, take a lifetime, take anything rather than keep up this maddening masquerade that makes us all ridiculous". I sympathize with them.'

All the same, Shaw's regard for Lawrence was unmistakable. Shaw gave him a copy of his *The Intelligent Woman's Guide to Socialism and Capitalism* with a specially printed title page reading, 'The Foundation of the Seven Pillars, being the Word of a Western Prophet to the Deliverer of Damascus: Shaw born Shaw to Shaw that took that name upon him.' Yet on another occasion, exasperated by him for some reason, Shaw bluntly demanded, 'What is your game, really?'

Charlotte and Lawrence had none of these ups and downs. As their friendship deepened into complete trust, she revealed herself and her thoughts and doubts to him as she probably did to no one else. This was not easy for her and it did not happen before Lawrence had bared his own emotional scars—something that before he met Charlotte Shaw he found was a painful process. Gradually she drew him out, consciously helping to exorcise his shyness by talking to him about it. He became able to tell her about his moods, especially when he was depressed:

'I've changed, and the Lawrence who used to go about and be friendly and familiar with that sort of people is dead. He's worse than dead. He is a stranger I once knew. From henceforward my way will lie with these fellows [in the RAF] here degrading myself (for in their eyes and your eyes and Winterton's eyes I see that it is a degradation) in the hope that some day I will really feel degraded, be degraded, to their level. I long for people to look down on me and despise me, and I'm too shy to take the filthy steps which would publicly shame me, and put me into their contempt. I want to dirty myself outwardly, so that my person may properly reflect the distress which it conceals ... and I shrink from dirtying the outside, while I have eaten, avidly eaten, every filthy morsel which chance threw my way.

I'm too shy to go looking for dirt. I'd be afraid of seeming a novice in it, when I found it. That's why I can't go off stewing into the Lincoln or Navenby brothels with the fellows. They think its because I'm superior, proud, or peculiar, or "posh", as they say: and its because I wouldn't know what to do, how to carry myself, where to stop. Fear again: fear everywhere.'

At the end of 1926, when Lawrence was posted to India and the distance from Charlotte increased, their letters became more personal. Lawrence told her the story of his family and in return, on 17 May 1927, Charlotte wrote Lawrence what was probably—because of its emotional honesty—the most significant letter of her life:

> I'd like to make this a real letter, if I can. I want to tell you something about myself. I had a perfectly hellish childhood and youth, after I got old enough to take things in at all. My father was Irish, in the sense that your father was: his family had lived in Ireland for generations and had married into families of which the same was true. But I had the (to me) misfortune of having an English mother. Her father came from a goodish Yorkshire family, her mother from a set of lawyers and small country gentlemen in Shropshire, and she was a fairly typical representative of what the English call 'middle class'. Now here I must make a parenthesis to emphasize what you—on account of your one great misfortune—that of having passed your childhood in England—probably don't know. It is this. In Ireland we have had, up to now, no middle class. It came partly from having in the country two races and two religions. We had The Gentry and The People: nothing else. You will say 'but the in-betweeners?' They belonged to the people. . . . We had none of the infamous snobbery of 'the Nobility' and 'the upper middle class'. The Duke of Leinster and Provost Mahaffy of Trinity and myself and the doctor's daughter were all equally The Gentry. You will laugh: but it is important; it is a great distinction between England and Ireland; and Ireland, losing this now, will greatly change.
> That is the end of the parenthesis.
> My mother was middle-class, my father was . . . gentry.
> My mother was a terribly strong character—managing and

domineering. She could not bear opposition; if it was offered she either became quite violent, or she cried. She constantly cried. She felt (genuinely felt) she had sacrificed her life for us and my father (we were two, my sister and myself) and she never ceased telling us so. She felt (quite genuinely) that we none of us loved her enough, or considered her enough, or helped her enough (she would not be helped—ever) or respected her wishes sufficiently, or cared to spend our time with her.

My father was gentle and affectionate, well educated and well read: very, very good—honourable and straight. Trying to live with because he was slow and blundering about little things. He was a marvel of patience with my mother, which was terribly bad for her. I think, now, she ought to have been beaten: it would have been better for us all, especially for herself. As it was my father led a most unhappy life, and died comparatively young out of sheer tiredness.

It was a terrible home. My sister is as hard as nails, she takes after another branch of the family, and got through it best. I am, in some ways, like my father, but I have a lot of my mother's managing, domineering strain in me. I used to stand between my father and her, and stand up against her on my own account. But I have in me (what you have so much more strongly) a fearful streak of conscience, and sense of duty; complicated by a sensitiveness that is nothing less than a disease. The conscience has been my undoing! At that time I thought "she is my mother: I owe her respect and devotion: I must bow to properly-constituted-authority" (fearful little prig that I was, I used to go about mouthing that phrase to myself—I got it from some accursed book— and crushing down all that was best in me with it. 'Properly-constituted-authority'. Lord!) and so I was a kind of buffer she hurled herself against. (I wonder are you dreadfully shocked!)

You see it is so much worse for a girl: and a Victorian girl! A boy goes out in the world: even in his childhood he has the consolation of knowing he will so go out. But a girl of those days was supposed to live at home until she married; and, if she didn't marry, to live at home always and 'make herself useful'. And even in my earliest years I had determined I would never marry.

Well, I needn't go on with that. It warped my character

and spoiled my life and my health and my mind. The older
I got the more I felt it and the more I longed for freedom.
We were comparatively poor when I was young and lived
in one of the most lovely spots in the world, in a rather big
rambling family house all set round with yards and stables
and gardens and woodlands and lawns, and 'our own people'
(tenants!) for miles in every direction. My father loved his
home; but my mother constantly railed about 'exile' and
'this accursed country'. Later we became rich by the death
of relatives and she took us away to Dublin and London—to
'marry' us. One very vivid recollection of my London life
is of her saying to me after my father had committed what
she considered some little social gaffe (he had beautiful and
considerate manners, but occasionally they were just a
tiny trifle too good. You know.) She said 'who could get
into society dragging such an incubus as that . . .' I have
never told a soul that before . . .

It is my belief she first killed my father and then killed
herself. Oh! not murder in any legal sense—though it ought
to be. But separated (mostly) from his home and his interests,
and constantly snubbed and corrected he began to be often
ill, and then he got internal trouble, and died, I think of
pure unhappiness. Afterwards she died: of brooding, and
self-pity, and . . . well . . . and selfishness. It is really awful
to think how glad I was. I sometimes still wonder whether
my constant longing for her death had anything to do with
killing her.

Well. That's that.

Now what about it all.

You see it couldn't really happen now: or it is very unlikely it could; even in the remotest and most primitive
locality. Girls have emancipated themselves and expect to
go out into the world and live their lives as boys do. And
yet, how burning a question this of the exactions of parents
remains . . .

Then another thing.

I don't believe, as far as I can remember, that I was born
with a dislike for children—perhaps I was. But, anyway,
my own home life made me firmly resolve never to be the
mother of a child who might suffer as I had suffered. As I
grew older I saw many, and better, reasons for sticking to
my resolution. The idea was physically repulsive to me in

the highest degree, and my reason did not consent to any of the arguments brought to bear upon me. I was told it was my duty to contribute my share to the maintenance of the race. I said I was living in what I considered to be an over-populated country, and I saw no immediate prospect of the disappearance of the race: also I did not desire to produce cannon-fodder. Then they said I was a remarkable person and I should hand on my qualities. I said it did not appear that distinguished people had distinguished descendants: great men and women are 'sports' usually. And so on.

But there is another side to this question. No one must say 'Because of my heredity, I will not have children'. The finest people come from the most unexpected and, apparently, the most unlikely and unfortunate combinations. You and I and G.B.S. are all instances of this . . .

There! I feel so much better for saying all that . . . The fatal mistake, I find, is to keep these things locked up like guilty secrets and brood upon them. Bring them out to the surface: let the daylight shine on them and the Sun of Rightness will shrivel up all the pettiness, and meanness, and make Wisdom and Beauty.

Ever,

C.F.S.

There were few secrets left between them now, and the letters seem to have taken a fresher and more open turn. The talk was mainly on the topic most dear to both of them—literature. Lawrence brimmed with ideas for Shaw and criticism of his plays. He praised *St Joan*, but chided GBS for publishing his correspondence with Ellen Terry. In turn, Charlotte revealed that she had once written a criticism of a book about Christian ethics and sent a copy to Lawrence for his opinion. More important, she presented him with her common-place book.

This moved Lawrence to respond in kind. On 17 November 1927 he sent her his private anthology of poetry. He called it *Minorities*.

For many years there was doubt as to whether or not *Minorities* ever existed. It was first mentioned by Lawrence in a letter to Robert Graves when, almost as an aside, he asked, 'Did I ever show you my private anthology? Minorities, I called it.' And his colleagues in Arabia recalled sometimes seeing Lawrence copying into a little red notebook a few lines or so from one of the three other books he carried with him: an Aristophanes in the original

Greek, Malory's *Morte d'Arthur*, and the *Oxford Book of English Verse*. So the red notebook could well have been *Minorities* and the Oxford anthology the source of many of the items he chose for his personal anthology of poems in a minor key. This is the view of the few people who always believed that *Minorities* existed outside Lawrence's imagination. Others dismissed it as a Lawrentian fantasy, or as a project he had meant to undertake, or as something very different. For example, in 1955 Richard Aldington remarked, 'There is talk of Lawrence having compiled an Anthology. Could this be the collection of mostly forgotten poems torn from the pages of issues of the *English Review* between February 1913 and March 1914, and preserved in the Clouds Hill Library?' This is a surprising statement, for Aldington had access to the letters to Charlotte Shaw in the British Museum and is hardly likely to have overlooked Lawrence's letter of 17 November 1927, in which he described the appearance, content, and significance of *Minorities* in these terms:

'This week I send you a book. I've been trying to look at it with your eyes: realizing its shabbiness and dirtiness, outside and inside, after seven years of keeping me company. I found that not even the "Oxford Book of English Verse" quite fitted my whim. So I took to copying, carelessly, in a little Morell-bound* notebook (a decent plain binding, one), the minor poems I wanted. Some are the small poems of big men: others the better poems of small men. One necessary qualification was that they should be in a minor key, another that they should sing a little bit. So you will find no sonnets here.

'The worst is you do not like minor poetry: so that perhaps the weakness of spirit in this collection will only anger you: and then my notebook will not be a fair return for your notebook. In my eyes it is: for I'm not so intellectual as to put brain-work above feeling: indeed as you know, I don't like these subdivisions of that essential unity, man . . .

'The book had only three or four empty pages when I sailed from Southampton [for India] and these I filled with a [Humbert] Wolfe poem and a scrap of Blake. In the last year I have slowly copied [all the poems] into another book (with a few more blank pages) which will last me for another seven years.

'You live always within touch of shelves, and can keep so many poets on tap that you won't feel how necessary a friend is such a

* Morell was a well-known nineteenth-century English binder and printer.

notebook as this. Its poems have each of them had a day with me. That little, hackneyed Clough, for instance, about light coming up in the west ... I read that at Umtaiye, when the Deraa expedition was panicking and in misery: and it closely fitted my trust in Allenby, out of sight beyond the hills. There's all that sort of thing, for me, behind the simple words'.

After Lawrence died, *Minorities* came into the possession of his friend, J. G. Wilson, for many years the manager of Bumpus, the booksellers. Shortly before his death in 1963 Wilson sold *Minorities* to W. M. L. Escombe, a book collector, by whom it was shown to us, thus proving that *Minorities* does indeed exist.

While Lawrence was in India, Charlotte took care of certain of his interests in Britain. She became worried, for example, about the future of Clouds Hill and persuaded Thomas Hardy's wife, Florence, to write to the original owners of the cottage, to enquire if any payments were outstanding and offering to meet them if there were. When Lawrence came back from India the Shaws were among the first people he called on.

As the Charlotte–Lawrence relationship developed, it was inevitable that Bernard Shaw was more involved, particularly on the literary side of the collaboration. A central character of his play *Too True to be Good*, Private Napoleon Alexander Trotsky Meek, is based on Lawrence; and Charlotte's correspondence shows that Lawrence collaborated with Shaw on the technical details of the play. Shaw sent Lawrence each of his subsequent plays in either typescript or proof, and although Lawrence was ignorant of stagecraft, he criticized them freely and usually with reason. He did not like the preface to *St Joan*, and he wrote to Charlotte: 'I have written to G.B.S. about the preface. It wasn't as good as I would have liked ... G.B.S. has not enough flippancy in his make-up.'

Heartbreak House was Lawrence's favourite Shaw play, and Act I he described as 'the most blazing bit of genius in English literature. There is not one decent sentence. The stuff is all lit by lightning, and there's a devil's kitchen in the background, and a chorus of hyenas. I'd rather have produced that than anything in the English language.'

Lawrence's pet project for Shaw, however, never materialized, but there is a suggestion that he might have tried it himself when he left the RAF. He first mentioned it in a letter he wrote to Charlotte on 26 August 1927:

'I say, don't you think you could some day, when G.B.S. was sleeping in the Garden, whisper to him that he should write a life of Roger Casement?* The drama of the man's life was so beautiful . . . his early Congo work, his difficult Putamayo work . . . his life in Germany, his trial and death. Those diaries . . . provide all the man's very words and thoughts. To mirror him properly calls for a Cervantes-of-the-first-part-of-Don-Quixote. Not the official life, of course, in two volumes: but just a living portrait of a queer knight . . .'

But Shaw had an Olympian disregard for Irish heroes, let alone queer knights, and rejected the project. 'He feels for all the Irish leaders,' wrote Charlotte, 'a slightly amused contempt, and a semiconscious dislike.' At the end of September 1927, she wrote to Lawrence:

> When Casement was arrested and brought to England we were, of course, much moved, but really did not pay exceptional attention to the matter, as we only knew him in a general way, our paths never having run together. But very shortly there appeared at Adelphi Terrace a Miss Gertrude Bannister and asked for an interview. We saw her. She was an Irishwoman of a fine type: sensible, shrewd, capable, responsible; at that moment teacher in a girl's school near London. She told us that she was Roger Casement's cousin: that their two families had been brought up together as children and were like brothers and sisters, but that she and Roger had been special friends. It was evident she was deeply attached to him. She said she had just come from the prison where she had taken a change of clothes and some little comforts . . . She came to us, in the first place for some money help, and, in the second, to ask if we would work with her to get together a little group of people to attempt to work up some real defence for him.
>
> Well—I liked her—and it was not difficult to persuade G.B.S. to do everything in his power. We got a little knot of people together . . . we had many meetings. G.B.S.

* Sir Roger Casement, after a distinguished career in the British Consular Service, espoused the cause of Irish independence. In April 1916 he landed in Ireland from a German submarine, but was captured and tried for high treason. Diaries said to be his and containing references to homosexual behaviour inflamed influential opinion against him; he was condemned to death and executed on 3 August 1916. The diaries, now in the Public Record Office, can be examined only on the authority of the Home Secretary.

wrote out what he thought Casement ought to do. That was, not to employ Counsel: to defend himself (he was a fine speaker); not to deny anything, to acknowledge the facts and to say they did not make him guilty: that his country had declared herself free and that he had a right to work for his country's freedom and be treated as, what he was, a prisoner of war. [Shaw's speech for Casement began 'I am not trying to shirk the British scaffold. It is the altar on which the Irish saints have been canonized for centuries'.]

Casement wouldn't take this advice. He was just not big enough.

He sent most grateful messages but said he was in the hands of his legal advisers and that they said they must conduct the case, but that he, Casement, should make a statement afterwards from the dock.

They did for him. When the trial came of course precisely what we feared happened. F. E. [Smith],* was damnable: treated the whole with consummate insolence, de haut en bas ... They passed sentence, and then ... Casement got up and made the speech G.B.S. had sketched for him. He made a profound sensation with it, and several of the jurymen said afterwards that if they had heard all that before retiring the verdict would have been different. Of course it was too late and could do nothing to change the result.

It will always be one of my deep personal regrets that I did not go to that trial. I felt at the time it was like running after a sensation—thinking of myself, you see, and not Casement! ...

Well—now—there is this dreadful thing to tell you.

During the meetings at Adelphi Terrace of our little gang, after it had been going on for some time, suddenly a shattering piece of "information" was flung into the middle of us. There were diaries: Casement's diaries had been seized: found in some trunks he had left in some lodgings— somewhere. And these diaries ... ! There were dark hints [of homosexuality]. The diaries had been written in— Putuamayo, I think it was—'notes-n-observations—impossible to describe—could not be mentioned before a lady—

* Frederick Edwin Smith (1872–1930). 1st Earl of Birkenhead. Politician and lawyer. Lord Chancellor, 1918–22, Secretary of State for India 1924–8.

most unfortunate . . . !' Of course we got angry and said 'suggestions, hints, to injure him'. Then Mr [H. W.] Massingham
(of whom you may have heard: an intimate friend of ours:
Editor for years of The Nation, a paper he made famous for
a sort of knight-errantry, taking up the case of every under-
dog and going for every highly-placed littleness and meanness and inefficiency) one of our little party, doing all in his
power to help, went to Scotland Yard and demanded, as a
prominent journalist, to be told the truth of this matter.
And he came back and said they had shown him the diaries
. . . and he told us they were as bad as it was possible to
conceive, and they undoubtedly appeared to be in Casement's handwriting.

It was a crushing blow. We were (or rather our little
committee was) rather knocked to pieces . . . To this day I
have not solved this mystery. These diaries were never
mentioned at the trial. Some of his enemies took great credit
to themselves for this and made it out to be very generous (no
doubt the diaries would have appeared quick enough (if
genuine) had there been any chance of acquittal) but you
could go nowhere in London at the time without hearing this
scandal whispered. It was put about in influential people's
houses, discussed in low tones in drawing rooms: shouted in
clubs . . . I do not know . . . I wish I did. The thing
entirely killed any English sympathy there might have been
for Casement; and I myself think, had it not been for
this, even in war time, they would not have dared to
hang him . . . I am so glad you are a friend of Casement.
Perhaps some day you will find out about those diaries for
me.

Blessings always, C.F.S.

Lawrence told Charlotte that he might write a short book about
Casement one day. But the idea was eventually put aside in favour
of the major project of his retirement—a book to be called *Confession
of Faith*. The idea came to him in the early hours of 9 December
1933, when he was stationed at Southampton. He wrote to Charlotte:

'Something happened to me last night, when I lay awake till 5.
You know I have been moody or broody for years, wondering
what I was at in the R.A.F. but unable to let go—well, last night I
suddenly understood that it was to write a book called "Confession of

Faith", beginning in the cloaca* at Covent Garden, and embodying The Mint, and much that has happened to me before and since as regards the air. Not the conquest of the air, but our entry into the reserved element, "as lords that are expected, yet with a silent joy in our arrival" . . . I see the plan of it. It will take long to do. Clouds Hill, I think. In this next and the last R.A.F. year I can collect feelings for it. . . . I wonder if it will come off. The purpose of my generation, that's really it.'

It can be seen from all this how Charlotte acted as an inspiration for Lawrence and how, under her influence, he tended to view his future with optimism. He had started to prepare Clouds Hill for the day when he would leave the RAF. 'The kitchen is being shelved for books,' he wrote to Buxton, his bank manager. 'And then only the bath remains to be installed. I hope to put in the bath, a pump for water and a boiler out of the profits of the U.S.A. Odyssey.'†

But until the idea for *Confession of Faith* occurred to him he had been worried about the significance of retirement. Former aircraftman Shaw might be prepared to 'potter about like any other retired Colonel', but for Lawrence of Arabia, the man who had helped to mould the future of the Middle East, the end of an active life smacked of a surrender to Time. As he wrote to Lady Astor, 'Nature would be merciful if she would end us at a climax and not in the decline'.

Despite Charlotte's encouragement he tended to have periods when he was preoccupied with growing old, a worry accentuated by the visible ageing of the great men he had admired. His Chief of Air Staff, Sir Geoffrey Salmond, was dying. Allenby now devoted his time to bird-watching and fishing; Churchill was spending his period in the political wilderness, bricklaying and painting. Even Trenchard, still active as Commissioner of Police, wrote in an old man's slightly querulous tones because Lawrence had not kept in touch with him: 'How are you? You never come and see me and I hear little of you . . .'

On 26 February 1935 A/C Shaw, who had been serving in Yorkshire, left the RAF for good. He packed a saddle bag, put on his

* The public lavatory on the south-western side of Covent Garden, where Lawrence went before going to the RAF recruiting centre nearby.

† In 1927 Lawrence had been introduced to the American typographer, Bruce Rogers, as the ideal man to make a new translation of the *Odyssey* for an edition which Rogers had been commissioned to produce. Lawrence began the work in Karachi in 1928 and finished it in 1931. A limited edition was published by the Oxford University Press in England in 1932 and a cheaper edition in New York the same year.

trouser-clips and a check muffler and got on his bicycle. He paused by a wall at Bridlington to let a friend photograph him—an ordinary-looking man of forty-seven with deep lines round his mouth and eyes. Then he rode off, heading south for Clouds Hill.

His last months in the service had been extremely tiring and it was with a certain pleasure that he wrote to Liddell Hart: 'I am going to taste the flavour of true leisure. For 46 years I have worked and been worked. Remaineth 23 years (of expectancy). May they be like Flecker's, "a great Sunday that goes on and on".'

18 Death in a Minor Key

As Lawrence tries to settle down in retirement, he alternates between periods of optimism and a sense of emptiness. His friends try to interest him in projects that will occupy his talents. Then death comes in a minor key. While riding his motorcycle he is involved in an accident and seriously injured. Rumours that he has been murdered spread rapidly. For six days he hovers between life and death, heavily guarded at an RAF hospital, then dies without regaining consciousness. An inquest is held, but the cause of the accident is not satisfactorily explained. Mourners at the funeral include Winston Churchill and friends from Lawrence's Arabian days. The King sends a message to Professor Lawrence—'Your brother's name will live in history.'

In the weeks after he left the RAF, Lawrence tried to settle down to life at Clouds Hill. But he had had the worst possible training for idleness: 'It feels so queer and aimless here,' he wrote to a friend in the RAF. 'I potter about all day, picking up jobs and laying them down, to keep myself in an attitude of busyness ... Life here is quiet and good enough but a very second best. I advise you all to hang on as long as you feel the job is in your power. There's such a blank afterwards.'

His friends sensed his loss of purpose and began all sorts of manoeuvres to get him to occupy his mind and his talents. Mr Pat Knowles, his Clouds Hill neighbour, believes—as a result of a conversation with Lawrence—that in March 1935, he was offered the job of reorganizing Home Defence. Something on these lines was certainly being mooted; only a few weeks before Lawrence's death Lady Astor wrote to him saying: 'Philip Lothian is right as usual. I believe when the Government reorganises you will be asked to help reorganise the Defence Forces. I will tell you what I have done already about it. If you will come to Cliveden Saturday, the last Saturday in May ... you will never regret it.'* She added that among others, the Prime Minister, Stanley Baldwin, would be there.

* Bodleian Library.

But Lawrence was not interested. 'No, wild mares would not at present take me away from Clouds Hill . . . there is something broken in the works, as I told you: my will, I think. In this mood I would not take on any job at all, so do not commit yourself to advocating me, lest I prove a non-starter.'

Retirement was not as sweet and trouble-free as he had imagined; also, the Lawrence of Arabia legend had returned to haunt him in the form of reporters who besieged Clouds Hill to see what the King-maker would do next. Was he going to meet Hitler? Would he be prepared to become dictator of England? Lawrence refused to see them, so they staked out a watch round the cottage. This led to a clash and Lawrence gave one of the reporters a black eye. He was upset afterwards and told his old RAF friend, Jock Chambers, 'It's years and years since I've hit anybody like that. I didn't think I could.' After the incident, he wrote to the Newspaper Proprietors' Association and from then on, except for an occasional intrusion by a more than usually determined reporter, he was left alone to lead the eccentric life he had chosen for himself.

With a bachelor's instinct for lessening chores, he examined the whole ritual of housekeeping. Much earlier he had decided that beds were unnecessary and instead had two sleeping bags, one for him-self and one for when he had a visitor. He did away with socks to avoid washing them and wore instead a pair of high sheepskin slippers with rubber soles. Washing up was done by placing the dishes in a sloping brick bath and pouring boiling water on them. Meals were like picnics, often eaten straight from tins. Bread, butter and cheese were kept under glass bells, as in an old-fashioned railway refreshment room. Lawrence considered keeping chickens so as to have eggs, but decided not to because of the noise. His wants were few—he neither smoked nor drank—and the small demands that the cottage made on him occupied him only for a few hours a day. For the rest of the time he appears to have alternated between periods of optimism when he was full of plans for his literary future— like the book, *Confessions of Faith*, or a life of Sir Roger Casement— and a sense of emptiness. He told Liddell Hart that perhaps his neap-tide might still lie ahead. Colonel Newcombe found him 'more normal and human and appearing to be less self-centred and self-examining than before . . . a little vague perhaps on his vocation in life for the future, but rather less self-critical and more ready to become as other men'. But he wrote to Robin Buxton, his bank manager and friend, 'What ails me is this odd sense of being laid aside before being worn out . . . I think in time I will get used to the feeling that nobody wants me to do anything today. For the moment it is a lost sort of life.' It need not have been. Lawrence could have had any one of a number of posts his friends would have found for him. Already the first warnings of the storm gathering in Europe were apparent and it is unlikely that the government would have allowed his talents to go unused once it had become apparent that war was inevitable. And there was his writing. If he had started work on one of the new books that he had been thinking about, the self-pity that he seemed to have felt might have disappeared. But fate had other plans. On 13 May, only ten weeks after his return to civilian life, Lawrence was injured in a motor-cycle accident and died six days later.

The manner of his death was such that almost inevitably a series of legends have grown up about it. There are people who believe to this day that Lawrence was not killed, that the accident was faked so as to allow him to undertake, incognito, important work in the Middle East during World War II and that he died of old age (or is still alive) in a villa outside Tangier. Others believe that Lawrence committed suicide because life no longer held any appeal for him. Lawrence himself wrote: 'Days seem to dawn, suns to shine, evenings to follow, and then I sleep. What I have done, what I am doing, what I am going to do, puzzle and bewilder me.'* Other people are certain that Lawrence was killed by agents of a foreign power; some say French, some German, some Arab. A more fanciful version is that he was killed by British agents because his next book would have exposed government secrets. A legend that has lingered longer than most is that Lawrence was a victim of his love of speed and of a death-wish, both expressed in a verse he wrote for his friend Lord Carlow:

In speed we hurl ourselves beyond the body.
Our bodies cannot scale the heavens except in a fume of petrol.
Bones. Blood. Flesh. All pressed inward together.

The facts are very different. They establish that Lawrence died after a road accident while trying to avoid a boy on a bicycle. Subsequent mystery about his death was due to the efforts of the authorities to avoid the publicity that any activity of Lawrence's inevitably attracted.

On the morning of the accident Lawrence decided to go into Bovington to do some errands, among them sending a parcel of books

* *Letters*, No. 579.

to Jock Chambers, and a telegram to another friend, Henry Williamson, the author, about his coming to Clouds Hill for lunch. The telegram read:

LUNCH TUESDAY WET FINE. COTTAGE ONE MILE NORTH BOVINGTON CAMP—SHAW.

Williamson has his own idea of why Lawrence sent him this message: 'The new age must begin: Europe was ready for peace: Lawrence was the natural leader of that age in England. I dreamed of an Anglo-German friendship, the beginning of the pacification of Europe. Hitler and Lawrence must meet. I wrote thus to him, shortly after he had left the R.A.F. He replied immediately by telegram, asking me to come the next day, wet or fine; but while returning from writing the telegram, swiftly on his motor-cycle, he saw suddenly before him over the crest of the narrow road across Egdon Heath two boys on bicycles, and braked and turned off lest he hurt them; and the temples of his brain were broken.'* This account, taken with the words 'wet fine' in Lawrence's telegram, suggests that he could not wait to talk to Williamson about meeting Hitler. There is, however, a less dramatic explanation of the words. On 10 May Williamson had written to Lawrence suggesting that he should call and see him at Clouds Hill to get his advice about the unfinished autobiography of V. M. Yeates, author of *Winged Victory*, the manuscript of which was entrusted to him after Yeates's death. Williamson concluded his letter by saying: 'I'll call in anyway on Tuesday unless rainy day . . .' To which Lawrence's reply on the Monday, 'Lunch Tuesday *wet fine* . . .' is perfectly logical, showing that overtones of urgency or indications of an interest in Hitler or Anglo-German fellowship existed only in imagination.

Clouds Hill is about a mile and a half from the few shops and the post office that serve Bovington Camp. The road between the cottage and the camp—much altered today—is straight and characterized by three dips at the Clouds Hill end. The dip furthest from Clouds Hill is the deepest, the second less deep and the third, just abreast of Lawrence's cottage, hardly perceptible. The first two, however, are both deep enough to hide approaching traffic from anyone at the bottom of them.

The first dip is about 600 yards from Clouds Hill, the second 200 yards nearer and the third about 100 yards from a gate leading to the cottage itself. When Lawrence went to Bovington, he usually rode

* *T. E. Lawrence by His Friends*, p. 455.

his Brough Superior. It was a noisy machine in first, second, and third gears, but much quieter in top gear.

Lawrence's neighbour, Pat Knowles, having lived in close proximity to his various Broughs, could tell by the sound of a motorcycle whether it was Lawrence's because of the sweet certainty with which he changed gear and the absolute regularity of his acceleration and decceleration. If the wind was in the right direction he could follow Lawrence's progress from a long way off. 'You could only hear T.E. on the bike when the wind was following him. The Broughs were awfully silent at speed. Normally all you would hear was him starting up and accelerating away, and on his return, the roar as he changed gear for the dips. As regular as clockwork he changed into third for the first dip and second for the one after. He would coast into his cottage so as not to frighten my mother when she was ill. . . .'

On the day of the accident Lawrence went across to Knowles's cottage at about 8.30 a.m. He had arranged with Mrs Knowles for her to cook lunch for Henry Williamson the next day, and he wanted to know if there was anything she needed from the shops. The postman arrived and Knowles and Lawrence sorted out the letters. When Lawrence left for Bovington at about 10.30, Pat Knowles was sowing some seed in his own garden beside the road. It was a bright, cheerful day with a strong wind blowing from Clouds Hill towards the Camp. He remembers the wind in particular because it was blowing away the fine tilth of his seed-bed. He did not see Lawrence leave because a hedge blocked his view of Clouds Hill, which was on the opposite side of the road, but he heard him start up the Brough and move off. Later he heard Lawrence returning. He heard him change down twice, then there was the usual silence which preceded his coasting into Clouds Hill. But he never arrived.

At 11.10 Corporal Ernest Catchpole clocked out of the guardroom of Bovington Camp and began to walk his dog across the heath in the direction of Knowles's cottage.

At 11.13 two delivery boys on bicycles left the camp and also turned towards Clouds Hill. A few minutes later, shortly before 11.20, Lawrence, having completed his errands, left Bovington for Clouds Hill. A few minutes after that Catchpole heard the sound of a motorcyclist changing gear on approaching the first dip in the road. It was Lawrence, and as he entered the first dip, Catchpole saw, emerging from the third dip—the one near Clouds Hill—a black car travelling in the opposite direction. Catchpole also saw the two boys on the crest of the road between the first and second dips. Then he saw Lawrence enter the middle dip and for a moment Lawrence, the car, and the two boys were all out of sight. Then the car emerged from the dip and went on towards Bovington. Almost simultaneously Catchpole heard the noise of a crash and then a riderless bicycle appeared turning over and over along the road. Catchpole described how he ran to the scene and found the motor-cyclist on the road. 'His face was covered with blood which I tried to wipe away with my handkerchief.'

At this moment an army lorry came along. Catchpole stopped it and told the driver to take Lawrence and one of the boys, who was injured but not seriously hurt, to Bovington Camp hospital. Lawrence was unconscious when he arrived there and after lingering in a coma for six days, he died.

As soon as his identity was discovered at the hospital, the War Office was told what had happened. Within an hour the accident had become an Affair of State. All ranks at Bovington were reminded that they were subject to the Official Secrets Act. Newspaper editors were told that all information about the accident and Lawrence's condition would be issued through the War Office. Even before the police had begun their investigations, an officer at the camp issued a statement saying that there had been no witnesses. Subsequently the two delivery boys spent more time with the army authorities than with the police, and Corporal Catchpole was instructed by a superior officer that he was to make no statement to the Press about the black car unless he had actually seen the collision, which he had not. To mention it otherwise would be misleading. It is difficult to understand why the matter came under army juris-diction. Lawrence was taken to the camp hospital only because it happened to be the nearest, but once he *was* there the army took charge.

The small hospital at Bovington became the centre of a struggle to save Lawrence's life—and to keep what had happened to him as quiet as possible. Four distinguished doctors, including two of the King's physicians, were sent for, and there was a constant procession, day and night, of despatch riders to and from the hospital. The King himself telephoned and asked to be informed the moment there was any news. A deluge of telegrams and telephone enquiries reached the camp, and a maximum security cordon was thrown round the hospital. The Home Office also took a hand in the arrangements and until Lawrence's death six days later, one of two plain clothes men sat by his bedside, while the other slept on a cot outside his room. Newspaper reporters besieged the camp until Newcombe arrived and persuaded the authorities to issue a statement twice a day about Lawrence's condition. Adding flesh to the bare bones of these bulletins some newspapers gave currency to a spate of rumours spreading throughout the country. The most widespread of these made Lawrence out to be a secret service agent and here the *Daily Express* led the field, quoting Professor Lawrence as saying, 'Whatever secret service he may have done in the past is over.' This statement, however, attracted less attention than rumours about foreign agents, consternation in Whitehall and the secret service, and alarm because 'Lawrence has the plans for the defence of England in his head.'

Lawrence's condition gradually grew worse and he died on Sunday, 19 May just after eight o'clock in the morning. On Tuesday 21 May an inquest was held at the hospital before the East Dorset coroner and a jury. It lasted two hours and in many ways was unsatisfactory. Corporal Catchpole, as the principal witness, estimated in his evidence that Lawrence, judging from the sound of his machine, had been travelling at between fifty to sixty miles an hour and had passed the black car safely. 'I heard a crash,' Catchpole said, 'and I saw a bicycle twisting and turning over and over along the road.'

The boys both said that they had heard the motor bicycle behind them, so had moved into single file, in which they had ridden for about a hundred yards when Lawrence crashed without warning into the boy riding in the rear. Both denied having seen or heard a car of any sort.

Catchpole was recalled and re-examined about the car, but insisted that he had not been mistaken. Dr C. P. Allen, of the Camp hospital, said death had been caused by a large fissured fracture nine inches long extending from the left side of the head backwards. There had also been a small fracture of the left orbital plate. 'Had Mr T. E. Shaw lived he would have . . . lost his memory, and would have been paralysed.'

The coroner was unhappy about the black car and told the jury that this conflicting point in the evidence, although it did not necessarily mean that the car had had anything to do with the accident, was rather unsatisfactory. The jury's verdict was that Lawrence had died from injuries received accidentally. The death certificate described him as Thomas Edward Shaw, male, 46 years, 'an aircraftsman (retired)', and gave as the cause of death, 'congestion of the lungs and heart failure following a fracture of the skull and laceration of the brain sustained on being thrown from his motorcycle when colliding with a pedal cyclist'. But left unanswered was the vital question: How did it happen?

A careful re-investigation of the occurrence suggests that what happened was this: it was quite possible that a black car was coming from the direction of Clouds Hill. Pat Knowles says a small black delivery van went past Clouds Hill at about this time every day, except on Sundays. Seen from where Corporal Catchpole was standing, the black van could easily have been mistaken for a car. The two boys were mistaken about the time at which they changed from riding abreast to riding in single file. Lawrence would have been at least a quarter of a mile away from them when they claimed that they had heard him and moved one behind the other. This, added to the fact that the wind was carrying the sound *away* from the boys, suggests that they could not have heard Lawrence's machine behind them until just before the collision. At that moment he could not have been going faster than 38 miles an hour because the Brough, which was badly damaged in the accident, was jammed in second gear, the top speed of which was 38 mph, so the gear could not have been engaged if the machine had been going any faster. It seems certain that Lawrence came upon the black van on the crown of the middle dip, coming out of it as he was about to go into it. The road was narrow and they passed close to each other. Lawrence pulled nearer to the left-hand side of the road and as he did so came suddenly on the two boys directly in front of him. Knowles says, 'I heard his engine suddenly rev up and I thought he must have been stopping suddenly to speak to someone on the road.' It is clear that the black van had nothing to do with what happened and locating it would not have altered the verdict that Lawrence died as the result of an accident. In the past, because of rumours and newspaper reports, the most ordinary events concerning Lawrence had become embarrassing to many government departments. Better, then, that the story of his death should be kept straightforward and incontrovertible. It should have been realized that nothing concerning Lawrence could ever remain uncomplicated. Discussion about the mystery of the accident has gone on for more than thirty years—and will no doubt continue—mainly because romantic minds find it hard to accept that a man who lived the extraordinary life of Lawrence of Arabia could die in such an ordinary manner.

The funeral was held on the afternoon of the inquest. It had been arranged from Whitehall and at the wish of Lawrence's family the public was requested not to attend. Lawrence's mother was in

China with his eldest brother, Bob. Professor Lawrence, who had been in the Mediterranean, hurried back on the day after the accident. Sir Ronald Storrs travelled down from London on the previous night and was allowed by Professor Lawrence to try to photograph his old friend lying in a plain oak coffin. 'Beyond a few small scars and a little discoloration of the left eye and region, Lawrence was looking handsomer and nobler than I had ever seen him. The nose sharp as a pen and more hooked and hawklike than in life and the chin less square . . . He was wrapped in white cotton wool with a tight bandage round the forehead and looser sheeting around him. He was, with almost no imagination, once more the Arab chieftain in Kuffiyah and Aigal lying in dark-stained ivory against the dead white of the hospital stuff.'

Storrs had had no experience in taking photographs under such conditions and had no idea what the exposure should be. He climbed a trestle, stood astride over the coffin and tried to hold the camera steady enough for a time exposure. He was interrupted half way through when the coroner came to view the body, but managed to take six photographs, one of which came out reasonably well. Storrs said he would like to have arranged for Kennington or Augustus John to sketch Lawrence but that there was not sufficient time.

At Lawrence's own request he was buried in the village church at Moreton. Storrs was chief pall-bearer, assisted by Eric Kennington, Aircraftman Bradbury, Private Russell, Pat Knowles and Colonel Newcombe. Only one hymn was sung, Lawrence's favourite, 'Jesu, Lover of my Soul'.

Many of his friends were there—Churchill, Lord Lloyd, Lionel Curtis, Thomas Hardy, Lady Astor, and Augustus John among them. The Shaws had left on a cruise in March and were in Durban. Friends from his Arabian days came from all over the country: Captain Dixon, Captain Brodie, Gunner Tom Beaumont, Gunner Bailey, Gunner Brown, and Driver Rolls. John Bruce, the man who had known a side of Lawrence different from that known by the others, says he was there too. As the coffin was lowered Gunners Beaumont and Bailey, on opposite sides of the grave, shook hands. Beaumont says he saw a name-plate on the coffin: T. E. Lawrence— but newspaper reports said the coffin carried no inscription. As the first earth fell into the grave, a girl of about twelve ran forward and threw in a little bunch of violets.

Afterwards the mourners gathered at Moreton House at the invitation of the owner. Lady Astor, her eyes still red from weeping, tried to cheer everyone up. Beaumont remembers her saying to Canon Kinloch, who had officiated at the funeral, 'That was a bloody fine sermon, the first time I've heard you sound really sincere'. But when Churchill, who had wept during the funeral, took his leave, Lady Astor's composure broke down again and she ran to his car calling 'Winnie, Winnie' and clasped his hands between hers. Perhaps it was a message to Professor Lawrence from the King that best expressed the feeling of those at the funeral: 'Your brother's name will live in history and the King gratefully recognizes his distinguished services to his country and feels that it is tragic that the end should have to come in this manner to a life still so full of promise'.

The tiny cemetery where Lawrence lies is barely half-full. His headstone is small and unpretentious. The inscription on it reads:

> To the dear memory of
> T. E. LAWRENCE
> Fellow of All Souls College
> Oxford
> Born 16 August 1888
> Died 19 May 1935
> The hour is coming & now is
> When the dead shall hear
> The voice of the
> SON OF GOD
> And they that hear
> Shall live

At the foot of the grave is an even smaller stone, carved in the shape of an open book. The inscription, in Latin, is from the twenty-sixth Psalm—

DOMINUS ILLUMINATIO MEA

Bibliography

ALDINGTON, Richard, *Lawrence of Arabia*: a biographical enquiry (Collins, 1955).

ANTONIUS, George, *The Arab Awakening* (Hamish Hamilton, 1938).

ARMITAGE, Flora, *The Desert and The Stars*: A Portrait of T. E. Lawrence (Faber and Faber, 1956).

BOURNE, K. and WATT, D. C. (editors) *Studies in International History*. Essays presented to W. H. Medlicott (Longmans, 1967).

BOYLE, Andrew, *Trenchard* (Collins, 1962).

BRODRICK, Alan Houghton, *Near to Greatness* (Hutchinson, 1965).

FLECKER, James Elroy, *Some Letters from Abroad* (William Heinemann, 1930).

GARNETT, David, *The Essential T. E. Lawrence* (Jonathan Cape, 1951).
(Editor) *The Letters of T. E. Lawrence* (Jonathan Cape, 1938).

GRAVES, Robert, *Lawrence and the Arabs* (Jonathan Cape, 1927).

GRAVES, Robert and HART, LIDDELL, B. H., *T. E. Lawrence to his Biographers* (Cassell, 1963).

HART, LIDDELL, B. H. '*T. E. Lawrence*'—*In Arabia and After* (Jonathan Cape, 1945).

HOWARTH, David, *The Desert King* (Collins, 1964).

KIRKBRIDE, Sir Alec Seath, *A Crackle of Thorns* (John Murray, 1956).

LAWRENCE, A. W. (editor) *T. E. Lawrence by his Friends* (Jonathan Cape, 1937).

LAWRENCE, M. R. (editor) *The Home letters of T. E. Lawrence and his Brothers* (Blackwell, Oxford, 1954).

LAWRENCE, T. E. *Oriental Assembly*, edited by A. W. Lawrence (Williams and Norgate, 1939).
Seven Pillars of Wisdom (Jonathan Cape, 1935).

LAWRENCE, T. E. *Revolt in the Desert* (Jonathan Cape, 1927).
The Mint (Jonathan Cape, 1955).

LESLIE, Shane, *Mark Sykes: His Life and Letters* (Cassell, 1923).

LÖNNROTH, Erik, *Lawrence of Arabia* (Vallentine, Mitchell, 1956).

MACPHAIL, Sir Andrew, *Three Persons* (John Murray, 1929).

MEINERTZHAGEN, Colonel R., *Middle East Diary* (The Cresset Press, 1959).

Military Operations, Egypt and Palestine, Vol. II (H.M. Stationery Office).

MONROE, Elizabeth, *Britain's Moment in the Middle East 1914–1956* (Chatto and Windus, 1963).

MOUSA, Suleiman, *T. E. Lawrence—An Arab View* (Oxford University Press, 1966).

NUTTING, Anthony, *Lawrence of Arabia—The Man and the Motive* (Hollis and Carter, 1961).

OCAMPO, Victoria, *338171 T. E. (Lawrence of Arabia)*, translated by David Garnett (Gollancz, 1963).

PAYNE, Robert, *Lawrence of Arabia* (Pyramid Books, New York, 1962).

PHILBY, H. St John, *Forty Years in the Wilderness* (Robert Hale, 1957).
Arabian Days (Robert Hale, 1948).

RICHARDS, Vyvyan, *Portrait of T. E. Lawrence* (Jonathan Cape, 1936).

ROTHENSTEIN, William, *Twenty-four Portraits* (Allen and Unwin, 1920).

SAMUEL, Viscount, *Memoirs* (The Cresset Press, 1945).

STEIN, Leonard, *The Balfour Declaration* (Vallentine, Mitchell, 1961).

STORRS, Sir Ronald, *Orientations* (Ivor Nicholson and Watson, 1937).

SYKES, Christopher, *Cross-Roads to Israel* (Collins, 1937).

THOMAS, Lowell, *With Lawrence in Arabia* (Hutchinson, 1924).

TOYNBEE, Arnold J., *Acquaintances* (Oxford University Press, 1967).

VILLARS, Jean Beraud, *T. E. Lawrence or the Search for the Absolute* (Sidgwick and Jackson, 1958).

WAVELL, Colonel A. P. *The Palestine Campaigns* (Constable, 1928).

WEINTRAUB, Stanley, *Private Shaw and Public Shaw* (Jonathan Cape, 1963).

YOUNG, Major Sir Hubert, *The Independent Arab* (John Murray, 1933).

ZEINE, Zeine, N., *The Struggle for Arab Independence* (Khayat's, Beirut, 1960).

Index